ALEXANDRIA, VIRGINIA
Town Lots

1749-1801

Together with
*Proceedings of the
Board of Trustees*
1749-1780

Compiler
Constance K. Ring

Production Editor
Wesley E. Pippenger

Contributors
Dr. James D. Munson
T. Michael Miller

Surveys Redrawn
William Sprouse

HERITAGE BOOKS
2008

HERITAGE BOOKS
AN IMPRINT OF HERITAGE BOOKS, INC.

Books, CDs, and more—Worldwide

For our listing of thousands of titles see our website
at
www.HeritageBooks.com

Published 2008 by
HERITAGE BOOKS, INC.
Publishing Division
100 Railroad Ave. #104
Westminster, Maryland 21157

Copyright © 1995 Constance K. Ring and Wesley E. Pippenger

Other Heritage Books by Constance K. Ring:
Index to Fairfax County, Virginia Wills and Fiduciary Records, 1742-1855
Index to the Fairfax County, Virginia Register of Marriages, 1853-1933
Constance K. Ring and Craig R. Scott

All rights reserved. No part of this book may be reproduced or transmitted in any form or by any means, electronic or mechanical, including photocopying, recording or by any information storage and retrieval system without written permission from the author, except for the inclusion of brief quotations in a review.

International Standard Book Numbers
Paperbound: 978-1-58549-323-4
Clothbound: 978-0-7884-7741-6

TABLE OF CONTENTS

LIST OF ILLUSTRATIONS iv

INTRODUCTION 1

ACT AND ORDER FOR SURVEY OF THE TOWN OF ALEXANDRIA AT
HUNTING CREEK WAREHOUSE IN FAIRFAX COUNTY 3

ABBREVIATIONS 4

LOT HISTORIES 4

PROCEEDINGS OF THE BOARD OF TRUSTEES, TOWN OF ALEXANDRIA . . . 119

APPENDIX 182

    An Act for Incorporating the Town of Alexandria in the County of Fairfax, and
        the Town of Winchester in the County of Frederick. 183
    Chronology 186
    Act for Erecting a Town at Hunting Creek Warehouse in the County of
        Fairfax 189

INDEX 193

LIST OF ILLUSTRATIONS

Figure 1 - George Washington's "A Plan of Alexandria now Belhaven," 1749. [Redrawn by Bill Sprouse] 2

Figure 2 - Plat of Lots 20, 21, 22, 26 and 27. [Record of Surveys, p. 210 (74), Redrawn by Bill Sprouse] 12

Figure 3 - Plat of Lots 31 and 32. [Alexandria Hustings Court Deeds, Bk. L, p. 362] 19

Figure 4 - Henry Salkeld's Division of Lots 38 and 39 (1760's?). [Constance K. Ring] 27

Figure 5 - Plat of Lots 69, 70, 77 and 78. [Record of Surveys, p. 146 (11), Redrawn by Bill Sprouse] 62

Figure 6 - Plat of Lots 80 and 81. [Alexandria Hustings Court Deeds, Bk. C, p. 15] 70

Figure 7 - George West's Map of Alexandria, March 10, 1763. (Delineates by dotted lines the new lots added in November 1762. Map was made for use by the Trustees in the sale of lots, May 9, 1763.) [Redrawn by Bill Sprouse] 74

Figure 8 - Drawing of Extended Lot Sequence. [Constance K. Ring, Redrawn by Bill Sprouse] . . 98

Figure 9 - Plat of Lots 168 and 181. [Alexandria Hustings Court Deeds, Bk. D, p. 258] 117

Figure 10 - Copy of First Page of the Proceedings, Board of Trustees, Town of Alexandria. 118

Figure 11 - Plat of Lots Rented to Messrs. Conway, Macrae, Mease and Adam, 24 FEB 1774. Scale by Jonathan Hall of 60 feet in an Inch. 168

Figure 12 - Plat of Lot Rented to Thomas Fleming, 1774. 170

INTRODUCTION

Prior to 1783, land and probate records for the town of Alexandria were recorded in the Fairfax County court. After 1782, records pertaining to the town appear in both jurisdictions. The transactions in this book are based mainly upon information from the Fairfax County Circuit Court records and the Proceedings of the Board of Trustees for the Town of Alexandria. They also include all pertinent deeds from the Alexandria Hustings Court. Fairfax County deed and will book references accompanying each transaction are for series I (1742-1797, and 1742-1855, respectively), unless otherwise indicated by a number following the book letter.

Much of the information pertaining to Alexandria lot sales is bewildering to the modern researcher. Lots were often subdivided into smaller numbered parcels. The Salkeld subdivision of Lots 38 and 39 contained parcels numbered one through eight, with a subsequent subdivision of parcel one into four sub-parcels numbered one through four. This overlapping numbering causes confusion in determining the exact location of a particular parcel. The pattern used to number new lots in the several additions to the original town departed from the early east-west plan to a "wrap-around" configuration. Lot numbers were not always used as part of the lot description. Therefore, some of the lot numbers in this book are conjectural and are noted by an asterisk (*).

Some records are missing, and many were not recorded. In the *Virginia Gazette*, May 9, 1766, William Black advertised "a lot well situated for trade, on which is a storehouse and other improvements," but court records do not tell us which lot he was selling, or how he came to own it. A deed, circa 1764, from the Trustees to Francis Dade, appears in the index to deeds, but the deed book is missing and no later transactions have been found to indicate which lot Dade owned. An advertisement in the *Virginia Gazette*, May 2, 1771, placed by John Alexander, Jr., offers few clues. It states "to be sold to the highest bidder for ready money, in the Town of Alexandria... a convenient lot in the said Town, whereon is a brick dwelling house... This lot was conveyed to me some time since by Francis Dade, Esq., attorney-at-law, and is to be sold to discharge certain debts of his for which I became security and am now obliged to pay." Notley Jones received a lot from the Trustees, but the deed is missing and no further transactions for Jones concerning the lot have been found. In the Proceedings (commonly referred to as the Trustees' Minutes), the amount paid for a lot is sometimes shown in pounds, shillings, and pence (e.g. £16.19.0), and sometimes in pistoles (a Spanish gold coin).

For some lots there is no information in the following list at all. The Proceedings do not account for the sale of Lot 142. Lots 143-181 were presumably laid out by John Alexander and his executors, but no information has been found for Lots 149, 161, 162, 170, 172, and 179 in Fairfax County records. Hopefully, information may yet be found in Alexandria records.

I am indebted to Wesley E. Pippenger, James D. Munson, and T. Michael Miller, whose contributions to this book, and to our collective knowledge of Alexandria history, are prodigious. A search for missing information should be undertaken by all interested parties, to produce a comprehensive history of Alexandria lot transactions. The information in this book is compiled as a step toward that goal.

Constance K. Ring
Archivist, Fairfax County
Circuit Court
December 1995

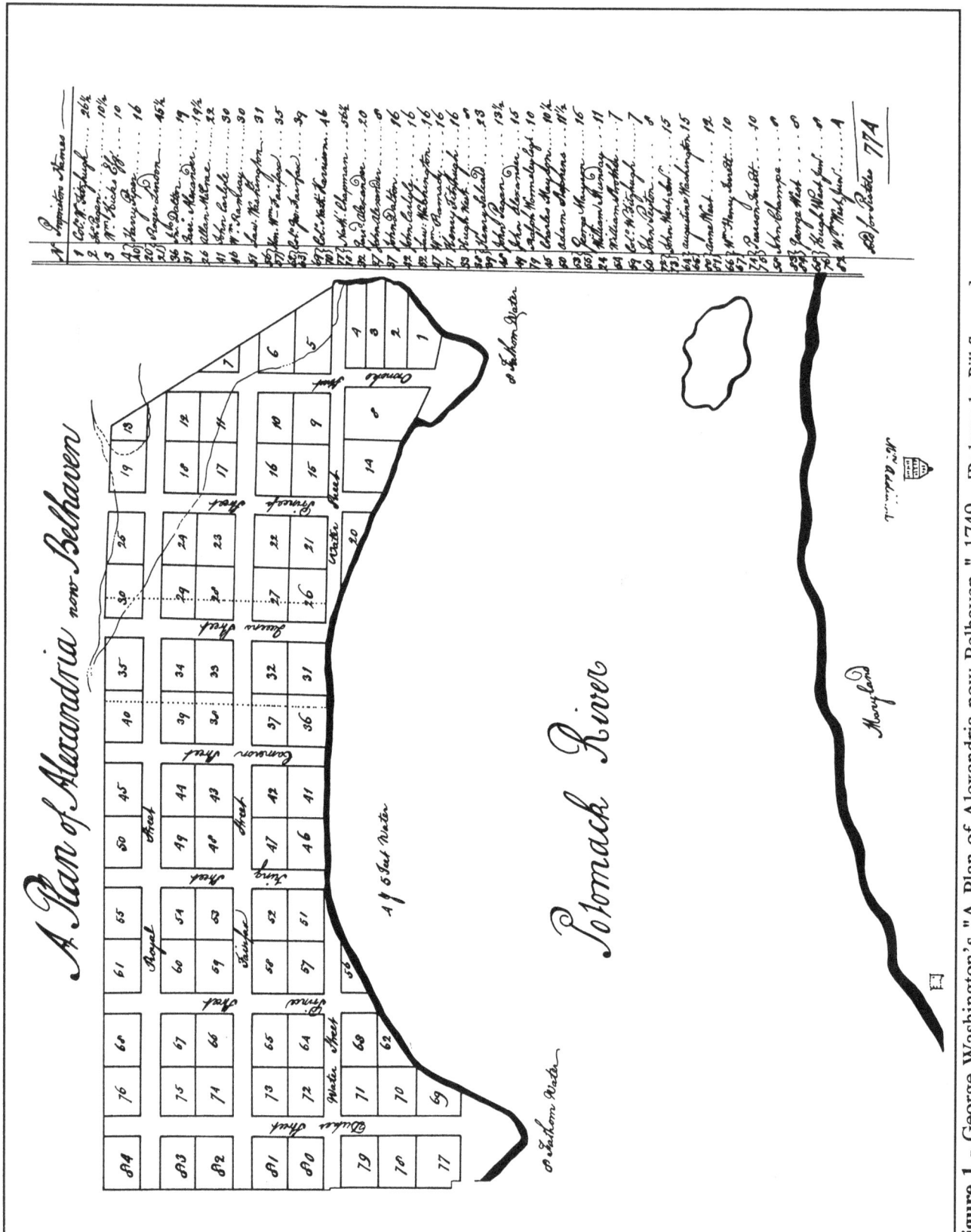

Figure 1 - George Washington's "A Plan of Alexandria now Belhaven," 1749. [Redrawn by Bill Sprouse]

Alexandria, Virginia Town Lots, 1749-1801

Act
for Erecting a Town at
Hunting Creek Warehouse
in the County of Fairfax[1]

The Virginia House of Burgesses and Council, on April 22 and May 2, 1749, respectively, enacted that a town called "Alexandria" was within four months to be established at Hunting Creek warehouse in Fairfax County. Sixty acres of land, from parcels of Philip Alexander, John Alexander, and Hugh West, located at the mouth of Great Hunting Creek on the south side of the Potomac River, were surveyed into lots and streets. Each lot was to contain no more than one half acre of ground. Directors and Trustees were appointed and given authority to effect lot sales, devise rules and orders, and nominate replacement Directors and Trustees. A lot purchaser could have no more than two lots and was required, within two years, to erect, build and finish on each lot a house of brick, stone or wood. The structure was to be twenty feet square with nine feet pitch, or proportionately similar. No wooden chimneys were allowed. The Act also prohibited the running at large of swine or hogs within town boundaries.

July the 18th 1749

Fairfax County

By virtue of an Act of the General Assembly made at the College in the City of Williamsburg in the twenty second year of the Reign of our Sovereign Lord George the second, by the Grace of God of Great Britain, France, and Ireland King defender of the faith...and in the year of our Lord one thousand seven hundred and forty eight, Entitled an Act for erecting a Town at Hunting Creek Warehouses in the County of Fairfax.

And persuant to the directions and order of Richard Osborne, Lawrence Washington, William Ramsay, John Carlyle, Gerrard Alexander and Hugh West Gentlemen, by the said Act appointed Trustees for the Town to be called Alexandria; I the subscriber did Survey and lay of [sic] sixty acres of land to be for the said Town and divided the same into lotts streets...as per the plan thereof.

Jno. West, Jr., Depy. S.F.C.

A true Copy by Daniel Jennings
Mem° The General Assembly in
which the Act was made began the
27th day of October 1748.

---

[1] Waverly K. Winfree, comp., The Laws of Virginia; Being a Supplement to Hening's The Statutes at Large, 1700-1750 (Richmond: The Virginia State Library, 1971), pp 443-446, October 27, 1748 to May 11, 1749, "An Act for erecting a Town at Hunting Creek Warehouse in the County of Fairfax." **See page 189 for complete text of the Act.** Additional information about the chain of title of the property on which was ultimately situated the Town of Alexandria, can be found in the following sources: Alexander v. Birch, in Prince William Co. Land Causes, 1789-1793, pp. 89-99, 226 et seq.; Birch v. Alexander, in Bushrod Washington, Reports of Cases Argued and Determined in the Court of Appeals, Vol. 1, pp. 34-9; and Charles W. Stetson, Four Mile Run Land Grants (Washington: Mimeoform Press, 1935), pp. 1-38, "Howsing Patent." Order by John West found at Fairfax Co. Record of Surveys, Bk. 1, p. 29 (57).

LOT HISTORIES

Abbreviations:
Alex.	=	Alexandria Hustings Court Deeds, book:page
FDB	=	Fairfax County Deeds, book:page
FWB	=	Fairfax County Wills, book:page
msg	=	Missing
Patents	=	Virginia State Land Office Patents, book:page; e.g. Patents [Grants], Book E, 1775/6-1780/1, is found on microfilm reel 46 at The Library of Virginia
Quit Rents	=	Fairfax County Quit Rent Rolls, 1761-1774
TM	=	Proceedings of the Board of Trustees, Town of Alexandria, commonly referred to as the "Trustees Minutes," TM:page

LOT 1
Oronoco & Potomac River

1749, JUL 13	Trustees to William Fitzhugh, for £28.9.9 (TM:1).
1760, MAY 21	William Fitzhugh, of Md., to Charles Digges, merchant, for £80 (FDB D:697).
1784, APR 19	George Digges, of Prince Georges Co., Md., Gent., to John Fitzgerald[2], merchant (FDB O:217; see Alex. L:267).
1793, DEC 29	John Fitzgerald and wife Jane to Henry Lee, for £750, all of Lot 1 (FDB W:402).
1799, FEB 2	Thomas Digges, of Warburton, Md., second son of William Digges, late of Md., deceased, and heir-at-law of his brother Charles Digges, to John Fitzgerald, to ensure clear title (Alex. L:267).
1799, SEP 2	Thomas Digges, of Prince Georges Co., Md., to Henry Lee, of Westmoreland Co., to clear additional doubts of title (Alex. M:279).
1800, FEB 10	Henry and Anne Lee of Stratford, Westmoreland Co., to William Herbert, for £550 of Va. (Alex. N:228).
1800, JUN 23	Edmund J. Lee, of Alexandria, to William Herbert, bond for £1000 of Va., if Anne Lee claims her 1/3 dower, Lee will reimburse Herbert for loss and damages (Alex. N:210).

LOT 2
Oronoco & Potomac River

1749, JUL 13	Trustees to John Pagan (TM:1).
1749, SEP 20	William Ramsay and Hugh West, Trustees, to John Pagan, for £11.5.9 (FDB C:20).
1780	Richard Conway apparently lived on Lot 2 in 1780 (Patents E:458).

---

[2] The Times and District of Columbia Daily Advertiser, 4/5 DEC 1799, notice that Colonel John Fitzgerald, of Alexandria, died on Monday last, he was an aide to General Washington and since the war has filled an important office under the Federal Government; his funeral was held 4 DEC 1799.

1786, SEP 28	Mordecai Lewis, of Philadelphia, to Dr. Elisha Dick, land adjoining Lot 2, "now or lately belonging to" William Hartshorne (Alex. B:394).

LOT 3
Oronoco & Potomac River

1749, JUL 14	Trustees to William Hicks, Esqr (TM:2).
1749, SEP 20	William Ramsay and Garrard Alexander, Trustees, to John Dixon, merchant, for William Hicks for £10.15. (FDB B:500).
1750, APR 7	Trustees to John Dixon for William Hicks (TM:7).
1757, JUL 20	John Dixon to John Carlyle and John Dalton (FDB D:444, part msg).
1780, AUG 28	Patent to William Herbert (Patents E:458).
1785, JUL 8	William Herbert and wife Sarah to Neil Mooney,[3] lease 137'6"x24' (Alex. C:86).

LOT 4
Oronoco, Water St. & Potomac River

1749, JUL 14	Trustees to Harry Piper (TM:2).
1749, SEP 20	John Carlyle and Hugh West, Trustees, to Harry Piper, for £10.15. (FDB B:503).
1757, AUG 6	Harry Piper to Robert Adam, for £20, 1/3 acre Oronoco frontage (FDB D:503).
1757, AUG 6	Harry Piper, merchant, to John Carlyle and John Dalton, for £10, 1/6 part of an acre being the remaining part of Lot 4, river frontage (FDB D:504).
1760	Note William Ramsay's mention (TM:39).
1780	Robert Adam apparently occupied Lot 4 (Patents E:458).
1795, MAR 18	James Irvin, guardian of John, Robert and Jane Adam, orphans of Robert Adam, dec.[4], to Andrew Jamieson and Robert Anderson, lease of Lot 4 with bake house and other buildings and improvements, and use and benefit of the river, for £25/annum (Alex. G:9, note on p. 11 states that a 25' square is excepted and contains a frame house).

LOT 5
Oronoco & Water St.

1753, MAR 20	Trustees to Samuel Mead, for £1.3. (FDB C:455 msg; see TM:20 for 1 MAR 1753).
1760, OCT 15	John Dalton and George Johnston, Trustees, to Robert Adam, for £1.3., formerly conveyed to Samuel Mead on 20 MAR 1753, as Mead failed to build (FDB D:799).

---

[3] <u>Virginia Journal and Alexandria Advertiser</u>, 19 APR 1787, Capt. Moone [sic] drowned some time ago; his body was recovered last Sun. and bur. in the Episcopal Burial Ground.

[4] <u>Virginia Gazette and Alexandria Advertiser</u>, 10 SEP 1789, Robert Adam of Alexandria, deceased, estate accounts with William Herbert, William Wilson, Roger West and William Hunter, Jr., administrators.

LOT 6
Oronoco & Fairfax

1763, MAY 9	Trustees to William West, for £1. (TM:52).
1791, MAY 27	Rev. William West's will, probated in Baltimore Co., Md., devised his real estate to son George William West (FWB F:300).

LOT 7
Fairfax & Oronoco
Unsold in this location. Lot 8 divided in 1763 into Lots 7 and 8.

Oronoco & Potomac River

1763, MAY 9   Trustees to Isaac Hughes, for £2. (TM:52; FDB F:449 msg).

This lot may have disappeared under water by 1786, or was absorbed into Lot 8 when part of Lot 8 was sold with the "right of wharfing" (FDB Q:362; see also Alex. M:197).

LOT 8
Oronoco & Water St.

1753, MAR 1	Trustees to Hugh West. Descended to Thomas West (TM:20; FDB C:456 msg; see FDB Q:362).
1763	Divided into Lots 7 and 8.
1783, NOV 25	William Bird to Baldwin Dade, for 5 shillings, part of Lot 8 (FDB P:24).
1786, SEP 30	Thomas West, Gent. and wife Ann to William Hunter, Jr. and John Allison, merchants, for £155, the lower part of Lot 8 with the "right of wharfing" (FDB Q:362).
1786, OCT 29	Baldwin Dade to Thomas West, part of Lot 8, 88'6"x123' (FDB Q:312).
1786, NOV 6	Thomas and Ann West to William Hepburn & John Dundas, for £250, 160'x123'5" (Alex. B:420).
178?, JUN 17	Baldwin and Catharine Dade to Jesse Taylor, part of Lot 8 (see Alex. M:197).
1796, AUG 2	John Allison (now of Wilkes Co., Ga.), power of attorney to "my friends" Robert Allison, of Alexandria, merchant, and Robert McCrea of Wilkes Co., Ga., to sell part of Lots 8 and 14, 105' frontage and extending into River (Alex. G:502).
1799, OCT 16	Jesse and Elizabeth Taylor to Richard Conway, for £300, 100'x160' (Alex. M:197). This deed mentions that Jesse Taylor purchased the property from Baldwin and Catharine Dade on June 17, 178?.

LOT 9
Oronoco & Water St.

1753, MAR 1	Trustees designated Lots 9 and 10 for warehouses (TM:20).
1786, FEB 24	Thomas West and Ann his wife to William Hepburn and John Dundas, for

£400, all of Lot 9 (FDB Q:115).

(See also Alex. A:44; recites that Lot 15 was next to one of the "Lotts whereon the public warehouses for inspecting Tobacco stand").

LOT 10
Fairfax & Oronoco

1753, MAR 1 — Trustees designated Lots 9 and 10 for warehouses (TM:20).

LOT 11
Fairfax & Oronoco

1763, MAY 9 — Trustees to John West for £5. (TM:52).

LOT 12
Royal & Oronoco

1763, MAY 9 — Trustees to John West, for £1. (TM:52).

LOT 13
Royal & Oronoco

1763, MAY 9 — Trustees to John [sic] Bushby, for £14.10. (TM:52; FDB F:305 msg).

1768, MAR 21 — William Bushby, painter, to Matthew Campbell, merchant, for £14.10., same lot he purchased from Trustees (FDB G:341).

LOT 14
Princess & Water St.

1750, APR 20 — George William Fairfax and William Ramsay, Trustees, to Hugh West, Sr., for £48.7.8 (TM:12; FDB C:354, dated 21 AUG 1752; see also Alex. C:186).

1782, NOV 21 — Sybil West rents lot to William Ward, for £80 per annum during her life (see Alex. A:222).

1783, DEC 12 — Thomas West and wife Ann to William Hepburn, for £650, 88'7½"x150' (FDB O:316).

1784, MAY 1 — Thomas West to William Hunter, Jr. and John Allison as tenants in common (see Alex. C:186).

1785, JUN 25 — William Ward to William Hunter, Jr. and John Allison, use of half lot, for £90 (Alex. A:222).

1786, JUN 21 — William Hepburn and wife Agnes to Monica and Jeremiah Clifford, part of lot, 88'7½"x36' (FDB Q:233).

1788, JAN 18 — William Hunter, Jr., merchant, to Josiah Watson, mortgage half the parcel granted Hunter and Allison (Alex. C:186).

1791, MAR 10	Nehemiah Clifford, late of Alexandria, now of Prince Georges Co., Md., to William Hepburn, for £8, 11'x88' (Alex. D:220).
1792, JAN 19	William Hunter, Jr. to John Hunter, part of lot, including ferry and landing (FDB U:233).
1793, JAN 26	John and Rebecca Allison to William Hunter, Jr., for £900, part of lot with ferry and ferry landing, and half the warehouse upon the wharf, "together with the Ferry and Ferry-landing" (Alex. E:22).
1796, AUG 2	John Allison, now of Wilkes Co., Ga., power of attorney to Robert Allison and Robert McCrea, to sell part of Lots 8 and 14, 105' frontage and extending into the river (Alex. G:502).

LOT 15
Princess & Water St.

1753, MAR 1	Trustees to William Yates (TM:20; FDB C:458 msg).
1754, DEC 18	William Yates, carpenter, to John West, Junr., Hugh West, George West and William West, Junr., sons of the late Hugh West, for £12.18; lot, woods and underwoods (FDB C:843; FDB P:74, deed of 1764, states Lot 16 [sic] was sold by Yates to Wests).
1780, MAY 30	Robert Rutherford to William Hepburn (see Alex. A:44).
1784, JAN 1	William Hepburn and wife Agnes to John Lomax, 80'x88', for $80 silver/annual rent; also 88'x43'5" (FDB A_2:311).
1784, JAN 1	William and Agniss [sic] Hepburn to James Adam, lease 123'5"x88'6", for $88½ specie (Alex. A:44).
1784, FEB 28	William and Agniss Hepburn to John Lomax, for £400 (Alex. A:29).
1793, APR 2	Occupied by Joseph Thomas (who married [Rachel] the widow of the said Mr. Lomax) (Alex. M:2).

LOT 16
Princess & Fairfax

1753, MAR 1	Trustees to John West, Jr. (TM:20).
1754, DEC 17	John Carlyle to Ralph Wormley, Esq., of Middlesex Co., for £20, bought by Carlyle from Trustees [sic] (FDB C:825; FDB D:16 msg, John West, Jr. to John Carlyle).
1788, MAR 22	William Hunter, Jr., merchant, to Rachel Lomax, widow of John Lomax[5], dec., for £213, 24'x100' (Alex. C:205; see FDB A_2:312).
1791, FEB 11	William Hunter, Jr. mortgage to John Dalrymple, of Fredericksburg, for £1200, two parcels of lot: 100'x51'5" and 123'5"x64'7" (Alex. D:306).
1793, JUL 8	William Ward and wife Celia, Town of Colchester, to Maurice Hurlihy for £120, part of lot (FDB W:249, deed recites that the piece was conveyed by Ralph Wormley to William Hunter, Jr. and by Hunter, Jr. to Ward in 1785;

---

[5] Virginia Journal and Alexandria Advertiser, 25 JAN 1787, John Lomax, for many years a noted tavern keeper in Alexandria, died recently. Estate accounts with his admx. Rachel Lomax (18 OCT 1787); his admx. and Joseph Thomas will petition the General Assembly to sell two of his unimproved lots in Alexandria (21 SEP 1791).

	Alex. D:306, recites date as 30 MAY 1785).
1800, DEC 27	Maurice Herlihy to William Smith, 48'x100' (Alex. O:171).

LOT 17
Princess & Fairfax

1760, FEB 20	Trustees to Thomas Brownly, for £8 (TM:33).
1760, FEB 21	John Carlyle and George Johnston, Trustees, to Thomas Brownly, joiner, for £8 (FDB D:665).
1773, JUL 22	Thomas Brownly mortgaged to John Muir (FDB L:5 damaged). Brownly failed to pay off note, Muir sued Brownly's estate.
1791, APR 20	Richard Weightman purchases from Charles Little, sheriff of Fairfax Co., for £136 at public auction (FDB T:264).
1791, MAY 16	Richard Weightman and wife Elizabeth to John Chew, of Loudoun Co., for £34 (FDB T:271).

LOT 18
Princess & Royal

1763, MAY 9	Trustees to George West, for £5 (TM:52). His will disposes of all his lots in Alexandria (FWB E:134).

LOT 19
Princess & Royal

1763, MAY 9	Trustees to Hugh Hughes, for £16.10 (TM:52; FDB F:453 or 459 msg).

LOTS 20 and 21[6]
Water St. & Potomac River

1749, JUL 13	William Ramsay and John Pagan, Trustees, to Roger Lindon of Whitehaven, Lot 20 for £24.9.1½, and Lot 21 for £20.9.1½ (TM:1; FDB C:302, 3).
1754, JUN 18	Escheated to Trustees for Lindon's failure to build (TM:21).
1754, SEP 9	Trustees to William Ramsay, for £2.5. (TM:22; FDB D:3, 4 msg).
1764, APR 21	William Ramsay and wife Ann to Jacob Hite, Lot 21 (FDB F:146 msg; see FDB L:257).
1766, DEC 16	Trustees Minutes show ownership of Lot 20 by Jacob Hite (TM:57).
1769, JAN 19	Jacob Hite, of Frederick Co., and Frances his wife to Robert Adam, one moiety of Lot 20 (FDB M:175, 211).
1773, DEC 2	Jacob Hite and wife Frances, of Berkeley Co., to Joshua Storrs, of Henrico Co., Lot 21 "with 2 houses on the same," for £400 (FDB L:257).
1773, DEC 3	Jacob Hite and wife Frances, of Berkeley Co., and Robert Adam convey to Joshua Storrs, of Henrico Co., for £400, part of Lot 20 or one equal moiety

---

[6] Also see Fairfax Co. Record of Surveys (1742-1856), pp. 191, 210 (plat), for Lots 20, 21, 22, 26 and 27.

Alexandria, Virginia Town Lots, 1749-1801

	of Lot 20. Storrs to receive the lower moiety (FDB L:269).
1774, JUL 30	Joshua Storrs to William Herbert and Andrew Stewart, merchants, for £850, Lot 21 and lower moiety of Lot 20 (see FDB M:2; Record of Surveys, 1742-1856:191-2, 210).
1775, AUG 16	Jacob Hite, of Frederick Co., and Frances his wife to Robert Adam, his share in upper half of Lot 20 (FDB M:211).
1778, OCT 21	Herbert & Stewart's executors to Richard Conway for the lower moiety of Lot 20, for £3000, "adjoining the lot whereof Thomas Kirkpatrick now seized and possessed" (FDB D$_4$:253).
1782, JUL 1	Richard Conway and wife Mary lease to John Lomax, part of Lot 21, 71'x72'2" (see FDB Q:195; Alex. A:10; see Alex. F:152, lease £17.15./annum).
1785, MAY 24	Robert Adam and wife Ann lease to Robert Evans, 52'x23½' (Alex. H:1).
1785, JUN 27?	John Lomax and wife Rachel to John Wise for £700, same part of Lot 21 as conveyed to them by Richard Conway on 1 JUL 1782 (FDB Q:195).
1786, MAR 22	Robert Adam and wife Ann lease to Ann McMachen, 23'x48' (FDB Q:262, deed appears to include part of Lot 20).
1786, APR 2	Robert Adam and wife Ann to Henry Gardner, 52'x23'6" (see Alex. C:194).
1786, APR 27	Robert Adam and wife Ann lease to James Myler, 84'x23'6" of Lot 21 (FDB Q:303, this deed appears to include part of Lot 20).
1786, JUL 21	James Myler and wife Elizabeth to William Sydebotham, of Bladensburg, Prince Georges Co., Md., mortgage to secure Myler's paying 10,000 lbs. tobacco, 84'x23'6" (Alex. B:403).
1787, JAN 26	Henry Gardner mortgage to John Reynolds and Alexander Smith, for 12 months (Alex. C:194).
1794, JAN 8	James Irvin, guardian of John Adam, Robert Adam, Jane Adam, orphans of Robert Adam, dec., lease to Robert Brockett, 52'x23'6" for 12 years, at £4.10.0 per year (Alex. E:188).
1794, MAR 1	Robert Evans and wife Drusilla, and Thomas White and wife Betty, to Lemuel Bent, 52'x23½' (Alex. H:1).
1794, JUN 8	James Irvin, guardian, etc. to James McHenry, lease 52'x23'6" with same terms as lease to Brockett (Alex. E:184).
1794, SEP 12/29	John Wise to Thomas West, 72'2"x71', part of Lot 21, lease £19.15/annum (see Alex. F:152, 290).
1794, SEP 13	Thomas West to Henry McCue, for £110/annum, same parcel with same rent (Alex. F:152).
1795, MAR 6	James Irvin, as guardian of John, Robert, and Jane Adam, orphans of Robert Adam, dec., lease to William Hodgson, for 7 years at £60 in quarterly payments, "all that Pier lying upon the south side of Princess Street... which was framed and finished by the said Robert Adam in his lifetime and commonly known by the name of Adam's Pier...and also the Warehouse thereupon erected..." (Alex. F:311).
1795, SEP 18	James Irvin, guardian, etc., lease to Robert Brockett, 92'x48' and 23'x52' and 84'x70'6", for 10 years at £24.7.6 annually; parcels devised by Robert Adam to his four children John, Robert, Jane and Mary (Mary now the wife of Daniel Barry) (Alex. F:379).

1796, AUG 27	Lemuel and Betsey Bent to Thomas Patten, for £130, 52'x23½' (Alex. H:1).
1798, SEP 17	John Harper gives deposition in suit of Thomas West versus Richard Conway, concerning common tides high water mark on Lot 20, and old warehouse said to have belonged to Thomas Kirkpatrick (Record of Surveys, 1742-1856:212).
1799, OCT 10	James Irvin, guardian, etc., and James Irvin and John Adam, trustees of Daniel Barry for Daniel's wife, Mary Barry, to Thomas White, recently of Alexandria, but now of the City of Baltimore, Md., for 7 years from 25 DEC 1798, paying quarterly $15 silver to Adam children's guardian and $5 silver to Daniel Barry's trustees, 23'6"x84' (Alex. M:202).

Note for Figure 2:

The plat on the following page was prepared for a suit in Chancery of Thomas West, plaintiff, against Richard Conway, defendant. The focus of the dispute was the west and south property boundaries of Lot 20 as they affected the wharves of West and Conway. Also delineated by points marked "C," "D," "F," and "G" is an unfinished wharf.

Structures and items of interest are identified on the plat:
1. store and brick warehouse on Conway's wharf.
2. warehouse of stone and brick on Conway's wharf.
3. an old house *said to be Thomas Kirkpatrick's old warehouse*, about 20 feet in length.
4. an old house that the middle was at about the common tide high water mark.

The common tide high water mark is indicated by the letter "I," and is shown across building number 4.

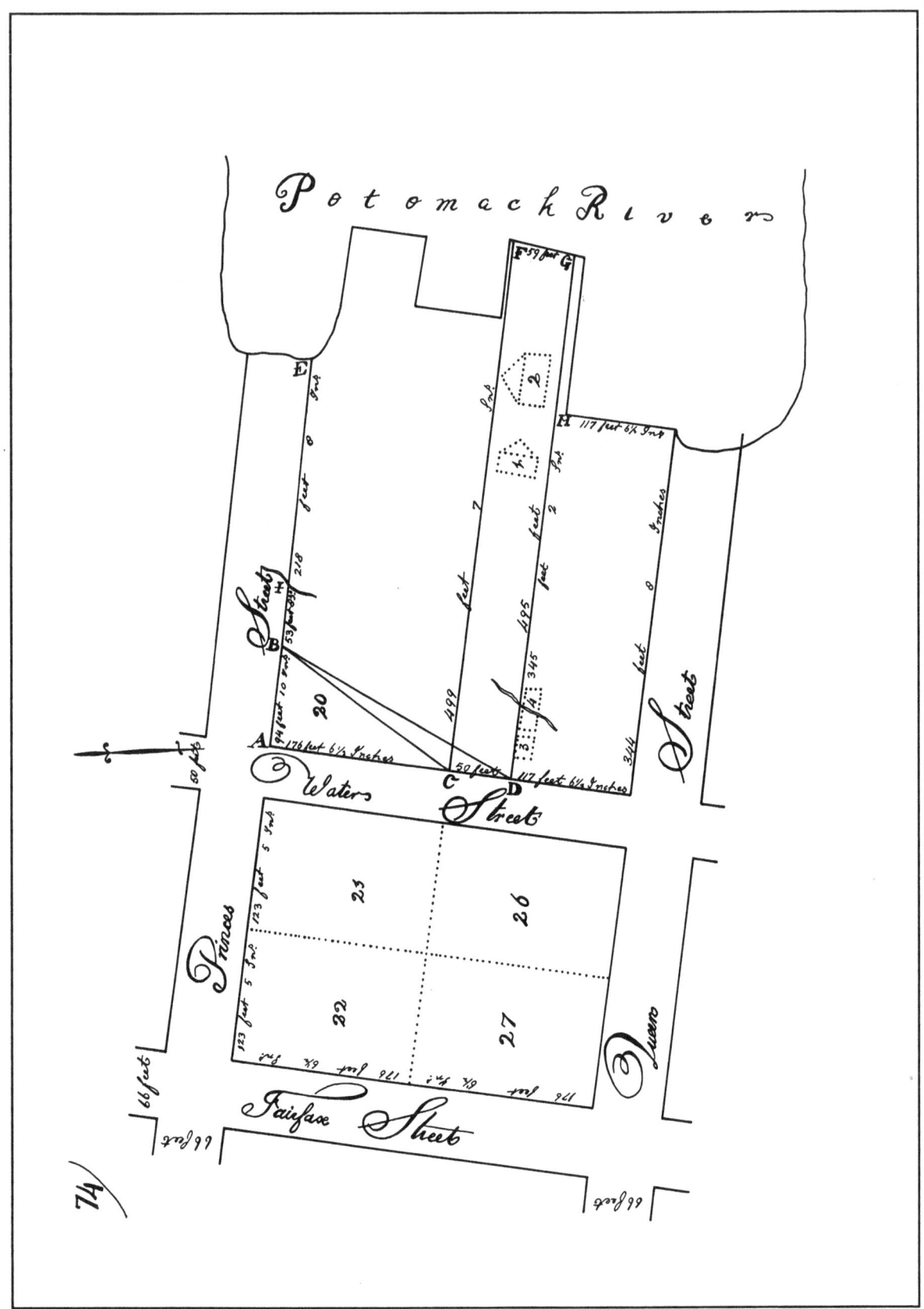

Figure 2 - Plat of Lots 20, 21, 22, 26 and 27. [Record of Surveys, p. 210 (74), Redrawn by Bill Sprouse]

LOT 22[7]
Fairfax & Princess

1753, MAR 1	Trustees to Josias Clapham, for £13.8.9 (TM:20, 39; FDB C:453 msg).
1755, APR 3	John Carlyle and John Dalton to George Johnston in trust for Mercy Chew (FDB D:81 msg).
1765, MAR 27	George Johnston to Lucas Garvey by power of attorney from Mercy Chew (see FDB L:295).
1774, MAY 17	Lucas Garvey and wife Ann, of the Island of St. Kitts in the West Indies but now in the Town of Alexandria, to Richard Conway, for £65, 56'6"x98' (FDB L:309).
1774, MAY 17	Lucas Garvey and wife Ann, to Lawrence Sandford, for £160, 34'2"x123'6" (FDB L:295).
1774, MAY 17	Lucas Garvey and wife Ann to Roger Chew, for £33, 28'3"x98' (FDB L:303)
1774, MAY 17	Lucas Garvey and wife Ann to John Lomax, for £31, 26'6"x144' (FDB L:304).
1774, MAY 20	Lucas Garvey and wife Ann, to George Fowler, merchant, for £45, 98'x28'3" (FDB L:300-1).
1774, MAY 21	Lucas Garvey and wife Ann, to Patrick Murray, for £35.10., 98'x28'3" (FDB L:305-6).
1782, JUL 1	Richard Conway and wife Mary to Roger Chew, for £14.2.6 per annum, lease 98'x56'6" of Lot 22, with purchase option, part of the northwest corner of lot purchased by Lawrence Sanford from Lucas Garvey and wife Ann (Alex. A:14).
1785, JUN 27	John Lomax and wife Rachel to John Wise, for £1200, 26½'x124' (FDB Q:192).
1785, AUG 25	Patrick Murray and wife Margaret to John Lomax, for £180, 98'x28'3" (FDB Q:25).
1790, Prior to	John Wise to Nathaniel Twining [Turning]. Wise transferred bond to Thomas West (see FDB S:250).
1793, JAN 7	Thomas West to Henry McCue, for £300, "contains the house in which McCue lives" (Alex. D:511; see Alex. F:150, this was before West had title).
1794, SEP 12	John and Elizabeth Wise to Thomas West (see Alex. F:150).
1794, SEP 13	Thomas West to Henry McCue, for £300, 26½'x124?, reiterates deed of 7 JAN 1793, but gives size and metes and bounds (Alex. F:150).
1794, SEP 29	John Wise and wife Elizabeth to Thomas West, for £500, same parcel as conveyed to Wise by Lomax (Alex. F:286).

---

[7] See also Fairfax Co. Record of Surveys (1742-1856), pp. 191, 210 (plat), for Lots 20, 21, 22, 26 and 27 (1798).

LOTS 23 and 24
Fairfax & Princess, and Princess & Royal

1749, JUL 14	Trustees to William Munday, Lot 24 (TM:2, 39).
1750, FEB 26	William Munday, joyner and carpenter, mortgage to John Dalton, merchant, to secure debt of £113.10. (FDB C:192).
1750, APR 20	Trustees to William Munday, Lot 23 (TM:12, 39).
1752, MAR 28	William Ramsay and John Pagan, Trustees, to Robert Dalton, for £17.15.9, Lots 23 and 24 (FDB C:308).
1765?	Robert Dalton to John Carlyle and John Dalton (FDB F:485 msg).
1780?	John Carlyle to Robert Lyle (FDB N:305 msg, could be part of Lot 23; see Alex. I:62, "to include the dwelling house formerly occupied by Robert Lyle").
1783, Prior to	Robert Lyle to Windle Bright (see FDB O:367, see Alex. C:160).
1783, FEB 19	Robert Lyle, merchant, to Joseph Greenway, merchant, "beginning 3' from the house now possessed by -- Bright on Lot 23," 25'x246'10", for $33-1/3 silver annual rent (FDB O:367).
1785, MAR 9	Joseph Greenway and wife Rebecca to Robert Lyle, for 5 shillings, 25'x246'10" (Alex. C:160).
1788, MAY 30	Robert Lyle, merchant, and wife Mary mortgage to Messrs. Robinson, Sanderson & Rumney, of Great Britain, merchants, 29'x84' of Lot 23, with dwelling house and use of alley (FDB R:259).
1792, NOV 12	William Herbert and John Dundas, as commissioners under decree of High Court of Chancery, to Benjamin Dulany, for £300, 29'x84' (Alex. D:461).
1792, NOV 15	Martha Lyle to Benjamin Dulany, for £80, her dower interest in above parcel (Alex. D:467).
1796, OCT 4	Robert and Elizabeth Lyle to Duncan Nevin, for £226, part of Lot 23, 31'x123'5" and part of Lot 24, 31'x123'5" (Alex. H:428, indicates same conveyed 10 MAY 1796 to Robert Lyle by Philip Marsteller and Peter Wise).
1797, MAY 5	Joseph and Elizabeth Forrest, of George Town, Md., to Jesse Simms, for £300, 29'x84' "so as to include the dwelling house formerly occupied by Robert Lyle," having been conveyed to Elizabeth by Benjamin Dulany (Alex. I:115).
1797, JUN 20	Jesse Simms to Francis Peyton, for £480, 29'x84'. Deed states Benjamin Dulany conveyed to daughter Elizabeth, later wife of Joseph Forrest. Forrest and wife to Jesse Simms (Alex. I:62).

LOT 25
Princess & Royal

1763, MAY 9	Trustees to Hugh West, for £5 (TM:52).
1767, JUN 18	Hugh West's will is probated. Will states lots to be sold by executors "whenever they shall think it fit..." (FWB C:7).

LOT 26
Water St. & Queen

1749, JUL 13	Trustees to Allan Macrae (TM:1).
1752, MAR 28	William Ramsay and John Pagan, Trustees, to Allan Macrae of Prince William Co., for £23.13. (FDB C:301). Macrae sold to William Black, but made no conveyance. Title remained with John McCrea (see Alex. B:357).
1770, MAR 17	Trustees lease to John and Thomas Kirkpatrick for 99 years.[8] Upon the death of John, lease became vested in Thomas. Thomas devised to his sisters Elizabeth Cutler, Katharine Coltart and Henrietta Kirkpatrick who appointed William Wilson and Roger Coltart their agents. The residue of the 99-year lease was purchased by William Hepburn who conveyed to Richard Conway (see FDB Z:352).
1773, MAY 4/5	William Black, merchant, to Thomas Kirkpatrick, half of Lot 26 (see Alex. B:357).
1786, SEP 20	John McCrea, of Prince William Co., son and heir-at-law of Allan McCrea, Prince William Co., merchant, dec. to Thomas Kirkpatrick's executors[9] (Alex. B:357, lot <u>west</u> of Water Street).
1791, SEP 20	Thomas West to Richard Conway (see Alex. H:437).
1792, NOV 16	(FDB Z:352, lot <u>east</u> of Water Street).
1793, AUG 20	Richard and Mary Condon [Conway] to James Young, lease for $40, 70'x40' (Alex. E:377).
1796, SEP 27	William Wilson and Roger Coltart as agents for Elizabeth Kirkpatrick Cutler, Katharine Kirkpatrick Coltart and Henrietta Kirkpatrick to William Hepburn, for £280 all the water property fronting Lot 26, including the unexpired 99-year lease (see Alex. H:437, 443).
1796, SEP 30	William Hepburn to William Wilson and Roger Coltart, 2/3 of property conveyed to Hepburn on 27 SEP (see Alex. H:437).
1796, NOV 16	Richard and Mary Conway to William Wilson, William Hepburn and Roger Coltart, part of that slip of ground adjoining the east side of Water Street and south side of Lot 20. This deed states "conveyed to Conway by Thomas West, Sept. 20, 1791." This parcel 67' distance to the River for 5 shillings (Alex. H:157).
1797, APR 12	Roger Coltart to John Dundas, half of what Hepburn sold to Wilson and Coltart, being 1/3 of what Wilson and Coltart, as agents for Kirkpatrick's heirs, sold to Hepburn, plus 1/3 of property sold by Conway to Wilson, Coltart and Hepburn (Alex. H:437). Alan McRea bought Lot 26 on the west side of Water Street, passed to son John who conveyed to Thomas Kirkpatrick's heirs and trustees, 20 SEP 1786, the water rights to Lot 26 as declared by the Trustees prior to sale on 12 SEP 1795 (see Alex. H:443).

---

[8] John and Thomas Kirkpatrick applied to the Trustees of Alexandria to build a warehouse on the east side of Water Street opposite Lot 26 and to the north side of Queen Street. Approved for 99 years beginning 25 DEC 1768 (TM:57).

[9] Alexander Henderson, Robert Adam, Robert McCrea, John Muir, William Hunter, Jr., John Gibson, all of Fairfax Co., all devisees and executors of the Last Will and Testament of Thomas Kirkpatrick, late of the Town of Alexandria, merchant, deceased.

(See also Alex. M:171, 178, 184, 473; N:43, 109; Record of Surveys: 191, 219).

LOT 27
Fairfax & Queen

1749, SEP 20	John Carlyle and Garrard Alexander, Trustees, to John Alexander of Stafford Co., for £8.12. (FDB B:499).
1753, by AUG	John Alexander and wife Frances to Nathaniel Smith (see FDB C:635, 768).
1753, AUG 23	Nathaniel Smith[10] to Joseph Chew, inn holder, for £144 (see FDB C:635; FDB C:768, another deed from Smith to Chew, 23 MAR 1754).
1753, SEP 1	Joseph Chew, inn holder, and wife Mercy, to William Digges, of Prince Georges Co., Md., in trust for Mercy (FDB C:635-6).
1756, DEC 9	Joseph Chew, inn holder, to John Muir, Robert Adams, John Dalton, merchants, Andrew Symmer, Thomas Mure [Muir], of Md., merchants, and William Gilpin and Thomas Thomson, mariners, for £200 (FDB D:447).
1760, FEB 5	John Dalton, John Muir and Robert Adam, merchants, to George Johnston, attorney at law, for £85 (FDB D:673).

(See also Record of Surveys, 1742-1856:191, 210).

LOT 28
Fairfax & Queen
(See also Lot 29)

1750, APR 20	Trustees to Anthony Ramsay, for £6.19.9 (TM:12, 39).
1752, MAR 28	William Ramsay and John Pagan, Trustees, to Nathaniel Smith, for £6.19.9 (FDB C:307).
1755, APR 11	Nathaniel Smith advertises for sale two lots with house and outhouses (*Virginia Gazette*, p. 3).
1757, MAR 2	Nathaniel Smith, inn keeper, to John Carlyle and John Dalton, merchants, for £150 (FDB D:444).
1761, JAN 8	John Carlyle and John Dalton, merchants, sell Lots 28 and 29 to Nathan Hughes, inn holder, for £262.10., called the "Long Ordinary" (FDB D:794).
1761, JAN 9	Nathan Hughes, inn holder, and Rachel his wife, to John Carlyle and John Dalton, Lots 28 and 29 for £266 (FDB D:796).
1768, APR 17	John Carlyle and John Dalton to Joseph Beeler, Lots 28 and 29 (FDB H:22 msg; recited in FDB K:65).
1771	Joseph Beeler to Christopher Beeler (FDB J:285 msg; recited in FDB K:65).
1772, JAN 17	Christopher Beeler and wife Henrietta Wilhelmina to John Graham of Chester Co., Pa., for £225, part of Lots 28 and 29, 167'2"x45'8" (FDB K:65).

---

[10] Maryland Gazette, 3 APR 1755, Nathaniel Smith, "going out as Sutler to the Camp" [probably Wills' Creek], has houses and lots for sale in Alexandria. Apply to Mr. Carlyle or Mr. Dalton.

1772, JUL 8	Christopher Beeler and wife Henrietta Wilhelmina to Joel Cooper[11], for £90, parts of Lots 28 and 29, 164'x63' (FDB K:252).
1772, JUL 23	Christopher Beeler and wife Henrietta Wilhelmina to Andrew Wales, for £150, parts of Lots 28 and 29 (FDB K:245, 247).
1785	John Tarbuck, alias Scott, mariner, to William Patterson, of Beaufort Co., N.C., £80 for part of lot "known by the name of the Long Ordinary" (Alex. C:199).
1785, MAR 10	Andrew Wales to Hugh McCaughen, 25'x167'2" with use of an alley 4'x100', for £300. McCaughen failed to complete payments; property sold 17 SEP 1794 to Thomas White for £200.5. (see Alex. E:409).
1785, JUL 29	Andrew and Margaret Wailes [Wales] to Robert Lyle, for £100, part of Lots 28 and 29, 86'8"x22' (Alex. B:136; see B:150).
1786, MAY 11	Robert Lyle, Sr. and wife Martha to Robert Lyle, Jr., part of Lots 28 and 29 (Alex. B:332).
1787, MAR 7	John Graham to daughter Mary Graham, parts of Lots 28 and 29, 123½'x45'8" (FDB R:213).
1794, SEP 19	Andrew Wales and wife Margaret to Thomas White, for £200.5., convey the former McCaughen property to Thomas White (Alex. E:409).
1795, SEP 28	Andrew Wales and wife Margaret to Andrew Fleming for £120, part of Lots 28 and 29 (Alex. G:2).
1796, JAN 30	Samuel Cooper and wife Elizabeth to John Limrick, for £93, "all that undivided fourth of land" 164'x63', "part of three [sic] Lotts known [as] the Long Ordinary Lotts" (Alex. G:1).
1797, SEP 27	John and Susannah Limrick to William Reynolds, for £93, fourth part of Lots 28 and 29, "generally called and known by the name of the long ordinary Lotts" (Alex. I:432).
1798, MAY 18	James and Elizabeth Gullatt to William Reynolds, for £400, Elizabeth's dividend (Alex. K:413).

LOT 29
Royal & Queen
(See also Lot 28)

1750, APR 20	William Ramsay and John Pagan, Trustees, to Nathaniel Smith, for £6.9. (TM:12; FDB C:307, deed dated 28 MAR 1752).
1755, APR 11	Nathaniel Smith advertises for sale two lots with house and outhouses (*Virginia Gazette*, p. 3).
1757, MAR 2	Nathaniel Smith, inn keeper, to John Carlyle and John Dalton, merchants and partners, for £150 (FDB D:446).
1761, JAN 8	John Carlyle and John Dalton, merchants, to Nathan Hughes, inn holder, for

---

[11] Alex. K:413, dated 18 MAY 1798, indicates the late Joel Cooper of Alexandria, in his will of 6 MAR 1786, left his estate to wife Elizabeth until son Samuel reached 21 (when the estate would be equally divided among the widow, and the children: Ann, Samuel, Sarah, and Elizabeth Cooper)... and Joel owned, among other things... part of three lots known by the name of the long ordinary lots... Elizabeth the wife having since died, the property goes to the children... daughter Elizabeth now married to James Gullatt...

Alexandria, Virginia Town Lots, 1749-1801

	£262.10., Lots 28 and 29 called the "long ordinary" (FDB D:794).
1761, JAN 9	Nathan Hughes, inn holder, and Rachel his wife, mortgage to John Carlyle and John Dalton, Lots 28 and 29, for £266 (FDB D:796).
1768, APR 17	Hughes evidently defaulted. Carlyle and Dalton conveyed Lots 28 and 29 to Joseph Beeler (see FDB K:65).
1772	See also Lot 28 for transactions to Beeler, Wales, Graham and Cooper.
1772, JUL 23	Christopher Beeler and Henrietta Wilhelmina his wife to William Shaw for £40, 42'x176' (FDB K:74).
1785, MAY 18	Division of lot among William Shaw's heirs (FDB Q:198).
1785, JUL 29	Andrew and Margaret Wales to Robert Lyle, part of Lots 28 and 29, 86'8"x22', for £100 (Alex. B:136; see B:150).
1786, MAY 11	Robert Lyle, Sr. and wife Martha to Robert Lyle, Jr., part of Lots 28 and 29 (Alex. B:332).
1787, MAR 7	John Graham to daughter Mary Graham, parts of Lots 28 and 29, 123½'x45'8" (FDB R:213).
1794, OCT 23	Eleanor Shaw and William Shaw her son to Jacob Fortney, for £141, part of Lot 29, 42'x176', same parcel sold by Christopher Beeler to William Shaw on 23 JUL 1772 (Alex. E:431).

362.

On Fairfax Street 176 feet 7 inches – 10 feet next Dalton's Lott, to be taken of for an Alley.

Dd. McHerbert

N° 1 55 feet 6 in. front by 90 deep WW	N° 2 55 feet 6 in. front by 90 deep IP	N° 3 Brick Stone WH
N° 22 IP	N° 4 22.4	WH
N° 23 WW	N° 5 22.4	WH
N° 24 IP	N° 6 22.4	IP
N° 9 WH	N° 8 IP.	N° 7 WW

10 feet Alley to be left on the back Wilson & Potts's Lott
10 feet Alley to be left in Mr. Dalton's Lott
On Queen Street 246 feet 10 inches to Water Street

On Water Street 176 feet 7 inches

N° 10 55 feet 6 inches front by 100 W.W.	N° 11 55 feet 6 inches front by 100 IP	N° 12 55 feet 6 inches front by 100 WH
N° 25 WW	N° 13 33 feet 4 in. WH	
N° 26 WH	N° 14 33 feet 4 in. WW	
N° 27 WH	N° 15 33 feet 4 IP	
N° 18 WW	N° 17 WH	N° 16 IP

10 feet Alley continued
Queen Street continued 200 feet to Union Street

Union Street

N° 19 56 feet 7 inches front IP	N° 20 60 feet front WH	N° 21 50 feet front WW

10 feet Alley continued
Queen Creek

Potomack River

~ We the Subscribers Joint Tenants of the Ground divided according to the above plott, do hereby acknowledge that in making partition of the same, the different Allottments marked with the Initial Letters of our Names are the parts, or divisions set apart for each of Us,—and that We hereby agree to the same each relinquishing to the others all Claim to any other part. Given under our hands & Seals, this 6th day of May 1799.

Wm Wilson (Seal)

Wm Herbert (Seal)

John Potts (Seal)

Sealed and Executed in presence of

Figure 3 - Plat of Lots 31 and 32. [Alexandria Hustings Court Deeds, Bk. L, p. 362]

LOT 30
Royal & Queen

1771, NOV 6	Trustees to Alexander Black, for £16.3. (TM:68; FDB J:186 msg).
1774, NOV 21	Sarah Black posts bond of £1000 as administratrix of Alexander Black (Fairfax Bond Book, 1752-1782:141).

LOT 31
Fairfax & Queen

1749, SEP 20	William Ramsay and John Carlyle, Trustees, to Garrard Alexander, for £20.19.4 (FDB B:496).
1760, AUG 9	In his will, Gerrard Alexander devised to his wife Mary for her life, Lots 31 and 32 (FWB B:327, probated 16 SEP 1760).
1767, MAR 11	Mary Alexander, widow, and son Philip with wife Catharine, lease and release to John Glassford and Archibald Henderson, merchants, of Glasgow, Lots 31 and 32 (FDB G:231; see Alex. O:76).
1776, OCT 1	John Glassford and Archibald Henderson of the City of Glasgow, Scotland, to John Gibson, of Colchester, merchant, for £1750, Lots 31 and 32 (FDB M:266).
1776, OCT 3	John Gibson, Town of Colchester, merchant, to Alexander Henderson, same place, merchant, for £1750, Lots 31 and 32 (FDB M:269).
1778, JAN 1	Alexander Henderson to William Herbert (see Alex. A:95).
1778, FEB 18	William Herbert and wife Sarah to Thomas May (see Alex. A:95).
1783, NOV 10	Thomas and Sarah May, of Cecil Co., Md., ironmaster, to William Herbert, merchant, for £1300 sell 1/3 interest in the land and in the improvements of the two-lot parcel (Alex. A:95).
1788, APR 14	Thomas[12] and Sarah May, of Wilmington, Del., to John Potts, Jr. of Montgomery Co. Pa., for £1250 of Pa. convey one third [interest] in the two lots (Alex. C:232).
1796, MAR 29	Articles of agreement between William Wilson, William Herbert, John Potts and Jonah Thompson, each party will contribute a 10' strip along their common dividing line to make one alley 20' wide (Alex. L:75).
1796, MAR 31	Partition of Lots 31 and 32, between William Wilson, William Herbert and John Potts as tenants in common (Alex. L:351, plat at p. 362).
1799, MAY 1	John Potts, merchant, and wife Elizabeth deed of trust to Ludwell Lee to secure payment of debts to the Bank of Alexandria (Alex. M:261).
1799, AUG 21	William Wilson deed of trust to James Keith for payment of debts to the Bank of Alexandria, including parts of Lots 31 and 32 (Alex. M:178).

---

[12] Alex. O:76, dated 9 FEB 1795, indicates Thomas May's last will and testament, dated 8 NOV 1791, was proved in Register's office of Newcastle, Del., on 29 FEB 1792.

LOT 32
Fairfax & Queen
(See also Lot 31)

1749, SEP 20	William Ramsay and John Carlyle, trustees, to Garrard Alexander, for £21.10 (FDB B:495).
1795, FEB 9	John Brooke, of Montgomery Co., Pa., and Robert May, of Chester Co., Pa., trustees and executors of Thomas May, of Wilmington, Del.,[13] to William Wilson, merchant, May's remaining 1/3 share of Lots 31 and 32 vested in trustees (Alex. O:76).
1795, NOV 16	William Herbert and wife Sarah to Leven Powell, for £500, 84'x55'6" part of Lot 32 (Alex. F:524, one reference in this deed is to Leven Powell, Jr.; see Alex. I:216).
1796, SEP 13	William and Sarah Herbert to Leven Powell, Jr., for £500, 1/2 of Lot 32, 84'x55'6" (Alex. I:312).
1797, JUL 4	William and Sarah Herbert to Leven Powell, for £250, part Lot 32 (Alex. I:216).
1796, MAR 29	See Lot 31 for articles of agreement this date (Alex. L:75).
1796, MAR 31	See Lot 31 for tripartite deed of partition this date (Alex. L:351, plat at p. 362).
1798, OCT 26	William Wilson lease to Alexander Latimer, beginning 1 MAY 1799 at $60 (silver) per annum (Alex. L:276).
1799, JAN 1	John and Elizabeth Potts, merchant, to James Carolan, carpenter, for £350 (Alex. L:333).
1799, MAY 1	John Potts, merchant, and wife Elizabeth deed of trust to Ludwell Lee, Gent., to secure payment of debts to the Bank of Alexandria (Alex. M:261).
1799, MAY 7	Andrew Ramsay and wife Catharine, with William Ramsay, deed of trust to Ludwell Lee, Esq., of "Shuter's Hill" (Alex. M:79).
1799, AUG 21	William Wilson deed of trust to James Keith for payment of debts to the Bank of Alexandria, including parts of Lots 31 and 32 (Alex. M:178).

LOT 33
Fairfax & Queen

1749, SEP 20	Garrard Alexander and Hugh West, Trustees, to Joseph Skelton, for £8.12. (FDB C:23).
1764, SEP 20	John Carlyle and John Dalton to John Semple (see FDB K:137).
1771, JUN 13	James Lawson says title may not be clear (*Virginia Gazette*, p. 3).
1772, OCT 6	John Semple, late of Charles Co., Md. but now of Prince William Co., merchant and ironmaster, and James Lawson, late of the city of Glasgow, Scotland, but now of Charles Co., Md., merchant, to Colin Dunlop & Son & Co., of Glasgow, 1/2 of Lot 33, for £168.10. (FDB K:137).
1772, OCT 6	John Semple, of Prince William Co. and James Lawson, at present of

---

[13] The Last Will and Testament of Thomas May, dated 8 NOV 1791, probated in the Register's Office in New Castle, Del. on 29 FEB 1792.

	Charles Co. Md, merchant, to Robert Adam, Matthew Campbell and James Adam, merchants and partners in trade, one half of Lot 33 for £300 (FDB K:142).
1777, APR 18	Colin Dunlop and James his son, City of Glasgow, James Wilson and James his son, and Cumberland Wilson, of Kilmarnock, Scotland, merchants, to John Gibson, Town of Colchester, merchant, one half of Lot 33 for £500 (FDB M:319).
1780, OCT 19	Hector Ross, Esq., escheator for Fairfax Co. to William Hunter, Jr., one half of Lot 33, formerly belonging to Colin Dunlop & Co., escheated as British property (see FDB R:196).
1780, AUG 28	Patent describes the escheated half as bounded on the north by Robert Adam's part of Lot 33 (Patents E:457).
1785, JAN 19	William Hunter, Jr. to William Wilson, 123'5"x39'1-3/4" for £650 (Alex. A:169).
1787, DEC 14	William Wilson to John Peter of Georgetown, Montgomery Co., Md., part of Lot 33 formerly belonging to Colin Dunlop & Co., 123'5"x39'1-3/4" (FDB R:196).
1788, MAY 12	Robert Adam and wife Ann mortgage to John Cooke, of Stafford Co., part of Lot 33 whereon his storehouse sat "now shut up," 44'x60' (FDB R:94).
1789, APR 20	John Peter and wife Ruth to William Wilson, for £650, same piece as above conveyed by Willson to Peter (FDB R:403, recites that on this half of Lot 33, there are two wooden houses and an old stable).
1789, AUG 27	William Hunter, Jr. to Robert Townshend Hooe[14], three parcels of Lots 33 and 151 (Alex. D:99).
1797, JUL 1	James Irvin, guardian of John, Robert and Jane Adam, orphans and devisees of the late Robert Adam, to Thomas Simms, lease of a tenement lately occupied by William Semple, adjoining house Irvin demised to Elizabeth Semple, for 8 years from 1 JUL 1797 for £21/annum in quarterly payments beginning 1 OCT 1797 (Alex. L:11).
1798, JAN 1	James Irvin, guardian, etc., and Daniel and Mary Barry (she a daughter/devisee of the late Robert Adam), to John Green, lease for 7 years, quarterly payments of £26/annum to James Irvin and £19.10./annum to Daniel and Mary Barry (Alex. I:440, and when this lease ends Green may within 1 month remove the "framed dwelling house erected thereupon by William Semple").
1799, FEB 28	William Wilson to Charles Jones, lease for 7 years from 1 APR 1799, [annual] payments of £40 to begin on 1 APR 1800 (Alex. L:294).

---

[14] <u>Maryland Gazette</u>, 29 MAR 1809, Robert Townshend Hooe, departed this life at Alexandria, on Thurs. evening, 16th inst., in his 66th year. At an early period of his life, he was selected as a member of the Maryland Convention. In 1776 he received from the Convention the appointment of Lieutenant Colonel in the 12th Battalion.

LOT 34
Royal & Queen

1750, APR 20	Trustees to Jonathan Ray [Rae] (TM:12).
1752, AUG 21	George William Fairfax and William Ramsay, Trustees, to Daniel McCarty, for £6.9. (FDB C:357).
1752, MAR 25	Jonathan Rae, joiner, to William Ramsay, for £17.4. by bill of sale (TM:71; FDB K:340).
1756, DEC 4	William Ramsay, merchant, and wife Anne, to Charles Green, clerk, and Daniel McCarty, lease for Lots 34, 46 and 47 (FDB D:380).
1757, JUL 21	William Ramsay, and Anne his wife, mortgage to John Dixon, of County of Cumberland in the Kingdom of England, merchant, for £810.7., parcel he purchased of Henry Awbrey, Frances Awbrey and Thomas Awbrey... 9 MAR 1749... on Four Mile Run adjoining lands of William Strutfield... containing 1261 acres, also Lots 34, 40, 46 and 47 in the Town of Alexandria (FDB D:450).
1773, MAY 15	Harry Piper and John Muir, Trustees, acknowledge conveyance and make deed to William Ramsay (FDB K:340).
1774, MAY 26	William Ramsay to John Dixon of Whitehaven. Ramsay defaulted on note. Deeded to Dixon one half of Lot 34 (FDB L:320).
1774, MAY 27	John Dixon to William Shaw, one half of Lot 34 (FDB L:326 msg, but loose copy filed in Drawer X in Circuit Court Archives).
1774, DEC 19	Will of William Shaw, probated 19 JAN 1775, devises his part of lot to his son Thomas Shaw and two daughters Isabel and Elizabeth Shaw, but first to his wife Eleanor for her life (FWB C:223).
1785, JAN 1	William Ramsay and wife Ann rent to Robert Harle, 123'5"x24' for £16/annum (FDB P:219).
1785, JAN 3	Daniel McCarty to William Ramsay, unrecorded deed for "the lot on which the widow Shaw now lives" (Drawer X, Circuit Court Archives).
1785, JAN 7	William Ramsay's will[15], probated 20 APR 1785, states that 123'5"x24' of Lot 34 to be sold by his executors (FWB E:69).
1785, MAY 18	Division among heirs of William Shaw's half of Lot 34 (FDB Q:198).
1785, MAY 20	Isabel [Shaw] Elton, daughter of William Shaw, to McKinsey Tallbutt (see Alex. C:93).
1787, MAY 16	John Steel, renter of Eleanor Shaw, at £6, mortgage to William Hunter, Jr., Esq. (Alex. C:147).
1787, JUL 20	McKinsey Talbutt to Jesse Taylor, for £100, 88'3½"x20' (Alex. C:93).
1795, MAR 20	William and Dennis Ramsay, Robert Allison and Michael Madden, executors of William Ramsay, dec., to Thomas Richards (Alex. F:240).
1795, JUN 23	Thomas Richards and wife Ann to John Turpin Brooks, for £100, 123'5"x24'3" (Alex. F:240).
1796, 17 OCT	Dennis and Jane Ramsay to James McGuire, for £165, 32'x123'5" (Alex. H:241).

---

[15] Virginia Journal and Alexandria Advertiser, 17 FEB 1785, William Ramsay, Esq., of Alexandria, died on 10 Feb. in the 69th year of his age; one of the first inhabitants of Alexandria, buried in the Episcopal Churchyard on 12 Feb.

1797, APR 24	Dennis Ramsay and wife Jane Allen to John Turpin Brookes, for $1, 123'5"x2' (Alex. I:95).
1797, MAY 16	John Steel, renter of Eleanor Shaw at £6, mortgages to William Hunter, Jr., Esq. (Alex. C:147).
1799, MAY 17	John Turpin Brooks to Charles Jones, lease for $66.66 (silver) in half-yearly payments, first due 1 DEC 1799 (Alex. L:471).

LOT 35
Royal & Queen

1753, MAR 1	Trustees to James Connell, for £5.7.6 (TM:20, 39; FDB C:460 msg).
1777, MAY 17	James Connell's will probated 16 JUN 1777 devises "my house and tenements... to John Sutton, watchmaker in Carlyle..." (FWB D:9).
1789, OCT 12	John Sutton mortgage to son John Davison Sutton (commonly called John Sutton, Junr.), for £100, 130'x166' of Lots 35 and 121. John Sutton had conveyed in 1778 to his mother Ann Sutton and children in trust (FDB S:146).
1790, MAY 4	John Sutton to John Mandeville, part of Lot 35, 42'6"x112' (FDB S:240).
1790, JUL 13	John Sutton to William Bird, in trust part of Lots 35 and 121, 130'x166' (FDB S:520).
1790, JUL 16	John Sutton to John Mandeville, in trust part of Lots 35 and 121, 130'x166' (FDB S:523).
1793, FEB 11	John Mandeville to Jonathan Mandeville, part of Lots 35 and 121, 130'x166' (FDB W:117).
1798, FEB 19	John Sutton to John Davison Sutton, for 5 shillings, parcel in trust to be disposed of and the proceeds thereof applied to debts listed (Alex. K:603).

LOT 36
Cameron & Water St.

1749, SEP 20	William Ramsay and John Carlyle, Trustees, to John Dalton, for £20.8.6 (FDB B:493).
1777, MAR 9	John Dalton's will probated 21 JUL 1777 devises to daughter Catharine part of Lots 36 and 37, "...ten feet beyond the house wherein John Page now lives" (FWB D:17).
1790, SEP 14	Thomas West to William Bird, for £16.4. annual rent, 60'x246'10" (FDB W:341).
1790, DEC 13	William Bird and wife Catharine [Dalton] to Thomas West, for £328, part of Lots 36 and 37, 60'x246'10" (FDB U:416).
1793, APR 24	William and Catharine [Dalton] Bird to Jonah Thompson and David Finley as tenants in common, for £1500, parts of Lots 36 and 37, "...reserving unto Lanty Crowe the house demised unto him" (Alex. E:63).
1793, AUG 22	Thomas West to William Hepburn and John Dundas, for £145.16., the rent on 60'x246'10", paid to West by Bird (FDB W:349).
1795, JUL 1	Amelia Finley, of Middlesex Co., Great Britain, mother and heir of David

Finley[16] (late of Alexandria) to Jonah Thompson (in place of C.R. Scott) for £1500.12., David's half of the joint holding (Alex. F:316).

(See also Alex. L:75).

LOT 37
Cameron & Fairfax
(See also Lot 36)

1749, SEP 20	William Ramsay and John Carlyle, Trustees, to John Dalton, for £17.4. (FDB B:494).
1777, MAR 9	John Dalton's will probated 21 JUL 1777 devises to daughter Jenny part of Lot 37 (FWB D:17).
1784, SEP 24	Thomas Herbert and wife Jenny [Dalton] to John Casey, of Prince Georges Co., Md. for £260, 28'x62' (FDB P:86).
1793, JUN 20	Thomas and Jane [Dalton] Herbert mortgage to John Casey, of Prince Georges Co., Md., 60'x46'4" (Alex. E:207).
1793, JUN 20	John Casey, of Prince Georges Co., Md. to Thomas Herbert, for £460, 28'x60' (Alex. E:474).

(See also Alex. L:75).

LOT 38
Cameron & Fairfax
(See also Lot 39)

1749, SEP 20	John Carlyle and Hugh West, trustees, to Henry Salkeld, for £12.7.3 (FDB B:504).
1771?	Henry Salkeld to Thomas Carson & James Muir (FDB J:305 msg; Patents E:457, recites Carson & Muir owned part of this lot).
[no date]	Henry Salkeld to David Gordon, Lot 4 of Salkeld's Division of Lots 38 and 39 (Alex. E:292).
1772, OCT 17	Thomas Carson's will probated 21 JUN 1773 provides for sale of his share of Lot 38 (FWB C:153). Carson's brother John, of Kirkenbright, Co. Galloway, Scotland, appoints agents to act for him when executors refused to qualify (FDB L:134).
c.1780	Robert Adam, executor of James Muir, merchant, dec., offered at auction to William Herbert, merchant, two parcels of Carson and Muir's part of Lot 38 (see Alex. E:2).
1783, FEB 25	Robert Adam as James Muir's executor to William Ramsay, 23'x123'5" (FDB N:656 msg; see FDB P:256; see FDB S:392).
1783, JUL 29	Robert Adam as James Muir's executor to William Herbert (Alex. C:201).

---

[16] The Columbian Mirror and Alexandria Gazette, 9 JUN 1795, David Finlay [Finley], deceased; James Patton, attorney in fact for Amelia Finlay, heir at law of David Finlay, will sell all of his real property in Alexandria.

Alexandria, Virginia Town Lots, 1749-1801

1783, JUL 30	William and Sarah Herbert to Robert Adam, for £250, 58'10-1/3"x41'1-1/3" (Alex. C:201).
1783, AUG 1	Robert Adam and wife Anne to John Hendricks, for annual rent of 4 oz. 13 pennyweight and 18 grains of gold, 58'10-1/3"x41'1-1/3" (FDB Q:80).
1784, MAR 1	"...that part of Lot 38 which [William] Duvall purchased of Adam Lynn..." (see Alex. A:38).
1784, MAR 1	William Ramsay assigns rent of £20 from [William] Duvall to Robert Allison and Dennis Ramsay in trust for Ann Ramsay (Alex. A:42).
1784, DEC 20	William Ramsay and wife Ann to John Allison, for £299, 23'x123'5", part sold to Ramsay by Robert Adam, executor of James Muir, dec., 25 FEB 1783 (FDB P:256).
1785, MAR 24	Ann Ramsay conveys, widow and relict of William Ramsay, Esq., dec., assigns £20 rent from William Duvall to her son Dennis Ramsay (Alex. A:194; see FDB R:446).
1787, SEP 10	John Allison to John Rumney, for £400, 123'5"x23' (Alex. C:121).
1788, JUN 13	John Rumney to William Hodgson, for £700, 23'x123'5" (Alex. C:237).
1789, JUL 20	Dennis Ramsay, gent., and wife Jane, to William Duvall, for £300, release from future rents due from Duvall to Ramsay. William Ramsay rented to Duvall part of Lot 38 for £20 annually, deed dated 1 MAR 1784 (see Alex. A:38, 42).
1790, JUN 1	William Hodgson to John Harper, for £1500, 23'x123'5" to the line of William Herbert (sold by James Muir's executor to William Ramsay who sold same to John Allison who sold to John Rumney who sold to William Hodgson) (FDB S:392).
1793, JAN 26	William and Nancy Duvall to Bank of Alexandria, for £100, 62'8"x41'1-2/3" (Alex. E:17).
1793, JUL 29	Robert Adam as James Muir's executor to William Herbert, merchant, for £570, title to two parcels bought by Herbert c.1780 (Alex. E:2).
1793, SEP 6	Deed of Henry Headley, Richmond Co., to Lawrence Hoof, recites that David Gordon's daughter Sarah inherited part of Lot 38 or 39. Sarah married George Headley. On 7 MAY 1793, Sarah and George conveyed to Henry Headley of Richmond Co. (Alex. E:292).
1793, SEP 24	William Duvall and wife Ann to William Downman, of Prince William Co., for £400, part of lot (Alex. E:238).
1794, FEB 21	William Downman, of Prince William Co., mortgage to John White, for £305, 82'x29'; at line dividing the two brick houses built by William Duvall (Alex. E:283).
1794, JUL 9	William Duvall and wife Ann, of Prince William Co., to John White, for £52.10., 82'x29' (Alex. E:287).
1794, OCT 13	William Duvall and wife Ann, of Prince William Co., to John White and Matthew Robinson, for £540, as tenants in common (Alex. F:44).
1796, JUL 19	John Harper to James Murray, for £215, 23'x123'5" (Alex. G:263).
1796, AUG 2	William and Sarah Herbert to Lanty Crowe, lease, 123'5"x35'6", for £30 annual rent (Alex. G:482).

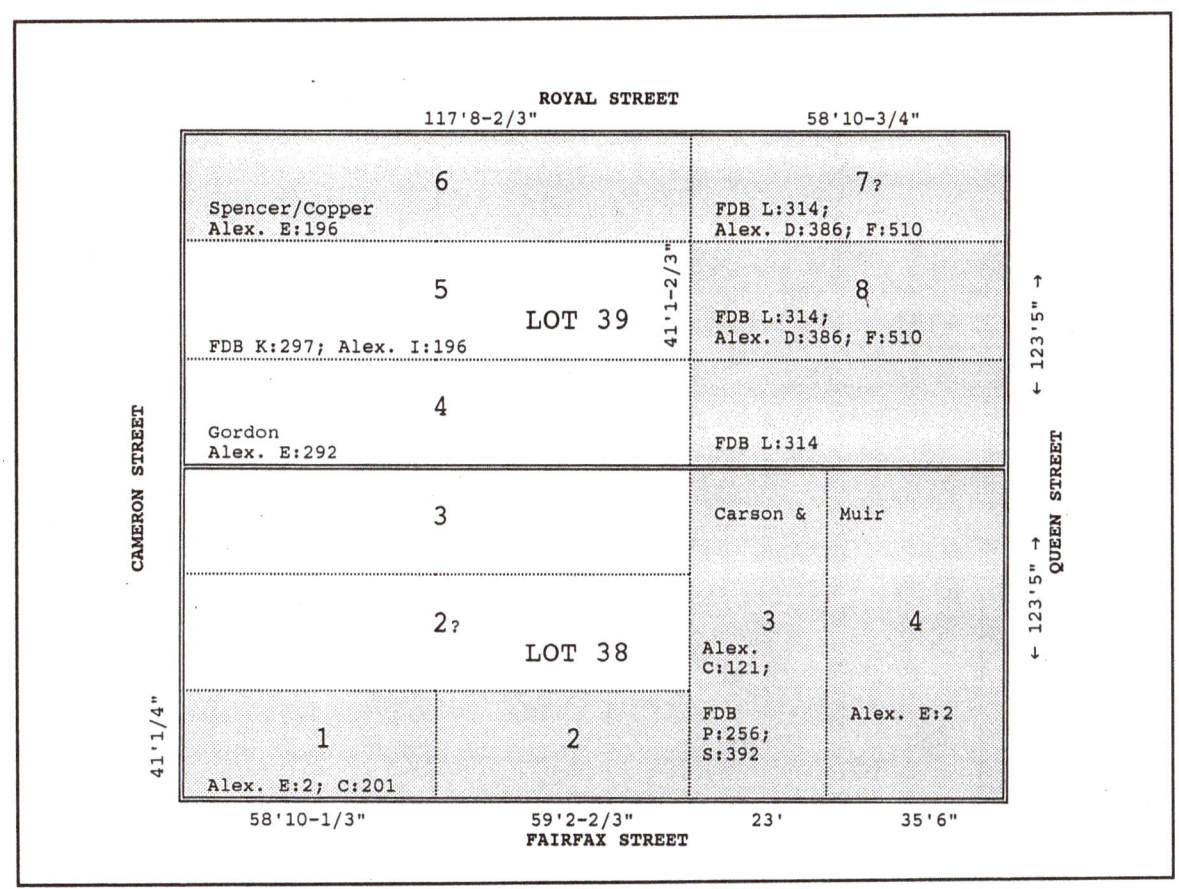

Figure 4 - Henry Salkeld's Division of Lots 38 and 39 (1760's?). [Constance K. Ring]

LOT 39
Cameron & Royal

1749, SEP 20	John Carlyle and Hugh West, trustees, to Henry Salkeld, mariner, for £12.7.3 (FDB B:505).
1771, AUG 29	Henry Salkeld to Robert Hall and Cyrus Copper, parcel 6 in Lot 38, 41'1-2/3"x117'8-2/3" (FDB J:293 msg; see FDB K:33; Alex I:196).
1771, SEP 29	Henry and Elizabeth Salkeld to William Spencer, 41'1-2/3"x117'8-2/3" (FDB J:335 msg; see FDB L:288; Alex. E:196, parcel 6?).
1771, NOV 21	William Spencer to William Smith, James Christie, Jr. and Thomas Ewing (see FDB L:288; Alex. E:196).
1772, MAY 23	Robert Hall to Cyrus Copper, merchant, for £27.15., for Hall's share of Parcel 6 of Lot 39 (FDB K:33).
1772, by SEP	Henry Salkeld to William Templeman, parcel 5 in Lot 39 (see FDB K:297).
1772, SEP 14	William Templeman, of Fredericksburg, to Henry Sheaffer, for £70, parcel 5 in Lot 39 (FDB K:297), 41'1-2/3" in front (Cyrus Copper had parcel 6; David Gordon parcel 4 of 39 (see Alex. E:292).
1774, APR 28	William Smith, James Christie, Jr., and Thomas Ewing, of Baltimore, Md., merchants, to Patrick Allison [of Baltimore], clerk, for £160 of Pa., 41'1-

	2/3"x117'8-2/3" (FDB L:288). This parcel was purchased by William Spencer from Henry and Elizabeth Salkeld, 29 SEP 1771 (FDB J:335 msg), sold by Spencer and wife Mary to Smith, Christie, Jr. & Ewing, 21 NOV 1771 (FDB J:360 msg; see Alex. E:196).
1774, MAY 16	Cyrus Copper and wife Elizabeth to Henry Stroman, of York Co., Pa., for £70, 58'10-3/4"x123'5" (FDB L:314).
1778, JUN 15	Henry and Mary Sheaffer to Frederick Henninger [parcel 5?] (see Alex. I:196).
1792, JAN 24	Henry Stroman and wife Elizabeth to Diederick Scheckel, for £96, part 123'x27'6" (Alex. D:386).
1793, NOV 21	Patrick Allison and wife Mary, of Baltimore, Md., to Jacob Fortney, for £450, 117'8-2/3"x41'1-2/3" (Alex. E:196).
1795, SEP 1	Dederick Scheckel to William Smith, for £100, 123'5"x27'6", sold by Stroman to Scheckel (Alex. F:510).
1797, JUN 6	Ann, widow of Robert Spadden, formerly widow of Frederick Henninger, dec., to nephew Thomas White, because of her natural love and affection and for 5 shillings, part of Lot 39 (Alex. I:196).

(See also Alex. L:339).

LOT 40
Cameron & Royal

1749, SEP 20	John Carlyle and Hugh West, trustees, to Harry Piper, for £6.9. (FDB B:504).
1757, JUL 21	William Ramsay mortgage to John Dixon (FDB D:450, see note for Lot 34).
1760, APR 24	Advertised for rent, the George Tavern at this location.[17]
c.1763	[Harry] Piper to William Ramsay (FDB F:142 msg).
1784, DEC 20	William Ramsay, Gent. to daughters Sarah and Amelia, 88'x123'5" (FDB P:372).
1793, MAY 20	William Ramsay, Dennis Ramsay, Robert Allison and Michael Madden, executors of William Ramsay, dec., to Thomas Richards, for £61, 24'2"x116' (FDB W:234; reiterated in Alex. G:150).
1794, JAN 21	Thomas Richards and wife Ann to Charles Cartlish, for £100, 116'x24'2" (FDB X:286).
1794, JUN 19	William Ramsay's executors to Thomas Richards, 96'8"x116' (see Alex. G:233).
1796, MAR 26	Thomas and Nancy Richards to Jesse Green, of Sussex Co., Del., for £300, 48'4"x116', half of the parcel conveyed by Wm. Ramsay's executors to Thomas Richards on 19 JUN 1794 (Alex. G:233).

---

[17] Maryland Gazette, 24 APR 1760; 22 MAR 1763; 23 AUG 1764. To be rented, the George Tavern, near the Court House, extremely convenient, has three rooms and a good bar, below stairs, and six rooms above; a kitchen adjoining, with two rooms below and one above; a large dining room; and a good London Billiard-Table above; a garden paled in; a well, smoke-house, stable, and necessary house; late in the possession of Patrick Byrn, deceased. The terms may be known by applying to William Ramsay.

Alexandria, Virginia Town Lots, 1749-1801

1797, MAY 1   Charles Cartlich to John Duff, for £130, 116'x24'2" (Alex. I:193).

(See also Alex. N:337).

LOT 41
Cameron & Water St.

1749, SEP 20   William Ramsay and Hugh West, trustees, to John Carlyle, for £32.5. (FDB B:501).

1780, APR 5   John Carlyle's will probated 17 OCT 1780 devises 50'x30' of Lot 41 to grandson Carlyle Fairfax Whiting to be rented out for his education (FWB D:203).[18]

(See also Alex. M:110 (13 JUN 1798)).

LOT 42
Cameron & Fairfax

1749, SEP 20   William Ramsay and Hugh West, trustees, to John Carlyle, for £17.4 (FDB B:501). In his will (FWB D:203), John Carlyle leaves to daughter Sarah Herbert, 30'x100' of Lot 42 including his "dry ware house" and the residue of the estate to his son George William Carlyle, or, in case of his death before age 21 years, to his grandsons John Carlyle Herbert and Carlyle Fairfax Whiting.

LOTS 43 and 44
Cameron, Fairfax & Royal

1753, FEB 2?   Trustees to the justices of Fairfax County for Lots 43 and 44, called the marketplace for the use of the court house and prison (TM:19; see also deed at FDB D:360 damaged, 18 JAN 1757, between John Carlyle and William Ramsay, trustees, and John West and Charles Broadwater).

LOT 45
Cameron & Royal

1749, SEP 20   John Carlyle and Garrard Alexander, trustees, to Charles Mayson [Mason], for £11.5.9 (FDB B:502).

1761, AUG 9   Ann Mason in her will, probated 15 SEP 1761, appointed John Dalton and John Carlyle her executors (FWB B:299). Dalton never qualified.

1761, SEP 3   John Carlyle and John Dalton apply to have lot escheated (Quit Rents:80).

1776, FEB 1   John Carlyle, as lone executor, conveyed to John Dalton, for £280 (FDB

---

[18] Virginia Gazette and Alexandria Advertiser, 2 NOV 1782, Colonel John Carlyle, of Alexandria, deceased, estate accounts with William Herbert and Charles Little, acting executors.

	M:188).
1778, OCT 14	John Carlyle, as co-executor of John Dalton, conveyed to Edward Owens, 125'5"x80' for £2000 (FDB D$_4$:251).
1778, NOV 16	John Carlyle, as co-executor of John Dalton, conveyed to Robert McCrea and Robert Mease, for £305, 125½'x24' (FDB D$_4$:247).
1780	John Carlyle, as co-executor, to Richard Clark (FDB N:254 msg).
1782, JAN 21	Edward Owens to John Wise (part of this deed appears in Fairfax Minute Book, 1756-1763, part 2, back, pp. 4, 24, 25).
1782, DEC 14	Adam Lynn[19] and wife Catherine to John Bryce, for £300, 24'x123'5" (FDB O:282). This deed refers to George Duncan's parcel of Lot 45. The deed from Carlyle and Dalton's executors to George Duncan (FDB N:164) is missing. Also missing is the deed from Carlyle and Dalton's executors to Adam Lynn (FDB N:163). FDB O:282 indicates "with a line of Robert McCrea to the beginning."
1783, SEP 25	Richard Clarke and wife Sarah to William Hunter and Samuel Arell, for £150, 24'x123'5" (FDB O:135).
1784, AUG 30	William Hunter and wife Christiana and Samuel Arell to Joseph Marie Perrin, for £210, 24'x123'5" (FDB P:160).
1784, NOV 19	John Bryce and wife Hannah to William Herbert and John Potts, Jr., 24'x123'5", "the same part of Lot 45 which Adam Lynn and Catherine his wife" conveyed to John Bryce (FDB Q:124). Deed also refers to George Duncan's parcel.
1789, JUN 23	Robert McCrea and Robert Mease, merchants, mortgage part of Lots 45 and 50 to Robert Peter, merchant of Georgetown [Md.] (FDB R:458).
1789, JUL 18	Joseph Marie Perrin to Mathurin Perrin his brother, for £105, "one moiety of an half acre or lot of land in the Town of Alexandria numbered in a plan of the said Town 45..." (FDB R:456). Deed describes the parcel as 24'x123'5".
1792, APR 9	Robert and Nancy McCrea and Robert Mease, merchants, to Robert Peter, of George Town, Md., 123'5"x44-1/4' (Alex. D:393).
1795, JUL 3	Robert Peter and wife Elizabeth to John Wise, 44-1/4'x123'5" of Lots 45 and 50, the same as mortgaged to Peter by McCrea and Mease (FDB Y:292).
1795, SEP 28	William Herbert and wife Sarah and John Potts and wife Elizabeth to Jesse Simms for £500, the same conveyed to John Bryce by Adam Lynn and wife (FDB A$_2$:230).
1797, AUG 23	Jesse Simms to Francis Peyton, for $5000, "all that Lot and houses Situate on Royal Street" (Alex. I:64).
1799, MAY 9	John and Elizabeth Wise deed of trust to Ludwell Lee, Esq. of Shuter's Hill, part of Lot 45, 123'5½"x80' (Alex. M:93).

---

[19] Virginia Journal and Alexandria Advertiser, 15 JUN 1786, Adam Lynn, of Alexandria, died; a lot belonging to his estate to be sold by Katherine Lynn, his executrix and his executors Peter Wise and Philip Webster (17 AUG 1786).

LOTS 46 and 47
King, Fairfax & Water St.
(See also below)

These lots initially were considered one parcel and later conveyed separately.

1749, SEP 20	John Carlyle and Hugh West, trustees, to William Ramsay, Lot 46 for £32.5., and Lot 47, for £17.4. (FDB B:506).
1757, JUL 21	William Ramsay mortgage to John Dixon (FDB D:452).
1777, FEB 13	William Ramsay to son Dennis, "being of full age," part of Lot 47, 75'7"x75' (FDB M:286).
1777, FEB 15	William Ramsay to son-in-law James Stewart, part of Lot 47, 34'4"x75'7", "adjoining the lot given to my son Dennis" (FDB M:284 "whereas a marriage is consumated between James Steuart, merchant in Alexandria, and my daughter Betty Ramsay, now Betty Steuart", see also FDB M:286).
1777, JUL 16	William Ramsay to Robert and Ann Allison, 77'x34'4" (FDB N:18 msg; see Alex. D:479; Alex. F:158).
1784, DEC 20	William Ramsay, Gent. to Dennis Ramsay, 30'x46'6½" (FDB P:348, 351). On the same date, William Ramsay made numerous conveyances to Dennis Ramsay in trust for William's wife Ann and daughters Betty Stewart, Ann Allison, Hannah Madden, Sarah Ramsay and Amelia Ramsay (FDB P:348, 351, 354, 357, 360). He also conveyed parts of Lot 46 to Hannah Madden, Amelia Ramsay and Sarah Ramsay (FDB P:374, 376, 378; see also FDB Y:254). Amelia died without issue before reaching 21 years; property passed to brothers and sisters (see Alex. H:36).
1785, JAN 15	William Ramsay, Gent. to daughter Betty Stewart and grandsons William Ramsay Stewart and James Montgomery Stewart, 75'7"x34'4" and other parcels of Lots 46 and 47 (FDB P:380).
1792, MAY 9	Betty [Ramsay] Stewart, widow, to son James Montgomery Stewart, two parcels; "the late William Ramsay, father of Betty, on 15 FEB 1777, 'soon after the marriage of... Betty with James Steuart' gave them three parcels which were devised by James' will" (Alex. D:423).
1792, MAY 23	Robert and Ann Allison, of Fauquier Co., mortgage to James and William Miller, of Philadelphia, merchants. Allison owes John Mease £250 (Alex. D:479).
1792, OCT 17	Robert and Ann Allison, of Fauquier Co., to James Patton and David Finley as tenants in common, for £240, 77'x30' (Alex. E:55).
1793, JAN 4	William Ramsay to Benjamin Augustus Hamp, for £180, 30'x81' (see Alex. E:242, 353).
1793, MAY 17	Benjamin Augustus Hamp to James Patton and James Kennedy, for £220, 81'x30' (Alex. E:242).
1793, NOV 4	James Patton and wife Mary Ann and David Finley to James Kennedy, for £500, 77'x30' (Alex. E:251).
1794, APR 12	Michael Madden and wife Hannah [Ramsay] to James Kennedy, for £120, 80'x15' part of Lot 46 (Alex. E:426).
1794, APR 16	Dennis Ramsay and wife Jane to Thomas Richards, for £274, 54'10½"x30' (Alex. E:274).
1794, OCT 20	Michael Madden and wife to James Wilson, Jr., for £240, 81'x30' (Alex.

	E:442).
1794, NOV 1	James Kennedy and wife Letitia to James Wilson, Jr., for £135, 81'x15' (Alex. E:446).
1794, NOV 3	Thomas Porter and wife Sarah to James Wilson, Jr., for £135, 81'x15' (Alex. E:451).
1795, MAR 20	James and Letitia Kennedy to Robert Brockett, for £270, 30'x65'7" (Alex. F:137). This deed states the parcel was conveyed to Kennedy by Allison on 12 FEB 1795; also two other parcels of Lot 46.

There are many later deeds for parcels below Water Street (extension of Lot 46): FDB T:29; U:46; X:411, 414, 443, 487, 567; Alex. B:168; Alex. C:288, 293).

Lot 46

1794, OCT 10	Dennis and Jane Ramsay to Thomas Richards, for £126, 30'x26'1½" of Lot 46 (Alex. G:12).
1794, OCT 10	Dennis and Jane Ramsay to Thomas Richards, for £211, 54'10½"x30' (Alex. G:16). Two additional parcels same parties, same date (Alex. G:49).
1795, FEB 6	Tripartite deed: Dennis Ramsay, Robert and Ann Allison to James Kennedy, 30'x65'6" of Lot 46 for £60 (Alex. F:162).
1795, FEB 9?	Frances Peyton and wife Sarah to Charles Simms, for £200, 123'4"x28' of Lot 46 (Alex. F:250).
1795, FEB 12	Robert and Ann Allison to James Kennedy, for £60, 30'x65'7" of Lot 46, conveyed to Ramsay to Allison on 16 JUL 1777 (Alex. F:158).
1795, MAR 18	Tripartite deed: Dennis Ramsay, Robert and Betty [Ramsay] Stewart Mease[20], to James Kennedy, 30'x65'6" of Lot 46 (same text as F:162 above) for £72.10 (Alex. F:179).
1795, JUN 24	Amelia Finley to James Kennedy, for £500 (Alex. F:324).
1795, JUL 1	Amelia Finley to Charles Robert Scott, for £370, 1/4 of the Stewart/Allison parcel, half of the half James Patton and David Finley bought together, Lot 46 (Alex. F:320). This deed says Patton and Finley conveyed to James Kennedy, but Finley died intestate before his portion was conveyed and passed to his mother Amelia. Patton, attorney in fact for Amelia, advertised the parcel 10 JUN 1795 (Finley's portion), and Charles Robert Scott was highest bidder at £370.
1795, JUL 2	Charles Robert Scott to James Patton, same parcel as conveyed by Amelia Finley to Scott for same consideration (£370) (Alex. F:352).
1795, OCT 10	Thomas Richards and wife Nancy to Joseph Riddle and James Dall, of Baltimore, Md., for £1600, 54'10½"x30' (same parcel conveyed by Dennis and Jane Ramsay to Thomas Richards on 16 APR 1794), also adjoining parcels of 54'10½"x30' and 26'1½"x30', plus two additional parcels conveyed to Richards by Ramsays on 10 OCT 1794 (Alex. G:49).
1796, MAR 7	James Wilson, Jr. and wife Elizabeth to Bryan Hampson, for £360, 81'x30'

---

[20] The Times & Alexandria Advertiser, 27 MAR 1798, Mrs. Betty Mease, consort of Robert Mease of Alexandria, died on Sunday morning last, she was buried in the Presbyterian Burying Ground.

	(Alex. G:246).
1796, MAY 3	William Ramsay's heirs[21] to Jesse Simms, for £300, parcel of Lot 46 conveyed by Ramsay to daughter Amelia (Alex. H:68).
1796, AUG 17	Jesse Simms to Richard Marshall Scott, for £900, 81'x34'4" of Lot 46. Deed indicates survivors of William Ramsay [Jr.], dec.,[22] conveyed 3 MAY 1796 to Jesse Simms (Alex. H:36).

Lot 47

1795, JUL 6	William Ramsay to Guy Atkinson, release for £100, Lot 47, from any and all responsibility for the property conveyed by Atkinson to Ramsay on 10 MAR 1795, 60'x25', adjoining parcel sold 28 OCT 1794 to Bernard Bryan by court decree (the same decree granted adjoining parcel to Atkinson). This deed releasing Atkinson states that Ramsay conveyed to Atkinson another 60'x25' parcel on 11 MAR 1795, overlapping the first parcel, that Ramsay sold to Daniel Moxley the remainder of the first parcel, receiving part of the price but title not conveyed, that the deed for the first parcel was lost. On the same day, 6 JUL 1795, Moxley conveys to Atkinson for £100 release of any and all claim or responsibility for the first parcel (Alex. F:331, 333).
1795, JUL 18	Dennis Ramsay and wife Jane Allen to Mathew Sexsmith, for £165, 17'8"x59'1½" of Lot 47, south of Ramsay's alley, conveyed by William Ramsay to Dennis on 15 JAN 1785 (Alex. F:259); Sexsmith mortgages to Ramsay for £100 (Alex. F:262).
1795, JUL 28	Dennis and Jane Allen Ramsay to Bernard Bryan, for £289, 59'1½"x24'1", Lot 47, includes agreement on alleys (Alex. F:335).
1795, JUL 29	Bernard Bryan mortgage to Dennis Ramsay above property, Lot 47 (Alex. F:339).
1795, DEC 24	Dennis Ramsay to Matthew Sexsmith, full title to property Sexsmith mortgaged on 18 JUL 1795. Sexsmith paid in full, same to Bernard Bryan (Alex. F:389, 391).
1796, OCT 12	Dennis and Jane Ramsay to Hugh Smith (see Alex. K:406).
1797, JAN 27	Jesse Simms to Alexander Smith (see Alex. K:235).
1798, JAN 22	Alexander and Rachel Smith to John Dunlap, for £600 (Alex. K:235).
1798, MAY 22	Hugh Smith to Joseph Riddle, for $1200 (Alex. K:406).
1799, JAN 26	James and Letitia Kennedy to John Ramsay, for £4000, this parcel sold by Benjamin Augustus Hamp to Patton and Kennedy as tenants in common on 19 MAY 1793 [sic], Patton sold his share to Kennedy on 25 JAN 1799 (Alex. L:192).
1799, 29 JUL	James and Letitia Kennedy to James Keith, deed of trust to secure $7620 Kennedy owes to the Bank of Alexandria (Alex. M:184).
1800, AUG 13	John and Clarissa Ramsay to Victor duPont, City of New York, for $4500; money paid to Ramsay by Anthony Charles Cazenove (Alex. N:361).

---

[21] Dennis and Jane Allen Ramsay, Robert and Betty Mease, Robert and Ann Allison, Michael and Hannah Madden, and Thomas and Sarah Porter.
[22] Complete Records [Alexandria], Liber A, fols. 169-70, dated 21 JUL 1787, probated 21 SEP 1795.

(See also Alex. K:110, M:425).

LOT 48
Fairfax & King

1749, SEP 20	Trustees to John Pagan, for £14.10.3 (FDB C:21).
c.1752	John Pagan to Benjamin Sebastian (FDB C:395 msg). Since this document is missing, no firm statement can be made as to its contents.
c.1754	Benjamin Sebastian and wife to Richard Arell (FDB F:326 msg). No firm statement can be made as to the contents of this document but a link between [John] Pagan and Arell is provided (Arell later subdivides lot).
1771, SEP 24	Richard Arell and wife Eleanor to William McCleery and John Allison, both of Frederick Co., Md., for $40 (Spanish milled) annual rent, 60'x60' (FDB J:315 msg; see FDB M:192, 195).
1772, APR 29	Richard and Eleanor Arell to James Rumsey, of Loudoun Co., for $50 annual rent, 50'x60' (FDB K:11).
c.1772	Richard and Eleanor Arell to Robert Hall and John Jones, probably for an annual rent (see FDB K:7).
1772, MAY 14	Richard Arell, inn holder, and wife Eleanor, to George Gilpin, for $40 (silver) annual rent, 60'x30'9" (FDB K:7).
1772, MAY 21	Court records for this date show that Robert Hall and John Jones swore to their account books, but no record has yet been found for conveyance of property (Fairfax Court Order Book 1772-1774, p. 49).
1773, JUN 16	Richard Arell, inn holder, and wife Eleanor to Angel Hart Couter, butcher, for $25 annual rent, 30'x60' (FDB L:229).
1773, AUG 27	Richard Arell, inn holder, and wife Eleanor to George Gilpin, merchant, for $10 annual rent for a parcel adjoining that previously conveyed to Gilpin, "a square of fifty five feet by twenty" (FDB L:217).
1773, AUG 27	Richard Arell and Eleanor his wife to John Butcher, hatter, 60'x35' for $30 annual rent (FDB L:220).
1773, DEC 17	Richard Arell, inn holder, and Eleanor his wife, to William Allison, joiner, for $30 annual rent, 27'7"x60' (FDB L:232).
1776, JAN 22	William McCleery and Isabella his wife, of Frederick Co., Md., and John Allison to Tobias Zimmerman, blacksmith, 30'x60' for $20 (Spanish silver) annual rent (FDB M:192). On the same day, McCleery and Allison to Adam Goose [Gantz] for $20 (Spanish silver) annual rent 30'x60' (FDB M:195).
1778, AUG 15	Richard and Eleanor Arell to John Rick of Baltimore, Md., part of Lot 48 (FDB N:441 msg; part of this deed appears in Fairfax Minute Book 1756-1763, part 2, back p. 3).
1780, JUL 20	William Allison to Alexander Pearce (FDB N:73 msg; see FDB Q:74).
1782?, APR 10	Alexander Pearce and wife Margaret to William Hunter (FDB N:355 msg; see FDB Q:74).
1782, APR 22	William Hunter to John Bryce (FDB N:531 msg; see FDB Q:74).
1782, APR 26	Adam Gantz [Goose] and wife Mary to William and Henry Lyles, for $20 annual rent (FDB N:560 msg; see FDB O:131).

1783, SEP 17	Will of Christian Longmarch, probated 16 DEC 1783 (FWB D:413), devises part of Lot 48 to Oliver Price, "conveyed by Indenture bearing date the 16th day of June 1773 from Richard Arel & Eloner [sic] his wife to Angle Hart Couter [sic] subjected to an annual rent of Twenty five dollars... which said part of lot number 48 was by Angel Hart Couter conveyed by indenture unto me..." The deed from Couter and wife Catharine to Longmarch on 27 OCT 1779 is missing (FDB N:319 msg; see Alex. G:416).
1783, DEC 16	William Lyles, Jr. and wife Sarah to Henry Lyles, for $20 (silver) annual rent (paid to Arell), 30'x60', same parcel William and Henry received from Adam Gantz and which Gantz received from McCleery and Allison (FDB O:131).
1784, JUL 22	John Bryce, merchant, and wife Hannah to Robert Bryce, merchant, for £500, all their part of the lot, 27'7"x60' (FDB Q:74).
1796, MAY 16	Oliver Price and wife Jane to John Limrick, for £350, 60'x30'; Limrick to pay $25 annual rent (Alex. G:416).

(See also loose 1796 deed from John Wise to Mandeville and Jamisson; FDB W:33; FDB Y:267; Alex. I:42, 462; Alex. L:186; Alex. M:26, 29).

LOT 49
Royal & King

1749, SEP 20	John Carlyle and Garrard Alexander, trustees, to John Alexander, for £16.2.6 (FDB B:498).
1753, JAN 26	John Alexander, of Stafford Co. and wife Susanna to Benjamin Sebastian, for £16.2.6 (FDB C:626).
1765, MAR 22	Benjamin Sebastian to son Benjamin except for 52'x42' (see Alex. H:13).
1768, FEB 22	Both men and wives all their interest to John Muir who, by his will dated DEC 1789, conveyed it to his sister, Elizabeth Muir (see Alex. H:13).
1796, MAY 16	Elizabeth [Muir] Donaldson, sister and devisee of John Muir, dec., to John Janney, for £700, 95'x35' (Alex. G:426).
1796, JUN 17	Elizabeth Donaldson to William and Charles McKnight, for £701, paid to Wm. Hartshorne, two parts of Lot 49, 111'x25'7" and 111'x25'6" (Alex. H:13).

LOT 50
Royal & King

1752, MAR 28	William Ramsay and John Pagan, trustees, to Adam Stephen for £12.7.3 (FDB C:310). In 1761, Stephen still owed the full amount (TM:37).
1756, JUN 1	George Johnston, attorney in fact for Col. Adam Stephen, conveyed to Jacob Frederick Curtius, Lot 50, for £26 (FDB D:290).
1757, OCT 8	Jacob Frederick Curtius to John Carlyle and John Dalton, for £32.13.4 (FDB D:508).
c.1773?	John Carlyle and John Dalton to Richard Lake (FDB L:331 msg; see FDB D:508 and W:373).

	62'x20' (Alex. H:86).
1796, MAY 23	Alexander Smith and wife Rachel to George Gilpin, for £283.10., 82'x31'6", adjoins property conveyed by John Fitzgerald to William Anderson, "upon which there is a brick dwelling house now in the seizin of Dedrick Sheckle" (see Alex. H:55), part of land conveyed by William Hodgson to Alexander Smith on 6 JAN 1796.
1796, JUL 21	Alexander Smith and wife Rachel to Jesse Smith, for £1200, two parcels: 42'x82' and 21'9"x82'; deed states parcels sold to Smith by William Hodgson on 6 JAN 1796 (Alex. H:101).
1796, AUG 24	Jesse Simms to Bernard Ghequiere, for £1300, same two parcels Simms bought from Smith (Alex. H:105).
1796, SEP 12	Joseph Dyson and wife Hannah to John Lumsdon and Daniel McLeod, lease 66'x20' for $60 silver annually (Alex. H:84).
1796, OCT 4	Alexander and Rachel Smith to Jonathan Swift, for £4000, 112'x67', the same parcel sold by Philip and Mary Fendall to Smith on 2 JAN 1796 (Alex. H:107).

(See also Alex. K:105; Alex. L:312, 405, 414; Alex. M:40, 62; and Alex. N:35).

LOT 52
Fairfax & King

1749, SEP 20	John Carlyle and Hugh West, trustees, to Lawrence Washington, for £17.4. (FDB B:497; see also note for Lot 51 regarding John Patterson's estate).
1784, MAY 10	Valentine Peers, merchant, and wife Margaret lease to Joseph Janney, Samuel Pleasants and John Field, of the City of Philadelphia, as tenants in common, 33'x100' (FDB O:436; see Alex. I:232).
1784, NOV 15	Valentine Peers, late of Alexandria, merchant, and now resident in Md., and Margaret his wife to Richard Chichester, Gent., for £750, 44'x80' (FDB P:98).
1786, JUL 23	Richard Chichester[23] and wife Sarah to Jonathan Swift, merchant, for £257.13., 23'x83' of Lot 52 (FDB Q:272).
1786, SEP 25	John Fitzgerald and wife Jane to William Anderson, lease 82'3½"x18', for 18 guineas from 1 SEP 1787 (Alex. B:399).
1790, JUN 1	William Hodgson to John Harper (FDB S:392). Deed recites a parcel 32'x82' sold by Valentine Peers to John Rumney who sold to William Hodgson. It also states Peers sold another parcel to Hodgson (see note for Lot 51, 1 JUN 1790).
1793, JUN 15	Richard Chichester and wife Sarah to Joseph Riddle and James Dall (FDB Y:93).
1794, OCT 10	Valentine Peers and wife Eleanor to Joseph Riddle and James Dall as tenants in common, part of Peers portion after division with Fitzgerald.

---

[23] The Columbian Mirror and Alexandria Gazette, 12 AUG 1797, Richard Chichester, Esq., deceased, estate accounts with his executrix Sarah Chichester.

1774, JUL 4	Michael Gretter and wife Elizabeth to Thomas Armat, 46'x246'10", parts of Lots 50 and 115 for £300 (FDB M:12).
1775, APR 30	Thomas Armat and wife Sarah to Robert McCrea and Robert Mease, merchants, same parts of Lots 50 and 115, for £360 (FDB M:159).
1782, FEB 25	Michael Gretter to John and Margaret Gretter's children, 130'7"x18' (see Alex. E:258).
1789, JUN 23	McCrea and Mease, merchants, mortgage to Robert Peter, parts of Lots 45 and 50 (FDB R:458).
1791, JUL 18/21	Michael Gretter and wife Elizabeth to Lawrence Hooff, for £150, part of Lots 115 and 50 (Alex. D:311, 317). Deed confirms sale by daughter Elizabeth Gretter and husband William Simpson to Lawrence Hooff.
1792, NOV 17	Division of the estate of Richard Lake includes part of Lot 50. Robert Mease, Michael Gretter, William McKnight, Charles Bryan, and Thomas Richards seem to hold leases or title in fee to parts of this lot, though the conveyances are unrecorded. The leases to Bryan and McKnight (1774) are extant (FDB W:373; Drawer X, Circuit Court Archives).
1793, JUL 22	Michael Gretter to George Deneale, 130'7"x16', mortgage for debt Gretter owes James [Craig] (Alex. E:147).
1794, FEB 17	Thomas and Casina Conn to Charles Bryan, 50'x19'3½"; Bryan lease to [Charles?] McKnight (Alex. F:169).
1794, APR 19	Parcel mortgaged 22 JUL 1793, reconveyed back to Gretter. Michael Gretter conveys to John and Margaret Gretter for £81.5.9, two parcels, 130'7"x16' and 130'7"x18", and to their children upon parents' death, reconfirming deed of 25 FEB 1782 (Alex. E:258).
1795, APR 4	Thomas and Casina Conn to William Hepburn and John Dundas, for £67.10., assignment of $22½ annual rent on parcel conveyed 17 FEB 1794 (Alex. F:169).
1795, JUL 2	Robert Peter and wife Elizabeth to John Wise, same parts of Lots 45 and 50 as were mortgaged to Peter by McCrea and Mease (FDB Y:292).

(See also Alex. N:317).

LOT 51
Water St. & King
(See also Lot 52)

1749, SEP 20	John Carlyle and Hugh West, trustees, to Lawrence Washington, for £33.6.6 (FDB B:497).
1760, MAY 20	George William Fairfax, John Carlyle and George Washington, surviving acting executors of Lawrence Washington, to John Patterson, joyner, for £150, Lots 51 and 52 (FDB D:693).
1765, OCT 6	John Patterson's will probated 15 AUG 1768, provides for sale of Lots 51 and 52 (FWB C:35).
1778, APR 25	Susannah, widow of John Patterson, dec., to John Fitzgerald and Valentine Peers, for £1400, Lots 51 and 52 (FDB D_4:196).
1781, DEC 20	Division between Fitzgerald and Peers (FDB N:497 msg; see FDB Y:85).

Alexandria, Virginia Town Lots, 1749-1801

1785, MAY 27	Ann Hooks to David Young, 18'x25'. Deed recites that John Longdon rents part of lot (FDB P:472).
1786, OCT 5	John and Jane Fitzgerald to John Jenkes, Olney Winsor, Joseph Jenkes and Crawford Jenkes, lease at $202½ (Spanish milled) at 6 shillings or 9 pennyweight Half Johanesses at 48 shillings each, part 40'6"x76'6" (Alex. D:227).
1787, OCT 9	Valentine Peers, of Charles Co., Md., to John Rumney, for £340, 82'x32' [deed indicates Lot 52 but description is clearly Lot 51] (Alex. C:140).
1788, JUN 13	John Rumney to William Hodgson, for £700, 82'x32' (Alex. C:237).
1789, FEB 18	Valentine Peers, of Charles Co., Md., to William Hodgson, for £180, 10'x82' (FDB R:346). Deed indicates that the parcel adjoins that sold by Peers to Rumney.
1789, OCT 28	Lease (see 5 OCT 1786).
1790, JUN 1	William Hodgson to John Harper, 32'x82' (FDB S:392). This parcel could be in Lot 52 (see Alex. F:155).
1790, OCT 2	Val. Peers, of Loudoun Co., to Thomas Porter in trust to pay Wm. Hodgson £290.19.3 (see Alex. E: 61).
1790, OCT 21	Valentine Peers, of Charles Co., Md., to William Hodgson, for £600, part 79'x82' (Alex. D:183).
1793, APR 17	Thomas Porter and wife Sarah to Valentine Peers, of Loudoun Co., 100'x73'3½" (Alex. E:61).
1793, MAY 16	Valentine Peers to Thomas Patten, 70'x40' (see Alex. G:140).
1793, NOV 10	Valentine and Eleanor Peers, Loudoun Co., to Thomas Irvine, for £270, 30'x70' (Alex. E:264).
1794, MAR 13	William Hodgson to John Robert Wheaton, 25'x82' (see Alex. F:118).
1794, JUL 9	John Harper to Alexander Smith, for £600, 82'x42' (Alex. F:155). This deed states the parcel is in Lot 52, but description is clearly for Lot 51.
1794, JUL 14	John Robert Wheaton and wife Elizabeth to Bernard Ghequire, for £400, 25'x82' (Alex. F:118).
1794, JUL 22	Alexander McConnell and wife Mary to John Dunlap, merchant, for £312, "from northwest corner of Rutter's lot...," 26'x70' (Alex. E:465).
1794, DEC 8	Valentine and Eleanor Peers to John Dalrymple Orr, part of Lot 51 (see FDB X:630).
1794, DEC 15	John Dalrymple Orr to Richard Marshall Scott, for £350, 40'x66', conveyed to Orr by Valentine and Eleanor Peers on 8 DEC 1794 (FDB X:630).
1795, APR 16	Richard Marshall Scott and wife Mary, of Prince William Co., to Matthew Franklin Bowne and Theodore James Hamilton, tenants in common, lease 66'x40', conveyed by Valentine Peers to John Dalrymple Orr and by Orr to Scott. Bowne and Hamilton to pay $126 silver annually and £400 within 5 years (Alex. F:349).
1795, SEP 24	Matthew Franklin Bowne and wife Elizabeth, and Theodorus James Hamilton and wife Eunice, to Joseph Dyson, 66'x40'; Dyson to pay rent to Scott (Alex. G:157).
1796, JAN 12	Thomas Patten and wife Mary, and Joseph May and wife Dorothy, to Jonathan Swift, 70'x40' for £5 (Alex. G:140).
1796, MAY 16	Joseph Dyson and wife Mary to John Lumsdon for £150 and $60 silver rent,

	Encumbered by Janney's right to "a water passage..." (Alex. F:56).
1795, MAR 7	Samuel and Mary Pleasants, City of Philadelphia, Pa., to John Field, for £500 Pa., one third of Peers parcel plus one third of the Finley parcel [see Lot 153], 100'x33' (Alex. I:232).
1795, MAY 15	William Hodgson to John Fitzgerald, for £36, 82'x4' part of a piece "lately conveyed by Valentine Peers to... Hodgson" (Alex. G:504).
1795, MAY 27	John and Jane Fitzgerald to Riddle and Dall, for $100, half of a 10-foot alley (5'x82') (Alex. F:253).

(See also FDB A_2:108, 333; B_2:72, 146, 173; U_2:188; Alex. I:381; L:260, 312; M:79, 212).

LOT 53
Fairfax & King

1752, MAR 28	William Ramsay and John Pagan, trustees, to George Mason, for £7.10.6 (FDB C:297).
1762, JUL 20/1	George Mason and wife Ann to Richard Arell, merchant, for £114.7.6 (FDB E:102, 104).
1773, DEC 17	Richard Arell, inn holder, and wife Eleanor to Benjamin Shreeve [Shreve], hatter, for part of Lot 53, 70'x40' for $50 annual rent (FDB L:223).
1774, MAY 16	Richard Arell and wife Eleanor to Philip Dawe, silver and copper smith, 20'x40', for $17 annual rent (FDB L:317).
1775, APR 3	Richard Arell and wife Eleanor to Martin McDermott, shoemaker, 30'x60', for $24 (silver) annual rent (FDB M:66).
1775, APR 3	Richard Arell and wife Eleanor to Lawrence Hooff, cartwright and butcher, 22'6"x60', for $20 annual rent (FDB M:70).
c.1778	Philip Dawe to Paton and Butcher (FDB N:30 msg).
1780, JUN 9	Richard and Eleanor Arell to Edward Mitchell Ramsay, part of Lot 53, for 1000 lbs. tobacco annually (see Alex. E:170; G:224).
c.1781	Martin McDermott to Robert Lyle (FDB N:306 msg).
1789, NOV 13	Edward Mitchell Ramsay to Benjamin Augustus Hamp, lease for 6 years (see Alex. E:170).
1793, JUN 11	Edward Mitchell Ramsay, merchant, mortgage to James Smith the younger, of Philadelphia, merchant, to secure payment of note (Alex. E:170; see FDB X:434).
1794, JUN 4	Edward Mitchell Ramsay and wife Mary mortgage to Abraham Usher and John Wolfenden, of Baltimore, Md., for £260.7.9, same parcel Ramsay leased from Arell (Alex. G:224).
1794, DEC 15	James Smith, Jr., City of Philadelphia, to Edward Mitchell Ramsay, release of mortgage for £1102.2.3 (FDB X:434). Edward Mitchell Ramsay and wife Mary to William Hartshorne, James Cavens and John Muir as tenants in common, 20'x90' (Alex. F:313).
1795, FEB 7	Richard and Eleanor Arell lease to John Norwood, 176'7"x63'5" (see Alex. I:46).
1795, JUN 22	James Cavens and John Muir to William Hartshorne, for £1209.6., two

	undivided third parts of 20'x90' parcel (Alex. F:313).
1797, APR 13	John Norwood to Francis Peyton in trust to secure debts owed to John Thomas Ricketts and William Newton, merchants, same parcel as leased by Norwood from Arell (Alex. I:46).

(See also FDB B$_2$:439; Alex. N:188).

LOT 54
Royal & King

1752, MAR 28	William Ramsay and John Pagan, trustees, to William Strother, for £7.10.6 (FDB C:305).
1754, SEP 9	Trustees to George Mason, for 10 shillings (TM:22).
1756, AUG 18	George Mason, Gent. to George Mercer, Gent., for £10 (FDB D:313).
1760, AUG 1	George Mercer of Frederick Co., to Harry Piper, for £115 (FDB D:784).
1777, AUG 20	Anthony Piper agreement with John Dixon of Whitehaven and agent for William Ramsay, whereby Piper to sell to Ramsay Lot 54, for £400, from the proceeds of sale of Fairgirth estate in Scotland (see FDB O:430).
1784, JAN 9	Anthony Piper, of Hall Catt, Parish of Hanington, Co. Cumberland, Great Britain, carpenter, to William Ramsay, Gent., for £400 (FDB O:430).
1784, FEB 23	William Ramsay, several conveyances to his children Betty, Hannah, Sarah and Amelia (FDB P:7, 9, 10, 12).
1785, APR 18	David Young to Ann Hooks, 18'x25', part of Lot 54 (this may be clerk's error; see information for Lot 55). Deed recites part of Lot 54 rented to John Longden (FDB P:395).
1785, JUN 14	Michael and Hannah [Ramsay] Madden lease to Alexander Smith, for 30-5/6 guineas per year, from 8 MAR, part of Lot 54 (Alex. B:190).
1786, APR 24	Sarah Ramsay lease to Hugh Mitchell, 100'x25'3", at 25¼ guineas per year, from 1 SEP 1786 (Alex. B:293).
1786, NOV 13	Hugh Mitchell to James Hendricks and Francis Peyton as tenants in common, same piece as leased from Sarah Ramsay on 24 APR 1786 (Alex. C:1).
1792, MAR 2	Michael and Hannah Madden to Alexander Smith, same piece as conveyed 14 JUN 1785, for £400, remitting rent and releasing the property (Alex. D:508).
1794, FEB 4	William, Dennis and Jane Ramsay, Robert and Betty Mease, Robert and Ann Allison, Michael and Hannah Madden, and Thomas and Sarah Porter to Alexander Smith. William Ramsay conveyed to daughter Amelia who died before reaching 21 years of age and without issue. Parcel descended to brothers and sisters (above). Now, for £295, convey to Smith, 123'5"x56' (Alex. G:31).
1794, MAY 14	Alexander Smith and wife Rachel to Joseph Ingle, lease 113'5"x25' at $50 silver annually (Alex. G:99).
1794, AUG 20	Thomas Porter and wife Sarah [Ramsay] to Francis Peyton, for £40, 100'x5'7-1/4" (Alex. E:401).

(See also FDB U:303; FDB W:170; Alex. I:446; Alex. K:69, 101, 376, 379,

Alexandria, Virginia Town Lots, 1749-1801

416, 425, 516; Alex. L:335; Alex. M:454).

LOT 55
Royal & King

1752, MAR 28	William Ramsay and John Pagan, trustees, to George Mason of Gunston Hall, for £8.12. (FDB C:296).
1762, OCT 16	George Mason of Gunston Hall and wife Ann to David Young, baker, for £120, half acre "whereon John Plummer lately lived" (FDB E:210).
1784, JUN 30	David Young, eldest son of David Young, dec., to Catharine Uhler, wife of Valentine Uhler, daughter of David Young, dec., sister of David Young, 33'6"x92'8", part of Lot 55 which descended to David Young as heir-at-law of his father whose will was not recorded because he was not in his "proper senses" (FDB O:354).
1784, JUL 1	David Young, eldest son and heir at law of the late David Young, to William Young, son of David Young, dec. and brother of David Young, 30'x123'6" (FDB O:349).
1784, JUL 1	David Young to half-brother Adam Longdon by his mother Dorothea, widow of David Young, dec., later wife of Ralph Longdon, 24'x123'6" (FDB O:352).
1784, JUL 1	David Young to brother Thomas Young, 30'x123'6" (FDB O:357). Thomas Young died without issue, parcel descended to David and Catharine (see Alex. I:258).
1784, JUL 8	David Young to John Longdon, 20'x90' for annual rent of $40 (Spanish milled) (FDB O:359).
1785, APR 21	David Young to Caleb Earp and George Wilson, for £155, 72'8"x16' (FDB P:469).
1785, DEC 22	Valentine and Catherine [Young] Uhler to Jacob Fortenay, for £250, 15'x92'8", part of piece conveyed to Catherine by David Young (FDB Q:112).
1786, JUN 27	David Young, eldest son and heir at law of David Young the elder, to Thomas Conn, for £160, 24'x72'6" (Alex. B:410).
1786, JUL 31	David Young to Benjamin Augustus Hamp, merchant of Alexandria, for £100. Deed describes "a brick house of Brown & Conn's" and "a new framed house... of David Young" (FDB Q:265).
1787, JAN 13	William Young to John Longdon, for £150, 30'x123'6", conveyed by David Young to brother William (FDB Q:318).
1787, MAR 8	Valentine and Catharine Uhler to Dederick Scheckel, remnant of parcel for £150; "reserving to [the Uhlers] the Privilege and Liberty of extending the upper Stories of any Building which they... may erect adjoining to the said Alley over the same" (Alex. B:406).
1787, MAR 13	David Young to John Weathers Harper, taylor, for £200, "a certain corner Lott," 51'6"x47' (Alex. C:71).
1787, APR 18	John and Elizabeth Longdon to Samuel Simmonds, for £75, 15'x123'6", conveyed to Longdon by William Young (Alex. B:415; see also FDB B$_2$:484).

1791, AUG 15	David Young, butcher, to Ann, widow of George Hyneman, butcher of Alexandria, 25'x51'10", "with a 2-story house on said lott," 25'x18', "with the privilege of a 3-foot alley from said house joining to John Harper's lott & the alley to run the depth of the said lott which is 51'10" (FDB T:317). Ann married Dixon Brittingham (see Alex. I:471).
1792, JUL 16	David Young to Samuel Simmonds, for £75, 12'6"x51'10" adjoining the north line of John Longdon's lot, with use of a 3-foot alley adjoining south line of John Harper's lot, alley to extend west 22 feet south 12'6" to be used jointly by Young and Simmonds (FDB W:230).
1792, DEC 20	Thomas and Casina Conn to Peter Wise, for £706, 72'6"x24' (Alex. D:505).
1793, JUL 18	Samuel Simonds and wife Jane to Ann Hineman, for £75, 51'10"x12'6" (Alex. E:107).
1793, OCT 8	David Young to Diederick Sheckel, for £120, part of house and lot adjoining "the part of the house & lott of Nancy Hineman... on Royal Street," 51'6"x12'6" (Alex. E:145).
1794, APR 10	Diedrick Scheckel, baker, to Joseph Thornton, baker, for £350, part of Lot 55 (Alex. E:455). Thornton mortgage same date to Scheckel for £150 (Alex. E:459).
1797, FEB 16	Catharine Uhler, widow of the late Valentine Uhler, to John Rigg, 1/3 of parcel which descended to her upon the death of her brother Thomas [Young], for £40 (Alex. I:258).

(See also Alex. I:471; Alex. L:263, 391; Alex. N:186, 284).

LOT 56
Prince, Water St.[24] & Potomac River

1749, JUL 13	Trustees to Hon. William Fairfax (TM:1).
1752, MAR 28	William Ramsay and John Pagan, trustees, to the Honourable William Fairfax, for £18.16.3 (FDB C:299).
1753, MAR 1	Trustees to George William Fairfax, for £37.12.6 for Lots 56 and 57 (FDB C:459 msg; see FDB G:116).
1766, DEC 16	Trustees to George William Fairfax, Lots 56, 57 and 58 (TM:56).
1767, JAN 30	John Carlyle and William Ramsay, trustees, to George William Fairfax, conveying Lots 56 and 57 as one lot (FDB G:116).
1771, DEC 3/4	Robert Adam to Andrew Wales, half of Lots 56, 57 and 58 (see Alex. D:300).
1771, DEC 10	Andrew Wales, brewer, and Margaret his wife, to Robert Adam, mortgage for half of Lots 56, 57 and 58, for £331.17.6 and interest (FDB K:302). This was the same land Wales bought of Adam (FDB J:429 msg).

---

[24] The lot later extended to Union Street; Hening, Vol. 11, pp. 44-5, May 1782, 6th of Commonwealth, Chap. XXIV, "An act to empower the mayor, recorder, aldermen and common council of the town of Alexandria to lay a wharfage tax, and to extend water and Union-streets."

Alexandria, Virginia Town Lots, 1749-1801

1771, DEC 11/12	Robert Adam to John Hough[25], of Loudoun Co., part of Lots 56, 57 and 58, remainder after sale to Andrew Wales (FDB J:379, 382 msg; see also FDB K:370).
1772, SEP 23	Hon. George William Fairfax, Esq., and wife Sarah to Robert Adam, merchant, for £350, part of Lot 56, and Lots 57 and 58 (FDB K:124).
1773, JUN 13	John Hough, of Loudoun Co., to George Gilpin, merchant, for £200, 1/4 part of Lot 56 (FDB K:378). Hough guarantees good title or will pay to Gilpin £500 if Hough's wife Sarah claims dower interest (FDB K:381).
1773, JUN 14	John Hough, of Loudoun Co., and wife Sarah to Capt. John Harper, of Philadelphia, for £780, part of Lots 56, 57 and 58 (FDB K:368, 370).
1774, JUL 28	Andrew Wales, brewer, and Margaret his wife to Robert McCrea and Robert Mease, merchants, and Matthew Mease, of Philadelphia, merchant, for £350, part of Lots 56, 57 and 58 and a nine-foot alley between Water and Fairfax streets along the north line of Lots 57 and 58, and a six-foot wide alley through Lot 56 from Water Street to the River (FDB M:4).
1774, AUG 11	Robert Adam to Robert McCrea and Robert Mease, of Alexandria, and Matthew Mease, of Philadelphia, merchant, the moiety of Lots 56, 57 and 58 which Andrew Wales mortgaged to Adam and which had been forfeited for nonpayment (FDB M:21).
1777, JUN 16	George Gilpin and wife Katherine to Josiah Watson, merchant, for £600, 1/4 part of Lot 56 (FDB M:299).
1783, JUL 1	John Harper, merchant, to Michael Thorn, merchant, 88'x40' of Lot 56 extended with use of a ten-foot alley, for $100 (Spanish milled silver) annual rent (FDB O:248).
1783, JUL 1	John Harper to John Brice, 88'x40' of Lot 56, for $106-2/3 (Spanish milled silver) annual rent (FDB O:264). This parcel adjoins that rented by Harper to Michael Thorn.
1783, DEC 6	John Harper to John Boyer and Christian Slimmer, 42'x83' for $126 (Spanish milled) (FDB D:343).
1784, MAY 11	John Harper to Thomas Tobin, 20'x88' of Lot 56 extended (between Union and Water streets) for $80 (Spanish milled silver) annual rent (FDB P:177).
1785, DEC 6	Thomas Tobin to William Wright, 20'x88', Wright to pay the $80 rent to Harper (see Alex. G:155). Harper, for £200, remitted further rent on 17 SEP 1794 (Alex. G:155).
1786, APR 26	Robert and Nancy McCrea and Robert Mease to Michael Thorn, lease 39'x40', for $40 (Spanish silver milled) from 1 MAY 1786 (Alex. B:349).
1786, JUL 30	Nicholas Bryce [Brice], brother and heir of John Bryce, dec.[26], to Hannah Bryce, widow of John, 20'x88' (Alex. B:392).

---

[25] Columbian Mirror and Alexandria Gazette, 27 APR 1797, John Hough, deceased, his executors William, Samuel and Mahlon Hough, will sell his plantation containing 700 acres in Loudoun County, near Fairfax Meeting House, 40 miles from Alexandria and also a house and lot in Leesburg, a 73-acre tract in Shenandoah Co., and a 200-acre tract in Hampshire County.

[26] Virginia Journal and Alexandria Advertiser, 13 JUL 1786, John Bryce died recently; his estate accounts to be settled with Robert Bryce and William Wilson, the administrators who are also selling several pieces of his property in Alexandria; his heir at law is Nicholas Bryce (10 AUG 1896, 30 AUG 1787).

1786, JUL 31	Nicholas Bryce to Robert Bryce and William Wilson, "sundry lots to sell at public auction, subject to dower of John Brice's widow [Hannah] who has married James Kenner" (see Alex. D:341).
1790, FEB 4	Michael Thorn to Thomas Vowell, for $47 (Spanish milled) annual rent, part of Lot 56 extended, 45'6"x19' with use of a 10' alley, part of the piece rented by Thorn from Harper (FDB S:260).
1790, MAR 20	Michael Thorn to John Harper, the annual rent of $47½ (Spanish milled) paid by Thomas Vowell to Thorn (FDB S:269).
1790, JUL 22	Robert Bryce and William Wilson to James Kenner, for 20 shillings and £91.0.9 rent in arrears. Kenner, highest bidder at auction, to pay £32 annual rent to Capt. John Harper (Alex. D:341).
1790, DEC 1	John Harper to Josiah Watson, ten-foot wide passage from Watson's part of pier they built onto wharf, through to Prince Street (see Alex. I:300).
1792, MAY 25	James Kenner and wife Hannah, of Botetourt Co., to Thomas Vowell, for £250, 40' on Prince and 88'3½" back (Alex. D:443).
1793, APR 10	John Harper to Edward and Charles Harper, William Hartshorne and James Keith, in trust for daughter Peggy [Harper], 22'x40' (Alex. E:111; see also Alex. D:119, 135). Also same date to daughters Elizabeth Harper (Alex. E:128), Frances Rush Harper (Alex. E:135), and Mary Harper (see Alex. E:119).
1793, JUN 25	Robert and Nancy McCrea, now of the State of Georgia, and Robert and Betty Mease of Alexandria, to Thomas Crandle, lease 38'x83' with use of alleys, for $114 in half yearly payments (Alex. E:224).
1794, JAN 11	Michael Thorn to Michael O'Mara [O'Meara], for £700, all that parcel from Harper that Thorn did not convey to Thomas Vowell, 4 FEB 1790 (Alex. E:174; see Alex. G:136).
1794, AUG 27	John Harper remits half annual rent due from John Boyer and certifies Christian Slimmer to be free of rent, owing only $63 Spanish milled (Alex. F:98). Deed indicates, "...beginning on Union Street at dividing line between McCrea & Mease (now belonging to Thomas Crandel), and John Harper..." and also "whereas Slimmer & Boyer made a partition..." Boyer to pay Harper half the rent.
1794, DEC 17	John Harper to William Wright, for £198, two parcels north Prince, west of Union (Alex. F:185).
1795, JAN 12	William Wright and wife Ann to William Hoye, 17'2-1/4"x88'3½", lease for £18 annual rent (Alex. F:142).
1795, FEB 23	John Harper to John Crips Vowell and Thomas Vowell, Jr., for £150, part of Lot 56, 24'6"x88'3½" (FDB Y:28).
1795, JUN 10	Robert McCrea and wife Nancy, now of Georgia, and Robert Mease and wife Betty to John Harper, for £105, 39'7-3/4"x30' (Alex. F:478). Deed indicates that Matthew Mease sold his interest to Robert McCrea and Robert Mease (no date given), that Harper sold a parcel to Josiah Faxon, and adjoins William Wright.
1795, JUL 21	John Harper to Cavan Boa, lease for £15 annual rent for Harper's life, beginning at the northeast corner of Harper's brick warehouse, 37'x16'3½", "to Christian Slimmer's line" (Alex. F:267).

1795, AUG 24	John Harper to Michael O'Mara [O'Meara], for £180, remits $52½ annual rent (Alex. G:136).
1795, SEP 1	George Gilpin to Robert Henderson, lease, "that Frame Warehouse lately occupied by... Gilpin as a Store... contiguous to Gilpin and Harper's Dock..." for 7 years at £97/year (Alex. G:219).
1796, JUN 23	John Harper lease to Aloysius and Joseph Boone, same parcel conveyed by Harper in trust for daughter Mary on 10 APR 1793 (see Alex. E:119) for £40 annually, payable to Mary. Boones to build brick house three stories high within 3 years (see Alex. H:186), same for parcel conveyed to daughter Frances Rush [Harper] now Riddle, lease to Boones at £22 annually (see Alex. H:203).
1796, AUG 24	Andrew Wales and wife Margaret to Jesse Simms, for £600, "part of the ground & wharf made & extended by... Andrew Wales..." Simms not to intentionally stop up the Trunk [the communication] from the Brew house to the River. Parcel 38'1-3/4" to river (Alex. G:493).
1796, SEP 9	Jesse Simms to John Crips Vowell and Thomas Vowell, Jr., same piece Simms bought from Wales on 24 AUG 1796 (Alex. G:499).
1796, DEC 30	John Harper to Charles Harper, part of property conveyed by Robert McCrea and wife Nancy and Robert Mease and wife Betty to John Harper; "ground recently William Wright's, now Joseph Dyson's" (Alex. H:451).
1797, MAR 19	Josiah and Jane Watson to George Slacum, for £2214, Watson's 1/4 of Lot 56 and his part of the wharf and pier (Alex. I:300).
1797, APR 28	William and Ann Wright to George Slacum, for £162, 88'3½"x17'2-1/4", assign £18 annual rent due from [William] Hoye (Alex. I:307).
1797, MAY 25	Thomas Tobin to William Wright, for £80, 20'x88' (Alex. I:5, cites transaction of 6 DEC 1785).

(See also Alex. E:224, 264, 344; Alex. G:140; Alex. H:454, 488; Alex. K:329; Alex. L:102, 108, 379; Alex. M:232, 351; Alex. N:153, 313, 388; FDB S:269, 400, 426; FDB X:630; FDB Y:28, 85).

LOT 57
Prince & Water St.
(See also Lot 56)

1749, JUL 13	Trustees to Hon. William Fairfax (TM:1).
1752, MAR 28	William Ramsay and John Pagan, trustees, to [George] William Fairfax, for £18.16.3 (FDB C:300).
1753, MAR 1	Trustees to George William Fairfax, for £37.12.6, for Lots 56 and 57 (FDB C:459 msg; see FDB G:116).
1766, DEC 16	Trustees to George William Fairfax for Lots 56, 57 and 58 (TM:56).
1767, JAN 30	John Carlyle and William Ramsay, trustees, to George William Fairfax, conveying Lots 56, 57 and 58 as one lot (FDB G:116).
1771?, SEP 23	George William Fairfax to Robert Adam (see FDB K:124, 370).
1771, DEC 3/4	Robert Adam to Andrew Wales, half of Lots 56, 57 and 58 (see Alex. D:300).

1771, DEC 10	Andrew Wales to Robert Adam, mortgage for half of Lots 56, 57 and 58, for £331.70.6 and interest (FDB K:302). This was the same land Wales bought from Adam (FDB J:429 msg).
1771, DEC 11/12	Robert Adam to John Hough, of Loudoun Co., part of Lots 56, 57 and 58 (FDB J:379, 382 msg; see FDB K:370). Deed recites that George William Fairfax conveyed the property to Robert Adam.
1772, SEP 23	Hon. George William Fairfax, Esq., and wife Sarah to Robert Adam, merchant, for £350 for Lots 56, 57 and 58 (FDB K:124). Deed is dated 1772, but the receipt is dated 1771.
1773, JUN 14	John Hough, of Loudoun Co., and wife Sarah to Capt. John Harper, of Philadelphia, for £780, part of Lot 56, and Lots 57 and 58 (FDB K:370).
1774, JUL 28	Andrew Wales, brewer, and wife Margaret to Robert McCrea, Robert Mease and Matthew Mease, of Philadelphia, for £350, part of Lots 56, 57 and 58, and a nine-foot alley between Water and Fairfax streets along the north line of Lots 57 and 58 and an alley six feet wide through Lot 56 from Water Street to the river (FDB M:4).
1774, AUG 11	Robert Adam to Robert McCrea and Robert Mease, of Alexandria, merchants, and Matthew Mease, of Philadelphia, merchant, the moiety of Lots 56, 57 and 58 which Andrew Wales mortgaged to Adam and which were forfeited for nonpayment (FDB M:21).
1778, NOV 16	Robert and Agnes McCrea and Robert Mease to Josiah Watson, all that parcel purchased from Wales (see Alex. D:294).
1781, AUG 7	Matthew Mease, of Philadelphia, to Robert McCrea and Robert Mease, his interest in the lots (FDB D_4:315).
1782, SEP 16	John Harper to William Lyles, Jr., for $80 (Spanish milled) annual rent, 40'x88' of Lot 57 (FDB N:583 msg; see FDB Z:51; see Alex. B:364).
1783, OCT 1	John Harper, merchant, to John Forbes, merchant of Md., 33'x88' of Lot 57, for $99 (Spanish milled silver) (FDB O:61). Deed recites that Harper's house was then occupied by Col. William Lyles.
1785, NOV 5	William Lyles, Jr. to John B. Murray, Obediah Bowen and John P. Mumford, for 40 guineas, £32 annual rent of part of Lot 57, 40'x88' (see FDB R:530 and FDB Z:51; original deed recorded in Alex. B:366).
1786, AUG 12	John Harper releases William Lyles, Jr. with proviso that Lyles "erect a larger frame house with brick or stone chimney..." (Alex. B:364).
1786, AUG 17	John Murray, Obediah Bowen and John Mumford to Lewis Deblois, Jr. and Edward Kennicutt Thompson, 15'x60' for 15 guineas annual rent (see FDB Z:52; Alex. B:370).
1788, MAY 28	John Forbes, of Md., to John Harper (FDB R:119). Deed recites that deed from Harper to Forbes was mislaid and cancelled. Forbes gives up all claim to the part of Lot 57 conveyed to him by Harper in return for release from payment of all rents due from this day.
1789, SEP 18	William Lyles, Jr. and wife Sarah to John Murray, Obediah Bowen and John Mumford (FDB R:530; see FDB Z:52). Previous deed of 7 NOV 1785, recorded in Alexandria Hustings Court, rented to grantees, 40'x88' for 40 £32 yearly. Deed releases the grantees from payment of the £32 yearly and provides for a payment of £400 additional.

Alexandria, Virginia Town Lots, 1749-1801

1790, MAY 22	Same transaction as 16 NOV 1778 (see Alex. D:294; FDB S:426).
1790, JUN 1	John Harper to William Hodgson, part of Lot 57, 31'x88' (FDB S:400).
1793, FEB 8	Josiah and Jane Watson to Jonah Thompson, for £250, 123'5"x31'6" (Alex. E:73).
1793, APR 10	John Harper to Charles and Edward Harper, William Hartshorne and James Keith, in trust for daughter Elizabeth [Harper], annual rent on parcel with three-story brick dwelling house "now in the occupation of Dr. Craik" (Alex. E:128). Deed recites "...a parcel sold by John Harper to Wm. Hodgson whereon is erected a 3-story brick house now in the tenure of... Wm. Hodgson."
1794, MAY 26	Andrew and Margaret Wales to Jonah Thompson, for £375, part of Lot 57 (Alex. E:296).
1795, AUG 24	George DeBlois, of Boston, Suffolk Co., Mass., merchant, to William James Hall, merchant, for £150, all his interest in 60'x15' of Lot 57, same parcel as conveyed to John Murray & Co. to Lewis DeBlois, Jr. and Edward Kennicutt Thompson, "with the buildings now thereon standing." Hall also to pay 15 guineas a year to John Murray & Co. George's wife Lydia DeBlois surrenders her dower rights (Alex. F:445).

(Other deeds for parts of Lot 57: FDB S:400, 439, 446; FDB Z:51, FDB B$_2$:299).

LOT 58
Prince & Fairfax

1749, JUL 14	Trustees to John Champ, for £8.12 (TM:3, 40, 43).
1767, JAN 30	John Carlyle and William Ramsay, trustees, to George William Fairfax, son of Hon. William Fairfax, for £18 (FDB G:115, 116). Deed indicates that Hon. William Fairfax had been deeded Lot 58 by the Trustees.
1771, DEC 3/4	Robert Adam to Andrew Wales, half of Lots 56, 57 and 58 (see Alex. D:300).
1771, DEC 11/12	George William Fairfax to Robert Adam; Robert Adam to John Hough (FDB K:370).
1772, APR 21	John Hough, of Loudoun Co., merchant, to Benjamin Shreve, hatter, for £50, 40'x61'7" of Lot 58 (FDB K:1).
1772, SEP 22/3	William Fairfax, Esq., and John Carlyle, Gent., executors of Hon. William Fairfax, dec., to Robert Adam, for £125, all of Lot 58 (FDB K:121).
1772, SEP 23	Hon. George William Fairfax, Esq. and wife Sarah to Robert Adam, merchant, for £350, part of Lot 56, and Lots 57 and 58 (FDB K:124).
1773, JUN 14	John Hough, of Loudoun Co., and wife Sarah to Capt. John Harper of Philadelphia, for £780, parts of Lots 56, 57 and 58, "being parts of 3 lots that the Trustees of said Town sold & conveyed to George William Fairfax, Esq., & by him conveyed to Robert Adams [sic] & by the said Robert Adam sold & conveyed to the said John Hough by deeds bearing date the 11th and 12th days of December... 1771" (FDB K:370).
1774, JUL 28	Andrew and Margaret Wales to McCrea, Mease and Mease (see FDB M:4,

	21; Alex. D:300)
1775, APR 15	Benjamin Shreve, hatter, and wife Hannah,[27] to Josiah Watson, merchant, for £355, 40'x123'5", "beginning on the east side of Fairfax Street upon the said street at the line dividing the said lott #58 beween the said Benjamin Shreve & Robert McCrea, Robert & Matthew Mease, to them conveyed by Andrew Wales..." (FDB M:158).
1783, NOV 6	John Harper, merchant, to James Lownes, 19'x58' to the line between Harper and Josiah Watson, for $38 (Spanish milled) annual rent (FDB O:254; see FDB S:366).
1786, by 29 DEC	John Harper lease to Aaron Hughes. John Harper to John Gill (see Alex. B:111).
1786, DEC 29	John Harper to William and John Hickman, for $38 (Spanish milled) annual rent (see FDB S:366).
1786, DEC 29	James and Sarah Lownes to William Hickman, Jr. and John Hickman, for £30, 19'x48', "...to line of Aaron Hughes" (Alex. C:112).
1787, JUL 6	John Harper to William and John Hickman, for $9-2/3 (Spanish milled), for 4'10"x48', adjoining first piece (Alex. C:98; see FDB S:366).
1789, OCT 15	William Hickman and wife Rebecca and John Hickman and wife Mary to William Hodgson, for £500, two pieces rented from Harper, the annual rent to be paid by Hodgson to Harper (FDB S:366).
1790, MAY 29	Josiah Watson to Jonah Thompson, small parcel of Lots 57 and 58 (see Alex. D:294).
1791, JUL 7	Andrew and Margaret Wales to Jonah Thompson, for 5 shillings, part 41'x1'6" (Alex. D:294).
1791, JUL 8	Andrew and Margaret Wales to Marcus McCausland, of Baltimore, Md. (Alex. D:300).
1793, FEB 8	Jonah and Margaret Thompson to Josiah Watson, for £5, 114'x4'4" (Alex. E:79).
1793, APR 10	John Harper to Edward and Charles Harper, William Hartshorne and James Keith, in trust for daughter Peggy [Harper] the annual rents from Aaron Hughes and John Gill, 48'x23'10", "to the line of ground belonging to Dr. Kennedy" (Alex. E:111). Deed states that the parcel is occupied by John Gill's storehouse.
1795, OCT 5	John Harper and wife Mary to James Kennedy, for £50, ...on a line of parcel conveyed by Josiah Watson to James Kennedy, 50'10"x5' (Alex. F:462).
1795, OCT 5	James Kennedy and wife Letitia to John Harper, for £50, part of Lot 58, adjoining the brick property occupied by David Easton and that occupied by Dr. James Craik (Alex. F:466).
1797, JUN 7	Marcus McCausland and wife Mary Ann, of Baltimore, Md., to Bryan Hampson, for £500, same parcel conveyed to McCausland (Alex. I:110).

(See also FDB S:392, 400, 439, 446; FDB U$_2$:188; FDB Y$_2$:4; Alex. H:451;

---

[27] Virginia Journal and Alexandria Advertiser, 30 DEC 1784, Mrs. Hannah Shreve, wife of Benjamin Shreve, merchant of Alexandria, died.

Alex. M:184, 289).

LOT 59
Prince & Fairfax

1749, JUL 14	Trustees to Col. William Fitzhugh (TM:2).
1752, MAR 28	William Ramsay and John Pagan, trustees, to John Peyton, of Stafford Co., for £7.10.6 (FDB C:311).
c.1781	John Peyton to Lawrason, Hunter and Arell (FDB N:558 msg).
1782, AUG 25	William Hunter and wife Christiana, James and Alice Lawrason, and David Arell to Jacob Hesse [Hess], for 11,000 pounds net of crop tobacco and £60, part of Lot 59, "beginning at a corner of a lot granted by Lawrason, Hunter & Arell to Samuel Simmons... to Valentine Peyton's lot...", 25'x80' (FDB O:126).
1782, AUG 25	William and Christiana Hunter, James and Alice Lawrason and David Arell to Samuel Simmons, 25'x60', adjoining William Farrell (FDB O:129).
1783, JUN 7	James and Alice Lawrason, William and Christiana Hunter, all of Alexandria, to David Arell, for £50, part of Lot 59, 100'x20' (FDB O:27).
1783, JUN 7	Same grantors with David Arell to Benjamin Shreve, for 25,400 pounds tobacco, parts of Lot 59, 25'x60' and 20'x100' (FDB O:29).
1783, JUN 7	James and Alice Lawrason and David Arell to William Hunter, for 40,000 pounds crop tobacco, part of Lot 59, 80'x75' and 20'x60' (FDB O:31).
1784, AUG 5	James Adam and wife Elizabeth to John Wise, 20'x100', for $66-2/3 (silver) annual rent (FDB P:43).
1784, NOV 16	Valentine Peyton and wife Mary Butler Peyton, of Stafford Co., to John Wise, for £351, 120'x38' (FDB P:345).
1784, DEC 1	William Hunter and wife Christiana to Robert Lyle, merchant of Alexandria, for £200, 20'x75' part of the piece conveyed by Lawrason and Arell to Hunter on 7 JUN 1783 (FDB P:259). Robert Lyle devised to son Robert Lyle who conveyed to Robert Evans on 13 JUN 1796, 20'x75' (FDB Y:519).
1785, MAR 28	William and Christiana Hunter to Joseph Greenway, 25'x60' (part of piece conveyed by Lawrason and Arell to Hunter on 7 JUN 1783), for 60 guineas annual rent (FDB P:465). Greenway back to Hunter (see Alex. D:380).
1786, MAY 15	Benjamin Shreve and wife Susanna to Thomas Whiting, of Gloucester Co., for £400, 20'x100' (FDB Q:240).
1786, JUN 19	John Wise and wife Elizabeth to Peter Wise, for £175, 19'x129' (part of piece conveyed to John Wise by Valentine Peyton on 16 NOV 1784) with use of nine-foot alley (FDB Q:182).
1787, DEC 4	John Wise to his wife Elizabeth Wise, to "enable his said wife Elizabeth to make provision for her children in case the said John Wise should die before her," 19'x120', "with 3-storied brick house theron in which Messrs. Saunderson & Rumney at present keep Store..." (Alex. C:150).
1792, JAN 5	William Hunter, Sr. and wife Kitty [Christiana] to George Slacum, for £350, 60'x20' (Alex. D:380).
1793, AUG 6	Samuel Harrison, of Charles Co., Md. and wife Barbara, "late Barbara

	Hess, relict of Jacob Hess," to Philip Marsteller, have for Barbara's lifetime, a brick house on Fairfax Street "adjoining... Mr. John Wise & Samuel Simmons respectively" (Alex. E:151). Deed recites that after Barbara's death, house and lot go to Jacob Butt, son of Jacob Hess' brother-in-law Adam Butt (Jacob now only about 5 years old), Jacob to pay executors £25 (see also FWB E:251 for will of Jacob Hess, dated 23 FEB 1788, probated 23 APR 1788).
1794, DEC 12	Thomas Whiting and wife Mary, of Gloucester Co., to Philip G. Marsteller, for £190, 100'x20' (Alex. F:235).
1795, JAN 24	Philip Godhelp Marsteller and wife Christiana to Jacob Resler, for £275, 100'x20', conveyed to Marsteller in DEC 1794 by Thomas Whiting (Alex. F:226).

(See also FDB U_2:188; Alex. L:61, M:204).

LOT 60
Prince & Royal

1749, JUL 14	Trustees to John Peyton (TM:2).
1749, SEP 20	John Carlyle and Hugh West, trustees, to John Peyton, for £8.12. (FDB C:19).
1754, SEP 9	Escheated by trustees and resold to Thomas Harrison, for £4.13. (TM:22, 49; FDB D:1 msg).
1763, FEB 1	Escheated again (TM:49). Resold to Richard Arell c.1764 (FDB F:230, 466 msg).
1775, APR 3	Richard and Eleanor Arell to Thomas Davis, 70'x70', "with all houses & buildings..." a 3-lives lease for $74 annual rent (FDB M:74).
1795, NOV 17	Richard and Eleanor Arell to Michael Steiber, lease part for $90 (silver) annually, "according to the present weight and fineness of the Dollar" (Alex. F:458).

(See also Alex. K:459; Alex. L:126, 133; Alex. M:127).

LOT 61
Prince & Royal

1749, JUL 14	Trustees to John Moncure, clerk, for 5/9 (TM:3).
1752, MAR 28	William Ramsay and John Pagan, trustees, to John Moncure, of Stafford Co., for £0.5.9 (FDB C:306).
1754, SEP 9	Escheated by trustees, resold to William Sewell, for £5.7.6 (TM:22; FDB D:169, from John Carlyle and William Ramsay, trustees).
1766, DEC 27	William Sewell, peruke maker[28], and wife Elizabeth, to Messrs. John

---

[28] Maryland Gazette, 13 SEP 1759, There will be sold, at Alexandria, Fairfax County, Virginia, a lot belonging to William Sewell, peruke maker, containing half an acre.

	Carlyle & John Dalton, William Ramsay, John Muir, merchants, Henry Ellison of Whitehaven, merchant, and Joshua Pollard of Liverpool, ship master, for £42.15.7 due Carlyle & Dalton, £83.14.4 due Ramsay, £23.7.9 due Muir, £62.10.7 due Ellison, and £17 due Pollard, plus interest, the mortgaged Lot 61, "with all buildings thereon" to be void when debts paid (FDB G:119).
1782, APR 17	Sold for debt by Court of Chancery to William Ramsay, the Elder (FDB N:565 msg; recited in later deed FDB O:117; see also Alex. E:41; Alex. H:6, 9, 181). Conveyance from sheriff Thomas Pollard to Ramsay dated 20 MAY 1782 (Alex. H:6).
1783, OCT 2	William Ramsay, Gent. and wife Anne to John Fitzgerald, merchant, for £205, 24½'x88' (FDB O:117).
1784, JUN 24	John Fitzgerald and wife Jane to David Keneday [Kennedy], of Berkeley Co., 24'x88', for $100 (Spanish milled) annual rent (FDB P:246).
1785, JAN 26	William Ramsay, Gent. and wife Ann to Colin McIver, 88'x24'6", for £225, adjoining piece conveyed by Ramsay and wife to Fitzgerald (FDB P:385).
1793, MAY 20	William Ramsay, Dennis Ramsay, Robert Allison and Michael Madden, executors of William Ramsay, late of Alexandria, dec., Gent., to Lemuel Bent and John Bass Dabney, for £130, 157'6"x40' (Alex. E:41).
1793, MAY 20	William Ramsay's executors to Samuel Simmonds, for £81, 123'5"x19' (Alex. E:102).
1793, MAY 21	Lemuel Bent and wife Betsey and John Bass Dabney and wife Roxa to John Horner, for £140, 157'6"x40' (Alex. E:50).
1794, APR 21	John and Jane Fitzgerald to George McMunn, lease for £16.10. annual rent, 88'x24'6" (Alex. F:244).
1795, AUG 17	John McIver to Charles Love, lease of house on Prince Street at present occupied by McIver, for 10 years, also the lot and out houses, the lot having a 25'8" front; McIver to build a stable and loft. Love agrees he will not let or sublet to any person of disreputable character. Love to pay £40 per year (Alex. G:222).
1795, NOV 7	John McIver and wife Margaret to William Crammond of Philadelphia, for £450, 88'x24'6" (Alex. F:483, 488, 498). Deed states that property passed from Colin to John McIver and upon Colin's death it was leased by John to James Kennedy for 5 years from 1 MAY 1796.
1796, MAY 4	Morris Worrell and wife Elizabeth, late widow of William Sewell, dec'd., to executors of William Ramsay "the Elder," dec'd., for $1, 127'6"x34'5", part of widow's dower (Alex. H:6, 9).
1796, MAY 17	William Ramsay's executors to Joseph Cary, 10'x88' (see FDB Z:74).
1796, MAY 17	William Ramsay's executors to Joseph Cary, 88'x34'5", for £182.8. (Alex. H:16).
1796, JUN 28	Joseph Cary to John Horner, same parcel conveyed 17 MAY 1796, for £100 (FDB Z:74).
1796, JUN 29	Joseph Cary to George McMunn, for £82.8., 88'x22'5" (Alex. I:106).
1796, SEP 22	Executors of William Ramsay, the Elder, dec'd., to William Summers, 83'5"x18', for £90 (Alex. H:181).

(See also FDB A₂:488; FWB E:298; Alex. I:486; Alex. K:259, 297; Alex. M:84).

LOT 62
Prince, Between Water St. and Potomac River[29]

1749, JUL 13	Trustees to Col. George William Fairfax, for Lots 62 and 63 (TM:1, 40).
1749, NOV 20	John Carlyle and Hugh West, trustees, to Willoughby Newton, of Westmoreland Co., Gent., Lots 62 and 63, for £41.18.6 (TM:7; FDB C:27).
1752, NOV 10	Willoughby Newton to George Johnston, Lots 62 and 63, for £64.0 (FDB C:382).
1769, Prior to	George Johnston's executors to Jonathan Hall and George Gilpin (FDB H:40 msg; see FDB K:5).
c.1769	George Gilpin to Jonathan Hall (FDB H:185 msg; see FDB O:104).
1783, NOV 18	George Gilpin, Gent. and wife Jane to Michael Maddin, merchant, 40'x44'4", for $80 (silver) annual rent (FDB O:104; see also Alex. C:278).
1783, NOV 18	George Gilpin, Gent. and wife Jane to Andrew Wales, 40'x44'4" for $80 (silver) annual rent (FDB O:110).
1783, NOV 18	George Gilpin, Gent. and wife Jane to Washer Blunt, 40'x44'4" for $80 (silver) annual rent, adjoining parcel rented by Gilpin and wife to Andrew Wales, and a parcel rented to Michael Madden, also a parcel belonging to the heirs of Jonathan Hall (FDB O:107).
1783, After	Andrew Wales to John Short (see Alex. C:154).
1786, MAR 20	George and Jane Gilpin lease to Isaac McPherson and Daniel McPherson, Jr., for £240 the Gilpins remit further rent from Isaac, 44'x40' (Alex. G:217).
1786, DEC 20	Michael and Hannah Madden mortgage 18'x44'4" to William Sydebotham[30], of Bladensburg, Md. (Alex. C:278).
1787, JUL 18	John Short and wife Anne to Thomas Richards, for £37.10., and annual rent to George Gilpin, 20'x44'4" (Alex. C:154).
1793, JUN 18	Isaac McPherson to daughters Jane and Elizabeth McPherson in trust, 44'x40'. This deed recites that the parcel was conveyed to Daniel and Isaac McPherson by Elisha Janney on 5 APR 1793 (Alex. E:34, 37).
1793, JUL 8	Michael and Hannah Madden lease to Patrick Burnes, 44'4"x22', adjoining [Jonathan] Hall and [Francis] Peyton; Burnes to assume Madden's obligations to Shreve and Lawrason. Patrick signs "Byrne" (Alex. F:368; see Alex. H:475).
1793, NOV 1	Samuel and Mary Hanson to Isaac McPherson, 123'5"x88'3½" (see Alex. G:238).
1794, Prior to	Parcel rented by George Gilpin and wife to Andrew Wales became vested in Robert Hamilton & Co., subject to annual rent. Robert Hamilton & Co. conveyed to Thomas Richards (see FDB X:469).

---

[29] Lot extended to Union Street.
[30] Virginia Journal and Alexandria Gazette, 1 AUG 1793, William Sydebotham, dec'd., his administrators are D. Ross and R. Cramphin of Alexandria.

1794, JUL 30	Joseph and Elizabeth [Hall] Massey and Abraham and Sarah [Hall] Falconer to John Walter Fletcher, for £625, 150'22½" (Sarah and Elizabeth daughters of Jonathan Hall), "the extreem [sic] part of a lot sold by Abraham Falconer to Francis Peyton" (Alex. E:356).
1794, AUG 5	Thomas Richards and wife Ann to John Crips Vowell and Thomas Vowell, Jr., for £350, 20'x44'4", adjoining Isaac McPherson's warehouse (FDB X:469).
1794, AUG 8	Thomas Richards and wife Ann to Francis Peyton, for £200, 44'4"x20' (Alex. G:44). Deed states John Short sold one part to Thomas Richards, and remainder to Samuel Montgomery Brown; Richards and Brown each paid half ($40) the annual rent; Richards acquired Brown's portion and now owns the parcel that Gilpins leased to Wales, the Gilpins remitting the rent requirement.
1794, DEC 24	George and Jane Gilpin to Benjamin Shreve and James Lawrason, for £510, remit all rent due from 51'x44'4" parcel (Alex. F:111).
1795, AUG 8	William Summers, sergeant of Town of Alexandria, to Benjamin Shreve. Deed states Michael Madden failed to pay off note of 20 DEC 1786 to [William] Sydebotham. Sydebotham died before a decree of sale could be executed. Sydebotham's executors revived suit and got judgment for £245.3.5 and interest against Madden who again failed to pay. Parcel sold to Benjamin Shreve for £390 (Alex. F:393).
1795, OCT 12	Francis Peyton and wife Sarah to Josias Milburne Speake, of Md., mariner, for £452, part of Lot 62. "This is the entire piece of ground conveyed to Peyton by Thomas Richards plus the west end of the parcel conveyed to Peyton by Abraham Falconer and wife" (Alex. G:4).
1796, JAN 1	Isaac McPherson to Elisha Janney and George Irish, mortgage on 123'5"x88'3½", the parcel conveyed by Samuel and Mary Hanson to Isaac McPherson on 1 NOV 1793 (Alex. G:238, 243).
1796, FEB 15	George and Jane Gilpin, for £240, remit to Isaac McPherson all further rent (Alex. G:217).
1796, FEB 18	John Crips Vowell and wife Margaret, Thomas Vowell, Jr., and wife Mary to Alexander McKenzie, for £450, 44'4"x20' (Alex. G:211). Deed states beginning "at that lot of ground & warehouse late the property of Isaac McPherson, but [now] the property of Elisha Janney & George Irish, being 129' E. of Water St."
1796, AUG 8	William Summers, by and for the Alexandria Hustings Court, to Benjamin Shreve (see Alex. I:149).
1796, SEP 1?	Benjamin Shreve and wife Susannah to David Ross and Richard Cramphen, of Prince Georges Co., Md., for £390, 18'x44'4", same property sold by William Summers to Shreve (Alex. I:149).

(See also Alex I:399; Alex. K:511, 546; Alex. M:443, 466; Alex. N:88, 356; and O:7, 41 and 53).

LOT 63
Prince & Water St.

1749, JUL 13	Trustees to Col. George William Fairfax for Lots 62 and 63 (TM:1, 40).
1749, NOV 20	John Carlyle and Hugh West, trustees, to Willoughby Newton, of Westmoreland Co., Gent., Lots 62 and 63, for £41.18.6 (TM:7; FDB C:27).
1752, NOV 10	Willoughby Newton to George Johnston, Lots 62 and 63, for £64 (FDB C:382).
1769, Prior to	George Johnston's executors to Jonathan Hall and George Gilpin (FDB H:40 msg; see FDB K:5).
c.1769	George Gilpin to Jonathan Hall, part of Lots 62 and 63 (FDB H:185 msg; see FDB O:104). Hall died intestate. Property descended to daughters Sarah and Elizabeth (see Alex. F:51).
1783, NOV 18	George Gilpin, Gent. and wife Jane to Samuel Montgomery Brown, merchant, 44'x44'4", for $88 (silver) annual rent (FDB O:101).
1786	Samuel Montgomery Brown and wife Mary to Nugent Ellis[31]. Deed mislaid and not recorded (see FDB Y:511).
1786, JUN 1	George Gilpin and wife Jane to Philip Marsteller, 44'4"x45' for 45 guineas annual rent (FDB Q:283).
1787, DEC 20	Philip and Magdalena Marsteller, store keeper, to John Korn, baker, 44'4"x23', lease for 23 guineas (Alex. C:225).
1790, APR 27	Brown and Ellis convey their interests to Gilpin (FDB Y:511).
1792, DEC 20	John Korn and wife Rosannah to Robert Hamilton, for £150, same parcel as conveyed by Marsteller to Korn (Alex. E:318). Korn to produce a grant from Gilpin for a 3½' alley.
1793, JAN 16	Abraham Falconer and wife Sarah [Hall], of Baltimore, Md. and Joseph Massey and wife Elizabeth [Hall], of Queen Anne's Co., Md. to George Gilpin, for £330, 150'x22'2" (Alex. F:51).
1794, JAN 22	George and Jane Gilpin to Robert Hamilton, 44'4"x36', lease for $72 (silver) annually each 31 DEC (Alex. E:305).
1794, MAR 19	George and Jane Gilpin to Philip Marsteller, 23'x44'4", for 230 guineas and 22 guineas rent (Alex. E:323).
1794, MAR 20	George Gilpin and wife Jane to Robert Hamilton, for $1, 44'4"x4' (Alex. E:301). Marstellers remit to Hamilton 23 guineas rent (Alex. E:328).
1796, MAY 10	Philip Godhelp Marsteller and wife Christiana to Alexander McKenzie, for £44, 22'2"x20' (Alex. G:506).
1796, MAY 13	Philip Godhelp Marsteller and wife Christiana to Elisha Janney and George Irish, for £96.16., 44'x22'2", "to Faulkner's [Falconer?] line." Marstellers to lay off a four-foot alley (Alex. G:510).

(See also FDB B$_2$:493; Alex. I:384; Alex. L:225, 401; and Alex. O:41, 53).

---

[31] Complete Records [Alexandria], Liber A, fols. 1-2, will of William Ellis, at present in the Town of Alexandria, mentions gift to his father Nugent Ellis of the County of Donnegall in the Kingdom of Ireland, *all my estate of watsoever kind or nature.*

LOT 64
Prince & Water St.
(See also Lot 65)

1749, JUL 14	Trustees to Augustine Washington (TM:3).
1752, MAR 28	William Ramsay and John Pagan, Trustees, to Augustine Washington, of Westmoreland Co., for Lots 64 and 65, for £16.2.6 (FDB C:309).
1754, SEP 9	Lots [64 and 65] escheated by Trustees and resold to William Ramsay, for £37.1.9 (TM:22, 23).
1757, JUL 21	William Ramsay mortgage to John Dixon, of Whitehaven, Lots 64 and 65 (FDB D:452).
1774, MAY 24	William Ramsay to John Dixon, Lots 64 and 65, now forfeited (FDB L:321).
1774, JUL 13	John Dixon, of the Town of Whitehaven, England, merchant, by Harry Piper, attorney in fact, to Robert McCrea and Robert Mease, of Alexandria, merchants, and John Boyd, physician of Baltimore, Md., for £280, part of Lot 64, 150'7"x123'8" (FDB M:18).
1776, MAR 23	John Dixon by Harry Piper to Daniel of St. Thomas Jennifer and Robert Townshend Hooe, merchants, of Md., for £300, for 98'7"x30'10" part of Lot 64 (FDB M:213) and the same size parcel in Lot 65.
1777, JAN 20	John Dixon, of the Town of Whitehaven, England, merchant, by Harry Piper, attorney in fact, to John Mills, merchant, parts of Lots 64 and 65, "beginning at the lot... sold to William Hartshorne [clerk's error?, should be Joseph Saunders?] on which Doctor Chapin is building on Fairfax Street..." (FDB M:259).
1778, JUL 17	John Dixon to Robert McCrea, Robert Mease and John Boyd, of Baltimore, part (see Alex. B:206).
1778, JUL 17	John Boyd, physician, of Baltimore, and wife Ann, to Robert McCrea and Robert Mease, for £400, his interest in Lot 64 (FDB D_4:218).
1784, DEC 22	Robert McCrea and wife Ann, and Robert Mease, to Michael Swope, for £253, part of Lot 64, 98'6"x23' (FDB P:226).
1784, DEC 22	Robert McCrea and wife Ann, and Robert Mease, to Paltzer Spangler, of York Co., Pa., for £253, part of Lot 64, 23'x98'6" (FDB P:237).
1785, OCT 26	[21 NOV 1785] Robert and Ann McCrea and Robert Mease to Robert Townhend Hooe [of Alexandria] and Richard Harrison [of Cadiz, Spain], 98'6"x23'3" (Alex. B:206, 210).
1785, OCT 28	Robert Townshend Hooe, of Alexandria, and Richard Harrison of Cadiz, Spain to Christian and Mary Slimmer, three feet along Lot 64 line with Lot 72 for an alley (Alex. B:197).
1785, OCT 29	Robert Townshend Hooe and Richard Harrison to Jacob Harman, part of Lot 64, 123'5"x26" (see Alex. F:173).
1785, NOV 8	Robert Townshend Hooe and Richard Harrison to Robert McCrea and Robert Mease, for £350, Jacob Harman's annual rent (Alex. B:214; see Alex. F:173).
1785, DEC 12	Robert and Nancy McCrea and Robert Mease to Sebastian Schiess, part of Lot 64, 98'6"x23'3" (see Alex. D:270).
1787, JAN 27	Sebastian Schiess to Joseph Cary, William Wilson and Philip Marsteller (see Alex. D:270; FDB W:376).

1787, MAR 23	Michael and Eve Swope to Jacob and Adam Simon Swoope, for £600, part of Lot 64, 98'6"x23' (see Alex. C:138).
1787, SEP 29	Jacob and Adam Simon Swope appoint Benjamin Augustus Hamp, attorney, to rent out for debt "that Lott of Ground and Brick house belonging to us upon Prince Street" (Alex. C:138).
1789, JUL 20	Robert McCrea and Robert Mease to James Miller and John Miller, of Philadelphia, Pa., for £156, part of Lot 64, 123'5½"x26' (FDB R:448).
1790, JUN 11	James Millar [Miller] and John Miller, City of Philadelphia, to Robert Townshend Hooe and Richard Harrison, for £156, part of Lot 64, 123'5"x26' (FDB S:385).
1790, DEC 22	Robert McCrea and Robert Mease assigned rent to Samuel Johnston (see Alex. F:173).
1791, FEB 3	Joseph Cary, William Wilson and Philip Marsteller to Christian Mayer, of Baltimore, Md., for £700, 98'6"x23'3" (Alex. D:270).
1795, APR 22	Samuel and Elizabeth Johnston, of Baltimore, to Robert Townshend Hooe, for £156, assignment of 26 guineas rent (Alex. F:173).

(See also FDB T:175; Y$_2$:5).

LOT 65
Prince & Fairfax
(See also Lot 64)

1749, JUL 14	Trustees to Augustine Washington (TM:3).
1752, MAR 28	William Ramsay and John Pagan, Trustees, to Augustine Washington, of Westmoreland Co., for Lots 64 and 65, for £16.2.6 (FDB C:309).
1754, SEP 9	Lots [64 and 65] escheated by Trustees and resold to William Ramsay, for £37.1.9 (TM:22, 23).
1757, JUL 21	William Ramsay mortgage to John Dixon of Whitehaven, Lots 64 and 65 (FDB D:452).
1774, MAY 24	William Ramsay to John Dixon of Whitehaven, merchant, Lots 64 and 65, now forfeited (FDB L:321).
1774, MAY 25	John Dixon of Whitehaven, merchant, by Harry Piper to William Hartshorne, merchant, for £65.10., part of Lot 65, 124'7"x30'10¼" (FDB L:322). By power of attorney from Dixon to Piper, dated 8 AUG 1757. John Dixon, of the County of Cumberland in the Kingdom of England, merchant, authorizes Harry Piper, merchant, to sell Ramsay's forfeited property (FDB D:455).
1774, MAY 25	John Dixon of Whitehaven, merchant, by Harry Piper, to Joseph Saunders, City of Philadelphia, merchant, for £134.10., part of Lot 65 (FDB L:324).
1774, JUL 13	John Dixon, Town of Whitehaven, England, by Harry Piper, attorney in fact, to Robert McCrea and Robert Mease, of Alexandria, merchants, and John Boyd, physician, of Baltimore, Md., Lots 64 and 65 (FDB M:18).
1775, FEB 4	Joseph Saunders, of Philadelphia, merchant, and wife Hannah to Edward Ramsay of the Town of Alexandria on the River Potowmack, house carpenter, 30'10¼"x98'5", with use of two 10' wide alleys for annual rent

	of 28 Spanish milled pieces of eight (FDB M:41). The parcel was bounded on the east by "land granted by Joseph Saunders to son John," and on the west by ground "then of William Ramsay, Esquire, but now of Joseph Harrison" (Alex. D:330).
1775, FEB 4	Joseph Saunders, City of Philadelphia, merchant, to John Saunders, of Town of Alexandria on the River Potowmack, house carpenter, 30'10¼"x114'5", for 33 Spanish milled pieces of eight... annual rent (FDB M:46; see FDB D_4:284).
1775, OCT 16	Joseph Saunders, of Philadelphia, to Benjamin Chapin, for £4 annual rent, 826-2/3 square feet (see FDB W:64).
1776, MAR 23	John Dixon, Town of Whitehaven, England, merchant, by Harry Piper, attorney in fact, to Daniel of St. Thomas Jennifer and Robert Townshend Hooe, of Md., merchants, for £300, part of Lot 64 (98'7"x30'10") and part of Lot 65, same size (FDB M:213).
1777, JAN 20	John Dixon, Town of Whitehaven, England, by Harry Piper, attorney in fact, to John Mills, merchant, parts of Lots 64 and 65, "beginning at the lot... sold to William Hartshorne [Joseph Saunders?] on which Doctor Chapin is building on Fairfax Street" (FDB M:259).
1778, FEB 18	Daniel of St. Thomas Jennifer sold his part to Richard and Joseph White Harrison (see Alex. K:8).
1778, SEP 21	Edward Ramsay to William Hunter, 98'5"x30'10¼" (see Alex. D:330).
1781, MAY 22	William Hunter to John Jolly, lease for parts of Lot 65 (FDB D_4:284; see also FDB S:1).
1781, OCT 15	Benjamin Chapin's will, probated 15 OCT 1781, devises house and lot to sons Hiram and Gurdin (FWB D:233).
1783, JUL 21	John Mills to William Brown, for £280, part of Lot 65 (FDB O:82), "beginning at the corner of a lott belonging to the estate of Dr. Chapin, dec'd., whereon his widow now lives... to a lott sold by the said John Mills to Col. Robert T. Hooe...", 26'x123'5" (FDB N:266 msg).
1786, JUN 29	Hiram Chapin to Gurdin Chapin, for £140, 51'8"x16' (Alex. B:231).
1790, MAY 2	William Hunter repossessed from John Jolly for Jolly's failure to pay rent (see Alex. D:330).
1791, APR 2	William Hunter, Sr. and wife Christiana to Joseph Thomas, for £51.10.0, lease of Jolly's parcel and annual rent of $40 Spanish milled (Alex. D:330).
1791, MAY 13	Joseph Thomas and wife Rachel to Richard Weightman, for £300, 30'10¼"x98'5", and use of two alleys (Alex. D:367).
1795, AUG 31	Gurdin Chapin and wife Margaret to Samuel Harper, for £640, 51'8"x16', adjoining William and Edward Ramsay (now belonging to Ricketts and Newton, and to Richard Weightman). Joseph Saunders' executors sold ground rent privileges to John Morton on 17 JAN 1793, and Morton sold to Mordecai Lewis on 18 JAN 1793. Lewis sold to Gurdin Chapin (Alex. F:450).

(See also FDB S:419; FDB W:24, 57, 64; FDB X:280, 407; FDB Y_2:5; Alex. K:96; Alex. N:126).

LOT 66
Prince & Fairfax

1749, SEP 20	John Carlyle and Hugh West, Trustees, to William Henry Terrett, for £5.7.6 (TM:4; FDB B:507).
1754, DEC 17	William Henry Terrett to John Carlyle, for £20 (FDB C:832).
1756, JAN 15	John Carlyle to Christopher Beeler, Lots 66 and 67, for £107.10. (FDB D:188).
c.1771	Christopher Beeler and wife to Naomy Ramsay and Catey Porter (FDB J:367, 370 msg; see FDB L:60).
1773, OCT 10	Naomy Ramsay and Catey Porter to Christopher Beeler, part of Lots 66 and 67, 154'x60' (FDB L:60).
1775, AUG 9	Christopher Beeler, yeoman, to George Keyger and wife Mary, part of Lots 66 and 67, for 5 shillings (FDB M:161).
1775, AUG 19	Christopher Beeler to William Hunter, merchant, for £4.11. annual rent, 90'x14'6", part of Lot 66, and use of an 8' alley (FDB M:187).
1775, OCT 23	George and Mary Keyger to William Hunter, merchant, for £4.18.2 annual rent, 90'x15'6" part of Lot 66 (FDB M:219).
1779, JUN 15	Joseph Beeler, Sr., of Westmoreland Co., Pa., son and heir of Christopher Beeler, late of Alexandria, dec'd.[32], to Dorsey Pentecost, "a 2-story brick house in the Town of Alexandria & part of Lots #66 & 67," it being the mansion dwelling of Christopher Beeler at the time of his decease (see FDB Q:351).
1783, FEB 20	William Hunter, merchant, and wife Christiana to William Brown, physician, for £160, 90'x15'6", and 90'x14'6"for £5 (Alex. A:1, 5).
1786, AUG 23	Dorsey Pentecost to Jesse Hollingsworth, of Baltimore, for £250 Pa. currency, and the original £15,000 in paper dollars (accounting dollars at 7/6 each) previously paid by Hollingsworth to Pentecost, for the property conveyed by Beeler senior to Pentecost (see FDB Q:351). Beeler senior never executed a deed to Pentecost.
1790, DEC 23	George and Mary Keyger, of Hampshire Co., to Josiah Watson, for £660, part of Lots 66 and 67 (Alex. D:277).
1791, MAR 29	George and Mary Kyger, of Hampshire Co., to Jacob Cox, for £5, 10'x25' (Alex. E:462).
1791, APR 5	George and Mary Kyger, of Hampshire Co., to Josiah Watson, for £60, assign Jacob Cox's rent of £6.6.8 to Watson (Alex. E:165, 168).
1793, DEC 18	Josiah Watson and wife Jane to Jacob Cox, for £65.17.3, their rights to rent from Cox (Alex. E:163).
1796, MAR 11	Jacob Cox to Henry Stanton Earle, for £480, 90'x20' (Alex. G:254).

(See also Alex. K:57, 263; Alex. L:32).

---

[32] The Virginia Gazette and Weekly Advertiser, 26 APR 1783, Beeler Family, Fairfax Co., September Court 1782 in chancery; Benjamin Beeler, administrator with the will annexed of Christopher Beeler, deceased, complainant against Joseph Beeler, son and heir of Christopher Beeler, deceased, defendant; the defendant cannot be found (also see Virginia Gazette and General Advertiser, 26 FEB 1799 for heirs of Christopher Beeler in suit against Stephen Hollingsworth, Joseph Beeler and Benjamin Beeler.

LOT 67
Prince & Royal

1749, SEP 20	John Carlyle and Hugh West, Trustees, to William Henry Terrett, for £5.7.6 (TM:4; FDB B:508).
1754, SEP 9	Escheated; resold to John Carlyle, for £5.7.0 (TM:22).
1756, JAN 15	John Carlyle to Christopher Beeler, for £107.10., Lots 66 and 67 (FDB D:188).
c.1771	Christopher Beeler and wife to Naomy Ramsay and Catey Porter (FDB J:367, 370 msg; see FDB L:60).
c.1771	Christopher Beeler to John Butcher, 62'2"x59', part of Lot 67 (FDB J:332 msg; see FDB M:13).
1773, OCT 10	Naomy Ramsay and Catey Porter to Christopher Beeler, part of Lots 66 and 67, 154'x60' (FDB L:60).
1774, MAY 30	John Butcher, hatter, and wife Ann, to Edward Mitchell Ramsay, joiner, for £35., 62'2"x59", part of Lot 67 (FDB M:13).
1775, AUG 9	Christopher Beeler, yeoman, to George Keyger and wife Mary, for 5 shillings, part of Lots 66 and 67 (FDB M:161).
c.1778	Edward Mitchell Ramsay to William Hartshorne (FDB N:169 msg; see FDB W:27).
1779, JUN 15	Joseph Beeler, Sr., of Westmoreland Co., Pa., son and heir of Christopher Beeler, late of Alexandria, dec'd., to Dorsey Pentecost, "a 2-story brick house in the Town of Alexandria & part of Lots #66 & 67," it being the mansion dwelling of Christopher Beeler at the time of his decease. Executed a deed to Pentecost (FDB Q:351).
1780, OCT 18	George and Mary Keyger, of Hampshire Co., to Christian Slimmer, of Alexandria, for £100, part of Lot 67, 29'4"x93'4" (FDB O:96).
1781, JUN 1	William Hartshorne and wife Susannah to Jacob Harman's executors, 93'5"x59', part of Lot 67 (FDB D$_4$:295).
1784, JAN 22	Christian and Mary Slimmer to William Hartshorne, for 5 shillings, 93'4"x29'4½" (Alex. A:21).
1786, AUG 23	Dorsey Pentecost to Jesse Hollingsworth, of Baltimore, for £250 Pa. currency, and the original £15,000 in paper dollars (accounting dollars at 7/6 each) previously paid by Hollingsworth to Pentecost, for the property conveyed by Beeler senior to Pentecost (see FDB Q:351). Beeler senior never executed a deed to Pentecost.
1790, DEC 23	George and Mary Keyger, of Hampshire Co., to Josiah Watson, for £660, part of Lots 66 and 67 (Alex. D:277).
1792, DEC 18	William Hartshorne, merchant, and wife Susannah to Mordecai Lewis, City of Philadelphia, merchant, same parcels of Lot 67 later conveyed by Lewis to Watson (FDB W:27; see Alex. E:422).
1794, JUN 30	Mordecai and Hannah Lewis, City of Philadelphia, merchant, to Josiah Watson, merchant, four parcels of Lot 67, for £1000 (Alex. E:422).

(See also FDB W:27, 51; Alex. K:57).

LOT 68
Prince & Royal

1749, DEC 28	George William Fairfax and William Ramsay, Trustees, to Hugh West, Jr., for £8.12., Lots 68 and 76 (FDB C:356). Deed dated 21 AUG 1852. West, Jr. refused deeds saying the persons for whom he bought the lots were under age and could not reconvey. Trustees considered reason insufficient and deeds were made (TM:5).
1784, MAR 15	John and Jane Fitzgerald to Andrew Hayes, 30'x80', for £15. rent (see Alex. E:351; Alex. I:455).
1786, OCT 5	John and Jane Fitzgerald to Thomas Redman, 18½'x80', for £55. annual rent (see Alex. E:351, I:455).
1794, JUL 24	John and Jane Fitzgerald, for £500, several parcels (Alex. E:351).
1795, MAY 1	John and Jane Fitzgerald to George McMunn (see Alex. G:487).
1795, MAY 15	John Fitzgerald[33] and wife Jane to George McMunn, for £16.10., lease 43'x78' (Alex. F:247).
1795, MAY 15	John and Jane Fitzgerald to George Spangler, lease for £14.10., 78'x20' (Alex. F:270).
1795, MAY 15	John and Jane Fitzgerald to Ludowick Tresseler, lease for £14.10, 78'x20', (Alex. F:275).
1796, FEB 27	George McMunn loaned George Spangler £60. To secure loan, Spangler mortgaged his parcel to James Keith for 1 year (Alex. H:124).
1796, JUN 17	George McMunn and wife Elizabeth lease to Jonathan Pancas, 78'x17', for $50 silver annual rent, to Spangler's line (Alex. G:487, 491).
1797, MAR 24	James Keith, trustee, to George McMunn, for £10.10., 78'x20' (Alex. I:37).
1797, SEP 19	George and Elizabeth McMunn mortgage to James Grimes, to secure payment of £260 McMunn owes Grimes, 74'x22' (Alex. I:304).

(See also Alex. I:484, 489, 491, 511; Alex. K:5, 80, 153, 525; Alex. M:84, 220; Alex. N:60, 270).

LOT 69
Duke & Union

1752, MAR 28	William Ramsay and John Pagan, Trustees, to Nathaniel Harrison, Gent., of Stafford Co., for £24.19.6 (FDB C:312).
1766, APR 19	Trustees fixed boundaries of lot (TM:55).
1775, MAR 6	Nathaniel Harrison, of Brandon, Prince Georges Co., [Md.] to Richard Arell, of Alexandria, Lot 69, for £300 (FDB M:33).
c.1784	Richard Arell to Aminadab Seekright [an alias], lease (Prince William Co. Land Causes, 1789-1793, p. 10).
1787, JUL 11	Richard and Eleanor Arell to William Hunter, Sr. who married Christiana (R. and E. Arell's daughter), part of Lots 69 and 70 (Alex. C:167).

---

[33] Also see Alex. I:455. This deed indicates the Fitzgeralds conveyed to Andrew Hayes on 15 MAR 1784, part of this lot, thought to be Lot 61, but may be Lot 68; also on 5 OCT 1786 to Thomas Redman.

1790, MAY 1   Richard Arell v. Town of Alexandria, concerning boundaries of Lots 69 and 70 (Record of Surveys, 1742-1856:145).

Numerous deeds (1778-1783) from Richard Arell were recorded in Deed Book N which is missing. (See also Alex. K:241; Alex. L:329; Alex. O:117).

LOT 70
Water St., Duke & Union
(Between Lots 69 and 71)

1752, MAR 28   William Ramsay and John Pagan, Trustees, to Nathaniel Harrison, Gent., of Stafford Co., for £24.19.6 (FDB C:312).

1775, MAR 6   Nathaniel Harrison to Richard Arell (FDB M:33).

1790, MAY 1   Richard Arell v. Town of Alexandria, concerning boundaries of Lots 69 and 70 (Record of Surveys, 1742-1856:145). Arell's house on the southwest corner of Lot 70.

1795, OCT 6   Richard Arell and wife Eleanor lease to Henry Walker, part of Lot 70, for £9.2.6 annually (Alex. F:402).

LOT 71
Duke & Water St.

1752, MAR 28   William Ramsay and John Pagan, Trustees, to Henry Fitzhugh, Gent., of Stafford Co., for £17.4. (FDB C:303).

1757, NOV 6   Henry Fitzhugh, Jr., of Stafford Co., to George Johnston, for 15 pistoles (FDB D:499).

c.1771   George Johnston's executors to Daniel Jenifer, of Charles Co., Md., and by Jenifer and wife Mary to Robert Hanson Harrison (FDB J:64, 251; FDB N:9 msg; see FDB K:35).

1772, JAN 27   George Johnston, son and heir-at-law of George Johnston, attorney-at-law, dec., confirms sale to Robert Hanson Harrison, for 5 shillings Sterling (FDB K:35).

1795, NOV 3   Sarah, daughter of Robert Hanson Harrison, and widow of Adam Craik, of Charles Co., Md., to her sister Dorothy Hanson [Harrison], wife of John Courts Jones. They divide Lot 71 (FDB Y:237). Sarah married David Easton (see Alex. K:29, 43).

1795, NOV 4   John C. Jones and wife Dorothy to Samuel Love, of Loudoun Co., for £300, 66'x25'4" (FDB Y:321).

1797, SEP 9   David and Sarah Easton [later of Philadelphia, Pa.] to James and Elizabeth Watson (see Alex. K:66).

(See also FDB Y$_2$:262; Alex. I:403, 411, 496; Alex. K:131; Alex. N:279; and Alex. O:64).

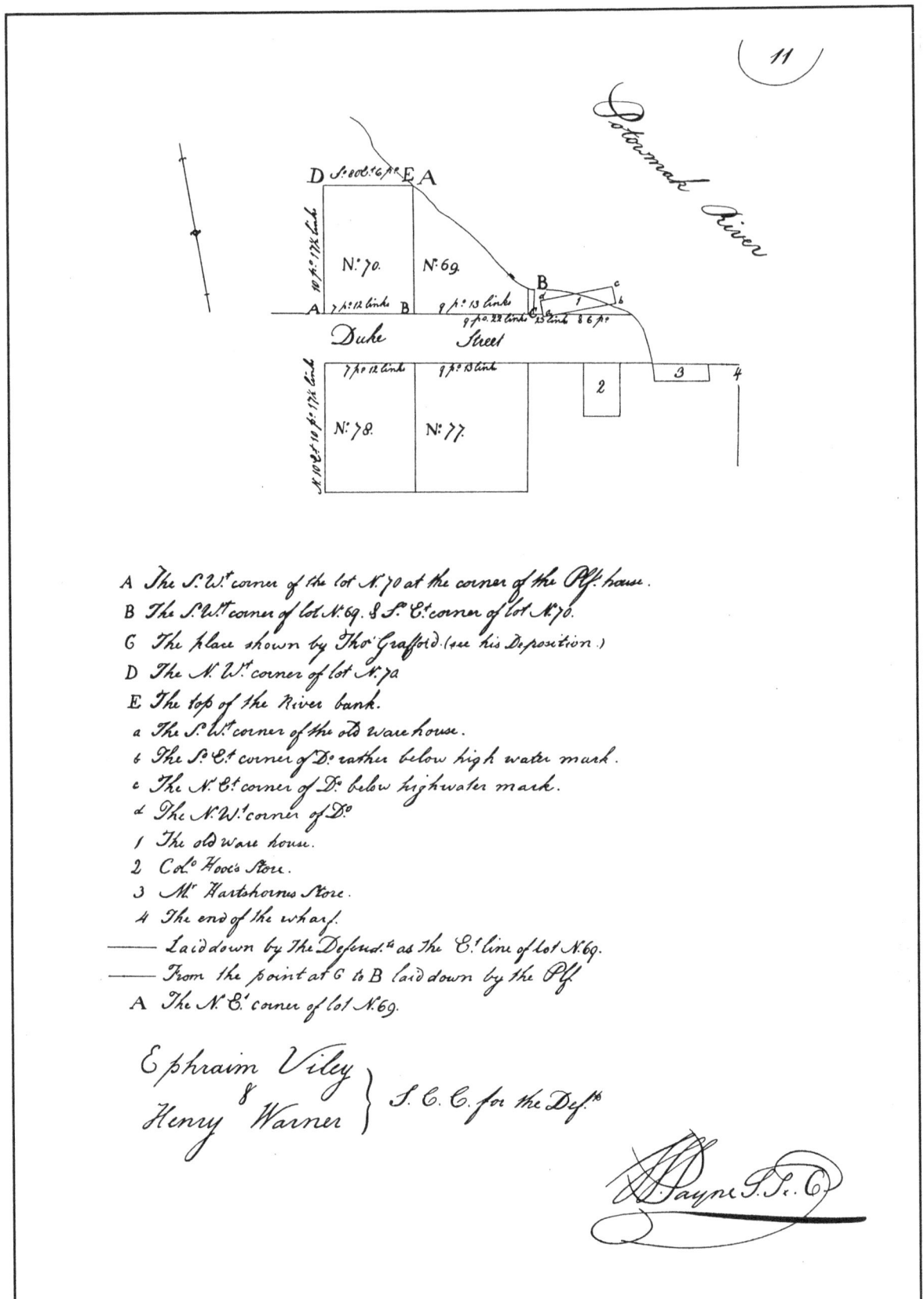

Figure 5 - Plat of Lots 69, 70, 77 and 78. [Record of Surveys, p. 146 (11), Redrawn by Bill Sprouse]

LOT 72
Duke & Water St.

1749, JUL 14	Trustees to Capt. John West, for £16.2.6 for Lots 72 and 73 (TM:3, 24, 25).
1759, NOV 19	John West and Mary his wife to Benjamin Sebastian, for £9.10. (FDB D:718).
1775, APR 3	Richard Arell and wife Eleanor to Lewis Weston, ship carpenter, lease for part of Lot 72, 123'5"x20', for $17 annual rent (FDB M:62).
1775, SEP 15	Richard Arell and wife Eleanor to John Hawn, wheelwright, of Alexandria, but late of Prince Georges Co., Md., part of Lot 72, 123'5"x30', for $25.50 annual rent (FDB M:203).
1780, JAN 17	Richard Arell to son David Arell (FDB N:302 msg; see FDB Y:51).
1783, JUN 18	David Arell to Henry Beideman, 76'7"x40' (FDB N:808 msg; see FDB P:39).
1783, JUL 7	David Arell to Richard Clarke, part of Lot 72, 123'5"x30' for $50 (Spanish milled silver) annual rent (FDB O:42).
1783, JUL 8	David Arell to Lewis Weston, part of Lot 72, 103'5"x20' for $33-1/3 (silver) annual rent (FDB O:1).
1783, SEP 6	David Arell to Henry Beideman, of Alexandria, part of Lot 72, 30'7"x63'5", for $105 (silver) annual rent, adjoining parcel granted by Arell to Christian Devillbiss (FDB N:8 msg; see FDB O:49).
1784, JUL 7	Henry Beideman and wife Charlotte to Jacob Butt, of York Co., Pa., for £150, same parcel as was conveyed to Beideman by Arell on 6 SEP 1783, for $105 (FDB P:35).
1784, JUL 7	Henry Beideman and wife Charlotte to Jacob Butt, of York Co., Pa., for £30 annual rent, 76'7"x40' (FDB P:39).
1784, DEC 21	David Arell to George Thumbler, of Alexandria, part of Lot 72, 20'x63'5" for $40 (silver) annual rent (FDB P:195).
1785, AUG 8	Christian and Mary Devilbiss, of Frederick Co., Md., and Jacob Pens of same Co., lease for $33-1/3 (silver) to David Arell, 20'x76'7" (Alex. B:94, 172).
1785, OCT 10	George Thumbler and wife Margaret to Peter Boyle, of Loudoun Co., for £50, subject to annual rent of $40 (silver) to David Arell (FDB Q:77).
1785, OCT 28	Christian Slimmer holds 30'x5' of Lot 72, gives three feet for alley (Alex. B:197).
1795, APR 26	Samuel Arell re-entered house rented by George Thumbler to Boyle for non-payment of rent; house empty (Alex. F:285).
1795, MAY 10	Samuel Arell, Phoebe (widow of David Arell), Christiana (daughter of David), Richard Arell (son of David) and Alexander McConnell, five-part deed.[34] McConnell to receive part of Lot 72 as devised by will of David Arell, dec. (FWB F:79), to son Richard, for $150 (silver) annual rent until Richard Arell reaches age 21 years or marries, 55'6"x63'5" (FDB Y:21).
1795, JUN 16	Jacob Butt to Jacob Leap, for £150, part of Lot 72, lease for $36-2/3 (silver)

---

[34] Shepherd, Vol. II, p. 65, Chap. 77, "An ACT authorizing Peter Caverley to lease, for the benefit of the orphans of David Arell, certain lots wherof he died seized, in the town of Alexandria," passed 10 DEC 1796.

	annual rent (Alex. F:279).
1797, APR 5	Alexander McConnell and wife Mary to John Dunlap, for £500 and rent of $88½ (silver), 32'9"x62'5" (Alex. I:75).
1797, MAY 5	Alexander and Mary McConnell lease to John Dunlap, 32'9"x63'5" (see Alex. I:156).
1797, MAY 10	Alexander and Mary McConnell lease to Jonathan Swift, for £900 and $61½ (silver) annually, 22'9"x63'5" (Alex. I:68, 82).
1797, JUN 20	Jonathan Swift and wife Ann to Robert Townshend Hooe and Richard Harrison, City of Philadelphia, for £900 and rents, plus "half the Necessary built by McConnell on the Arell-McConnell land..." (Alex. I:156).

LOT 73
Duke & Fairfax

1749, JUL 14	Trustees to Capt. John West, Lots 72 and 73, for £16.2.6 (TM:3, 24, 25).
1755, SEP 16	John West, Gent., and Mary his wife, to Going Lamphier, joiner, for £10.15., Lot 73 (FDB D:197, 198).
1780, JAN 17	Richard Arell to son Samuel, Lot 73 (FDB N:302; see FDB Y:51).
1790, MAY 27	Platt Townsend, formerly of Alexandria but now of New York, physician, to David Henley, late of Alexandria and now residing in New York, merchant, for $2500 (Spanish milled) (Alex. D:267).
1795, NOV 14	William Walter, D.D., Town of Boston, Mass., attorney-in-fact for David Henley, lease to Andrew Estave (Alex. L:94).
1798, SEP 26	Andrew Estave lease to John Lemoine, for $100, bake oven and house (Alex. L:93).

LOT 74
Duke & Fairfax

1749, SEP 20	George William Fairfax and William Ramsay, Trustees, to Pearson Terrett, Lots 74 and 75 (TM:3, 43). Deed dated 21 AUG 1752, for £10.15. (FDB C:358). The lots were actually bought by William Henry Terrett for use of his son Pearson (see FDB W:190).
1756, OCT 25	William Henry Terrett entered into bond to John Hunter, for £500, promising good deeds for the two lots (see FDB W:190).
1763, JUN 10	John Hunter's will, probated 17 JAN 1764, provides that his real estate be divided among his children after widow's dower is set aside (FWB B:364). Son Nathaniel Chapman Hunter received Lots 74 and 75 (see FDB W:190).[35]

---

[35] Much activity on this lot can be attributed to William Baker & Co., tenant of Nathaniel Hunter of Dumfries [1787 Tax List]. On 11 OCT 1787, William Baker announced in the Virginia Journal and Alexandria Advertiser that he "will move sometime in the next month to his plantation in Maryland" and proposed to either rent or sell his house "cheap credit for four or five years." In the same newspaper on 27 JAN 1791, is found an advertisement by William Baker to rent his dwelling house on Fairfax Street, and that inquiries should be made of Captain John Hawkins in Alexandria or of the Lodge in Prince George's Co. [Md.].

1793, APR 16	William Henry Terrett and wife Amelia to Nathaniel Chapman Hunter, of Prince William Co. Deed recites that William Henry Terrett, father of the grantor, received Lots 74 and 75 from the Alexandria Trustees for the use of his son Pearson Terrett, then an infant, who died without issue during his minority. Son William now conveying to Hunter the lots promised by his father (FDB W:190).
1794, SEP 23	Nathaniel Chapman Hunter and wife Sarah Ann, Town of Dumfries, to Aaron Hewes, for £156.5., 30'x118'; Hunter will lay off for his and Hewes' common use a 10' alley, 118' west of Fairfax Street from Jesse Hollingsworth's line (Alex. F:37).
1795, FEB 6	Nathaniel Chapman Hunter and wife Sarah Ann, Town of Dumfries, to Stephen Cook [Cooke], for £130, 118'6"x20'; Cooke to have use of alley (Alex. F:231, 357).[36] Deed on page 357 indicates "beginning at southeast corner of house built by Doctor William Baker... to Aaron Hewes' lot."

LOT 75
Duke & Royal

1749, SEP 20	(see history of Lot 74).
1794, MAY 9	Nathaniel Chapman Hunter and wife Sarah Anne, of Prince William Co., to Ephraim Evans, for £190, 100'x60' (Alex. F:127).

LOT 76
Duke & Royal

1749, DEC 28	Trustees to Hugh West, Jr., who refused, saying person for whom he bought lot was under age and could not convey. Trustees considered reason insufficient and made out deed (TM:5). Deed dated 21 AUG 1752, for Lots 68 and 76 (FDB C:356).
c.1752	Hugh West to William Digg [Digges] (FDB C:482 msg).
1782, FEB 20	William Diggs [Digges], of Prince Georges Co., Md., to John Fitzgerald (FDB N:464 msg; see FDB Q:107).
1786, JAN 16	John Fitzgerald, merchant, and wife Jane, to Arthur Lee, of Richmond Co., for £800 (FDB Q:107).
1798, APR 1	Edmund J. and Sarah Lee to Thomas Peterkin and John McIntosh, lease for $333.33 (silver) per annum from 1 NOV 1798 (Alex. K:498).
1799, JAN 5	Edmund J. Lee repossessed the 1/2-acre corner lot (Alex. L:306, dated 6 APR 1799).

(See also Alex. M:250, 357, and 384).

---

[36] On 6 MAR 1800, Stephen Cooke made notice in the Columbian Mirror & Alexandria Gazette of his intention to either rent or sell his house on Fairfax Street in which he lived at the time. Also see Alexandria Advertiser & Commercial Intelligencer for 3 AUG 1801, "TO LET..."

LOT 77
Duke & Union
(Point Lumley)

1749, JUL 13	Trustees to Nathaniel Chapman, of Stafford Co. (TM:1). Deed from William Ramsay and John Pagan, Trustees, dated 28 MAR 1752, for £30.7.4½ (FDB C:297).
1766, JUL 23	Pearson Chapman, of Charles Co., Md., to George Chapman his brother, of same place, Lots 77 and 79, conveyed by Alexandria Trustees to their father Nathaniel Chapman who died intestate[37] (FDB G:33). Lots descended to son Nathaniel who also died intestate [c.1762], descending then to brother Pearson Chapman.
1770, SEP 19	George Chapman to Thomas Fleming (FDB J:76 msg; see Alex. E:419).
1774, MAR 29	Trustees rent to Thomas Fleming for 63 years, part of Point Lumley adjoining Fleming's lot (see Alex. F:294).
1786, APR 7	Thomas Fleming's will, probated 18 SEP 1786 (FWB E:160), provides for the sale of Lot 77 for debts. George Hunter, Fleming's surviving executor, conveyed parts of Lot 77 on 6 JAN 1794 to Robert Townshend Hooe and George Slacum (see FDB X:428); see Alex. E:337, 419; see Alex. H:49).
1790, Prior to	Plat shows [William] Hartshorne's store on a wharf on Point Lumley (Record of Surveys:146).
1794, JAN 1	George Hunter, surviving executor of Thomas Fleming, dec.[38], lease to Robert Townshend Hooe, for £300, part of Lot 77 (Alex. E:419).
1794, JAN 6	George Hunter, surviving executor of Thomas Fleming, dec., to George Slacum, for £250, two parcels of Lot 77 (Alex. E:337).
1794, JAN 17	Mayor and Commonalty of Alexandria; George Hunter, surviving executor of Thomas Fleming; and Robert Townshend Hooe; in tripartite deed confirming Hooe's lease [Alex. E:419] for a term of 44 years. Trustees confirmed and acknowledged July and September 1794 and 1795 (Alex. F:294).
1794, APR 9	Thomas Fleming's daughter Betty, wife of Eli Valette, conveyed with husband, 1/5 part of Lot 77 to John Lockwood (see FDB X:125).
1794, JUN 11	John Lockwood to John Bass Dabney, for £240, same part of Lot 77 and a piece adjoining, and part of Lot 96 (see FDB X:428; see Alex. H:49).
1796, JUN 8	John Bass Dabney and wife Roxa to Thomas Patten, for £450 (Alex. H:49).

(See also Alex. B:153; Alex. I:287, 415, 419; Alex. K:284, 302, 360, 400).

LOT 78
Duke, Between Water St. & Union

1749, JUL 13	Trustees to Nathaniel Chapman, of Stafford Co. (TM:1, 43).

---

[37] FWB B:333, inventory; Nathaniel Chapman died intestate 1760 in Baltimore Co., Md.

[38] <u>Virginia Journal and Alexandria Advertiser</u>, 20 APR 1786, Thomas Fleming, ship builder, died in Alexandria, aged 63, he was one of the city's oldest inhabitants. His estate to be settled with Betty Fleming, his executrix, and George Hunter, his executor (14 JUN 1787). His lot in Alexandria to be sold (10 JUN 1790).

c.1751	Nathaniel Chapman to John Hunter (FDB C:479 msg).
1752, MAR 28	William Ramsay and John Pagan, Trustees, to Nathaniel Chapman, Gent. of Stafford Co., for £30.7.4½ (FDB C:298).
1763, JUN 10	John Hunter's will, probated 17 JAN 1764, mentions lots in Alexandria (FWB B:364).
1800, FEB 17	John C. Hunter, lease to negro Harry, 20' on an alley to back line of Lot 78 (FDB B_2:499).

LOT 79
Duke & Water St.

1749, JUL 14	Trustees to Ralph Wormley (TM:2).
1752, MAR 28	William Ramsay and John Pagan, Trustees, to Ralph Wormley, Esq. of Middlesex Co.,[39] for £10.15. (FDB C:304).
1766, JUL 23	Lot escheated? (see Lot 77). Pearson Chapman to George Chapman (FDB G:33).
1784, SEP 21	George Chapman, Esq., to Bernhard Mann, of Loudoun Co., 28'x90' with use of 6' alley, part of Lot 79, for £17.14., annual rent in gold or silver (FDB P:64). Chapman to John Ehrmin, 25'x82', £18.15. annual rent and use of 8' alley (FDB P:62).
1790, APR 27	George Chapman to Robert T. Hooe and Richard Harrison, 20'x90' (so as to include the house thereon built by James Grimes), adjoining Mann, with use of 6' alley and 8' alley for £13.16. annual rent in gold or silver (FDB S:380).
1794, OCT 8	Bernhard Mann and wife Johanna to Thomas Patten, for £136, 28'x90'; Patten paying Chapman the rent (Alex. F:193).
1796, MAY 1	Robert Townshend Hooe, and Richard and Ann Harrison, of Philadelphia, Pa. (but formerly of Alexandria) lease to John Muncaster, 20'x90', £13.16. per annum in gold or silver (Alex. H:226).
1797, MAR 17	Thomas Patten and wife Mary mortgage 28'x80' to William Hartshorne (FDB Z:483).

(See also Alex. M:5, 10).

LOT 80
Duke & Water St.

1761, FEB 10	Trustees to Ann West (TM:43).
1752, AUG 20	George William Fairfax and William Ramsay, Trustees, deed to John West, Gent., for £12.18., Lots 80 and 81. Escheated? (FDB C:355).
1754, SEP 9	Trustees to George Mercer, for £9.13.6 (TM:22, 23). Deed, same date, is from George Johnston and John Dalton, Trustees, for £10.4.3, Lot 80 (FDB

---

[39] Virginia Gazette and General Advertiser, 25 AUG 1790, Ralph Wormeley, Esq., died on Tuesday [or Thursday] the 19th inst. at Rosegill in his 75th year.

	C:794). Mercer died intestate, and lot descended to his brother James Mercer (see Alex. F:132).
1787, MAY 22	James Mercer to Leven Powell, 91'6"x40' (see FDB Y:507). James divided lot into parcels[40] (see Alex. F:132).
1787, MAY 22	Honorable James Mercer, Esq., to Daniel and Isaac McPherson, 103'5"x25' (parcels 2, 3 and 5 on James Mercer's plat[41]) (Alex. H:481; see FDB Z:53).
1787, MAY 22	James Mercer to William Lyles, 27'10"x91'6" (see FDB E_3:84; see Alex. H:481).
1787, MAY 22	Account of sales by James Mercer, of the estate of Col. George Mercer, dec.[42], for seven lots, to: William H. Powell for Leven Powell, John Murray for Daniel and Isaac McPherson, William Lyles, Jonah Thompson and George Slacum (Alex. C:16).
1790, MAY 29	Daniel and Isaac McPherson to John Murray, one moiety of the part of Lot 80 they received from James Mercer[43]. Daniel's will provides that property held in common with Isaac should be sold by executors (see also Alex. D:193).
1790, DEC 17	John and Patty Murray to John Walter Fletcher, for £100, 91'6"x27'10" (Alex. D:215).
1791, APR?	Daniel McPherson's[44] executors and Isaac McPherson to Isaac McPherson, the unsold moiety of Lot 80.[45]
1791, APR 11	Martha McPherson, executrix, and Edward Beeson and Isaac McPherson, acting executors, to James Wilson, Jr., for £70.10., at auction, undivided parcel; deed dated 13 APR 1791 (Alex. D:247).
1791, DEC 20	Daniel McPherson's executors to John Murray, 1/4 part of Lot 80, for £18, with the use of alleys.[46]
1794, JUN 6	William Lyles and wife Sarah to George Coryell (FDB E_3:84). This deed

---

[40] William Waller Hening, The Statutes at Large; Being a Collection of all the Laws of Virginia From the First Session of the Legislature, in the Year 1619 (Richmond: George Cochran, 1823), Vol. XII, pp. 365-69, October 1786, 11th of Commonwealth, Chapter LXXVIII, "An act for vesting in James Mercer, esq; certain lands whereof George Mercer died seized." James Mercer, esquire, eldest brother and heir at law of George Mercer, late of the city of London, where George departed this life in the month of April 1784, single and unmarried, without a will being located, was seized of certain small parcels of land within the Commonwealth.

[41] See Alex. C:15, detailed plat of lots at Duke and Water streets, made by James Mercer, 22 MAY 1787, for division into lots designated for William H. Powell, John Murray, William Lyles, George Slacum, and Jonah Thompson.

[42] Virginia Journal and Alexandria Advertiser, 3 MAY 1787, Colonel George Mercer, deceased, a lot in Alexandria formerly belonging to him, to be sold by his brother J. Mercer, of Fredericksburg.

[43] See certified deed from Daniel McPherson's executrix to John Murray, filed in Drawer X, Fairfax Circuit Court Archives.

[44] Virginia Journal and Alexandria Advertiser, 2 DEC 1790, Daniel M'Pherson, of Daniel & Isaac M'Pherson, dec'd., of Alexandria; Complete Records [Alexandria], Liber A, fols. 30-7, will of Daniel McPherson, dated 1 JUN 1790, probated 24 FEB 1791.

[45] See certified deed from Daniel McPherson's executrix to John Murray, filed in Drawer X, Fairfax Circuit Court Archives.

[46] See certified deed from Daniel McPherson's executrix to John Murray, filed in Drawer X, Fairfax Circuit Court Archives.

	provides chain of title up to 1838 for the parcel sold by James Mercer to William Lyles, 27'10"x91'6" (see Alex. F:132).
1794, JUL 25	John Walter Fletcher and wife Mary to Samuel Arell, 91'6"x29'10", for £82.16.8 (Alex. E:354).
1794, SEP 18	Samuel Arell to Thomas Richards, 91'6"x27'10" (see Alex. F:397).
1795, JUN 6	Thomas Richards and wife Ann to William Mitchell, for £100, 91'6"x27'10" (Alex. F:397).
1795, AUG 19	Levin and Sarah Powell to Daniel Douglass, 40'x91'6" (see Alex. M:340).
1795, OCT 2	Jonah and Margaret Thompson to Richard Veitch, 25'x103'6" (see Alex. M:230).
1796, NOV 19	Richard and Betsey Veitch to James Hartley, for £160, 25'x103'6" (see Alex. M:230).
1800, JAN 14	Daniel and Charlotte Douglass to Alexander Smith, for £1800, 40'x91'6" (Alex. M:340).

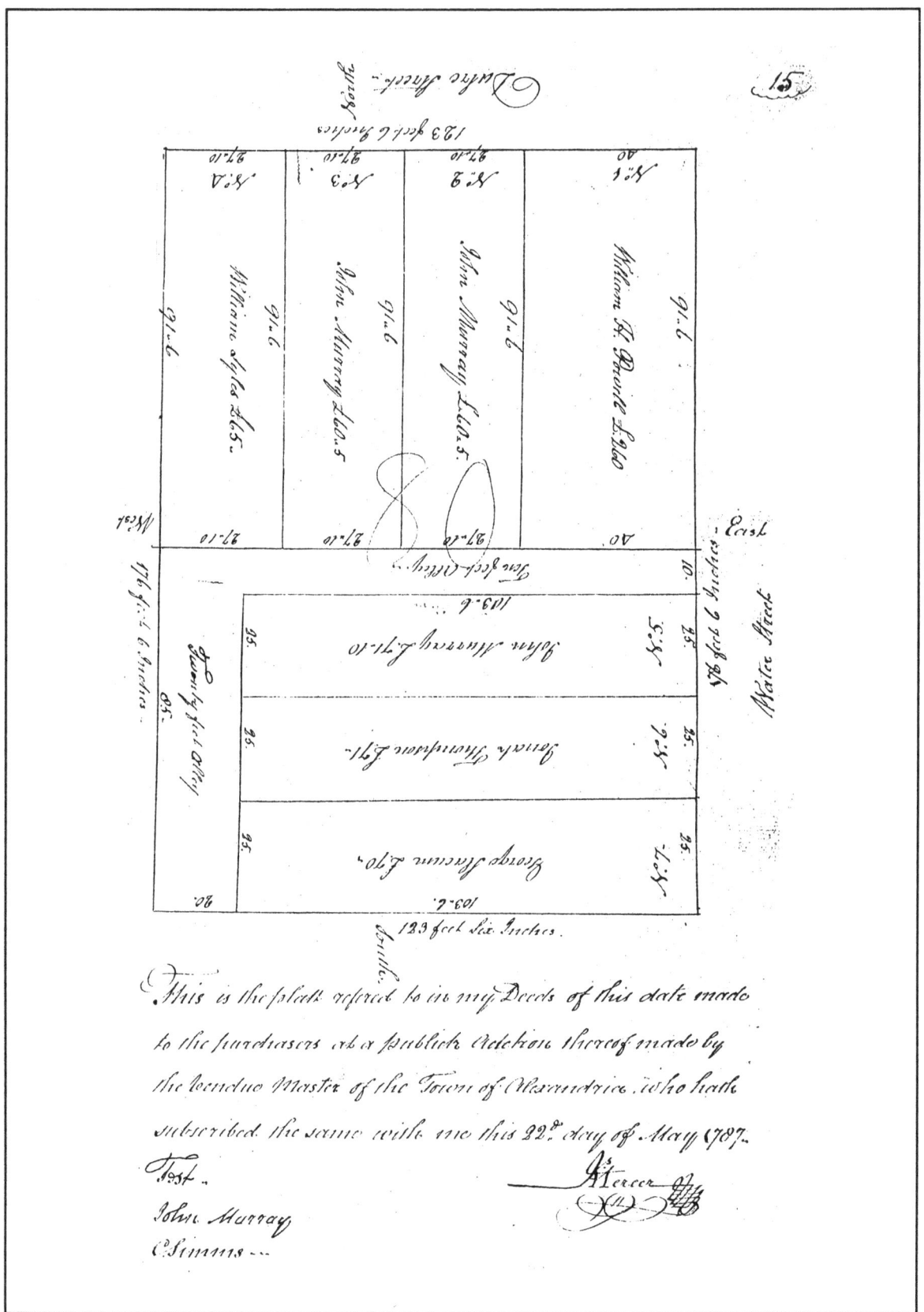

Figure 6 - Plat of Lots 80 and 81. [Alexandria Hustings Court Deeds, Bk. C, p. 15]

LOT 81
Duke & Fairfax

1752, AUG 20	Trustees to Ann West (TM:50) but deeded to John West, Gent. (FDB C:355, George William Fairfax and William Ramsay, Trustees, to John West, Gent., for £12.18.).
1754, SEP 9	Trustees to Daniel Wilson, for £10.10. (TM:22, 23). Escheated.
1755, SEP 9	George Johnston and John Dalton, Trustees, to William Young of Md., for £10.10.; same lot sold to John West, Senr. and for want of building thereon is lapsed (FDB D:194, part msg).
1767, JUN 16	William Young and wife Elenor, of Prince Georges Co., Md. to Richard Arell, merchant, for $175 (Spanish milled) (FDB G:239).
1783, JUN 1	Samuel Arell, merchant, lease to John Short, watchmaker, for $36-2/3 (silver) annual rent, 22'x96'6" (FDB O:15).
1783, JUN 1	Samuel Arell, merchant, lease to Joseph Robinson, sail maker, 116'6"x22' (FDB O:157).
1783, JUN 1	Samuel Arell lease to Ludovick Zimmerman, 20'x79'5" (FDB O:161).
1783, AUG 23	Samuel Arell lease to Michael Clarke, 20'x123'5" (FDB O:39).
1783, AUG 26	Samuel Arell lease to Nicholas Hannah for $36-2/3 (silver) annual rent, 76'6"x22' (FDB O:18).
1783, SEP 24	Samuel Arell lease to Peter Tartsepaugh, 20'x123'5" (FDB O:164).
1784, JUN 23	Samuel Arell to David Keneday [Kennedy], 25'x57'5", adjoining Nicholas Hannah, lease for £18.15. annual rent (FDB P:252).
1784, JUL 28	Lodowick Zimmerman and wife Mary reconvey to Samuel Arell, for £10 (FDB P:5).
1784, AUG 2	Michael Clarke and Elizabeth his wife reconvey to Samuel Arell, for £10 (FDB P:91).
1784, DEC 20	Samuel Arell lease to Shubael Pratt, for $50 (silver) annual rent, 123'5"x20' (FDB Q:56).
1785, MAR 4	Samuel Arell lease to Absolom Wroe, 20'x101'5" for $50 (silver) annual rent (FDB Q:84).
1785, JUN 9	Samuel Arell lease to Richard Craig, 25'x57'5" for $75 (silver) annual rent, adjoining Nicholas Hannah (FDB Q:45).
1787, MAY 3	John Short and wife Ann mortgage to John Harper, for £101, the parcel Short leased from Arell (FDB R:83).
1787, JUL 25	John Short and wife Ann mortgage to William Hartshorne and Peter Wise, executors of George Duncan, dec. (FDB S:100).
1788, FEB 8	Baldwin Dade and wife Catharine to James Lawrason, for £300, 123'5"x20", "conveyed by Samuel Arell to Thomas West, & by... West to Dade" (Alex. E:270).
1789, DEC 8	John Harper to John Murray, for £111.17. (FDB S:280).
1790, MAY 26	Samuel and Dolly Arell to John Murray, for £100, part of Lot 81 (Alex. D:201).
1792, SEP 7	Peter Tartsepaugh and wife Susannah to Mordecai Miller, for £66, 123'5"x20' (Alex. D:459).

(See also FDB S:285, 311; FDB T:146; FDB Y:224; FDB A_2:208; Alex.

K:216).

LOT 82
Duke & Fairfax

1749, DEC 28	Trustees to Hugh West. West refused on grounds person for whom he bought the lot was under age and could not reconvey. Trustees considered reason insufficient. Deed made bearing date 20 SEP 1749 (TM:5, 43), in name of [William?] West.
1750, JUN 25	Hugh West and John Dalton, Trustees, to Giles Rogers, carpenter, for £12.18., Lots 82 and 83. (FDB C:61).
1752?	Giles Rogers and John Rogers to Nathaniel Smith, Lots 82 and 83 (see FDB C:391, 417 msg).
1752, OCT 13	Nathaniel Smith to William Waite, for 5 shillings, Lots 82 and 83 (FDB C:391).
1767, JUN 3	William Waite and wife Jane, of Fauquier Co., to Joseph Thompson, Lots 82 and 83, held in trust by William Bronough (FDB C:512 msg; FDB G:263).
1783, JUN 18	Thomas Thompson, of Whitehaven, Co. Cumberland, England, mariner, cousin and heir of Samuel Thompson, only son of Joseph, mariner, dec., to William Bushby, surviving administrator of Joseph Thompson, Lots 82 and 83 (FDB O:55).
1786, DEC 21	William Bushby to William Hartshorne, part of Lot 82 (see FDB W:39; FDB Y:263).
1788, JUN 14	William Bushby and wife Mary mortgage to William Hodgson, merchant, and attorney in fact for Fisher & Bragg of Whitehaven, part of Lot 82, 24'x75'6", "whereon stands a framed house now in the tenure of Dennis McCarty, & another parcel, 24'x75'6"" (FDB R:265).
1792, FEB 3	William and Mary Bushby mortgage to George Suckley, for £79.6.2, 70'6"x22' (Alex. D:436).
1792, JUN 19	William and Mary Bushby mortgage to Anna Bell, of Frederick Co., for £82.5., 80'x24' (Alex. D:440).
1794, APR 30	William Bushby and wife Mary to William Reynolds, 70'6"x15' (Alex. E:416).

(See also FDB U:333; FDB W:39, 86; FDB Y:263; FDB A$_2$:327, 330; FDB Y$_2$:5; Alex. H:473).

LOT 83
Duke & Royal

1749, DEC 28	Trustees to Hugh West, charged to George West (TM:5, 43; see information for Lot 82).
1789, JUN 16	William Bushby and wife Mary to John Moss, William Adams, William Waters, Samuel Adams, James Morrison, William Rhodes and William Hickman, for 5 shillings, part of Lot 83, in the line of Chappell Alley and

north of the Presbyterian Meeting House, 43'x33' with use of the alley, in trust, "for a house for the worship of God for the use of the Rev. Thomas Cooke & the Rev. Francis Asbury, bishops for the time being of the Methodist Episcopal Church... & all other Methodist preachers" (FDB R:413).

(See also FDB A_2:208, FDB B_2:236; Alex. M:145).

LOT 84
Duke & Royal

1749, DEC 28	Trustees to Hugh West, Gent. (TM:5).
1752, SEP 20	George William Fairfax and William Ramsay, Trustees, to Francis Hague and John Hough, for £4.6. (FDB C:382).
1758, JUL 18	George Johnston and John Dalton, Trustees, to John Muir, merchant, for £10.5. (TM:30; FDB D:533). The Trustees Minutes (TM:43) shows this lot sold to George West.
1789, DEC	John Muir's[47] will, probated 19 APR 1791, directs that all his estate be given to his sister and executrix Elizabeth Muir (FWB F:17). Elizabeth married Robert Donaldson (see Alex. G:93; Alex. H:13).
1796, JUN 21	Elizabeth Donaldson, the former Elizabeth Muir, sister and devisee of John Muir, dec., to Elisha Cullen Dick, 176'7"x115'3", "to an alley" (see FDB Z:323; see Alex. G:420), 255'3"x177'1" (Alex. G:443).
1796, JUN 22	Elisha Cullen Dick and wife Hannah to William Hartshorne, deed of trust to secure payments Dick owes to Elizabeth Donaldson (Alex. G:420).

(See also FDB U_2:188; Alex. H:489; Alex. K:119, 475; Alex. N:27 power of attorney, 88; Alex. O:41, 53).

The caption on the map found at the following page is taken from Richard W. Stephenson, <u>The Cartography of Northern Virginia, Facsimile Reproductions of Maps Dating From 1806 to 1915</u> (Fairfax: Office of Comprehensive Planning, 1981), p. 27, Plate 13.

---

[47] <u>Virginia Gazette and Alexandria Advertiser</u>, 12 MAY 1791, John Muir, dec'd., estate accounts for him and for Robert Muir, dec'd., to be settled with Eliz. Muir of Alexandria, the executrix of John.

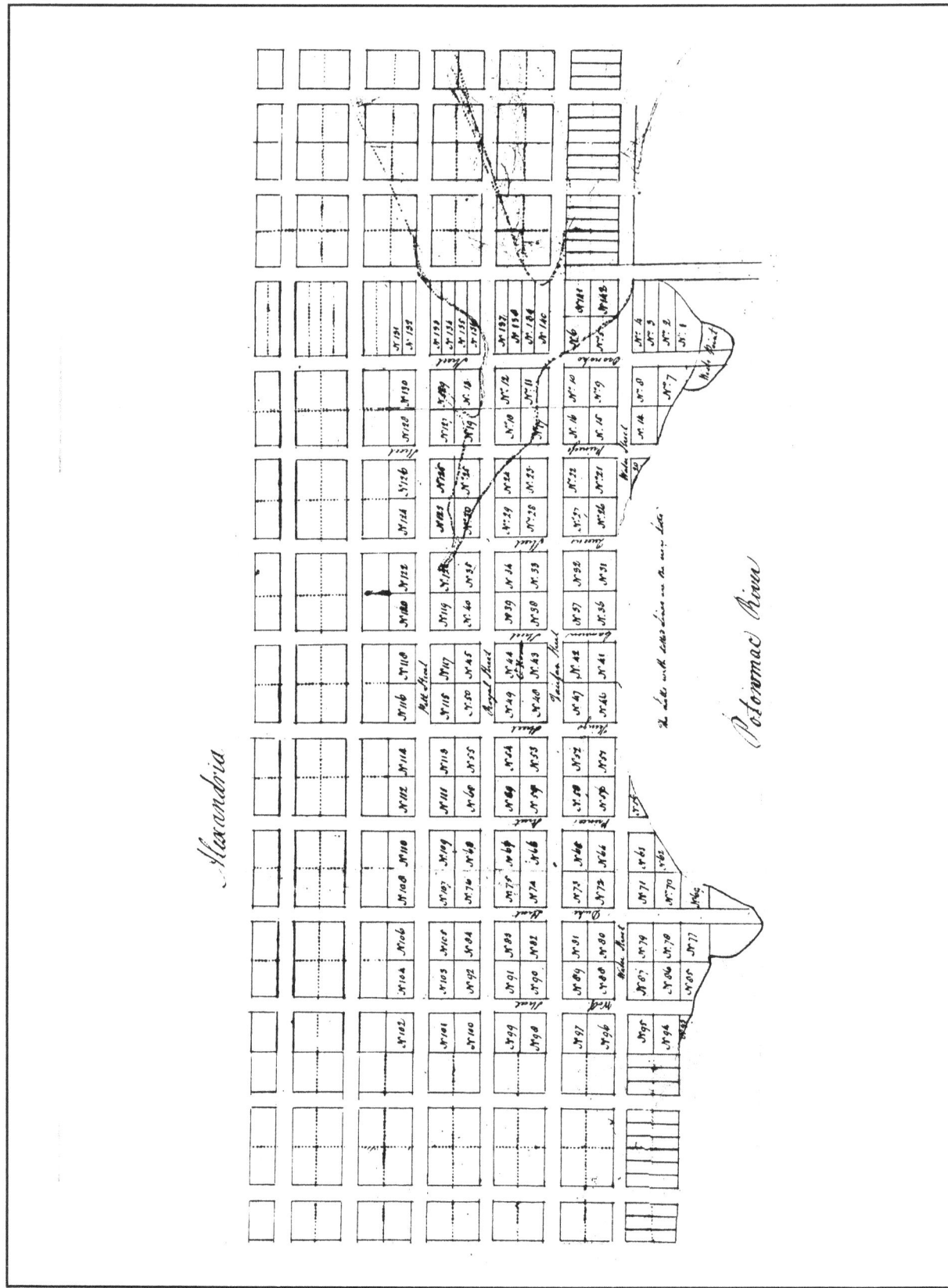

Figure 7 - George West's Map of Alexandria, March 10, 1763. (Delineates by dotted lines the new lots added in November 1762. Map was made for use by the Trustees in the sale of lots, May 9, 1763.) [Redrawn by Bill Sprouse]

LOT 85
Wolfe & Union

1763, MAY 9	Trustees to Thomas Fleming, for £50.10. (TM:50; FDB F:435 msg). For £90.10, Fleming received Lots 85 and 86 (Prince William Co. Land Causes, 1789-1793, pp. 12-23, 21 OCT 1765).
c.1770	Thomas Fleming to James Kirk (FDB H:335 msg).
1787, MAY?	Bridget Kirk, widow of James Kirk, to Joseph Caverley, 30'x123' and the wharf adjoining, lease for 15 years, "beginning upon the east side of an alley 21' wide laid out by the said Bridget Kirk upon the said wharf" (see FDB U:120).
1787, AUG 21	Joseph Caverley to John Murray & Co., merchants and partners, same parcel at annual rent, adjoining William Hartshorne (FDB U:120).
1791, MAR 3	Bridget Kirk, widow and relict of James Kirk, late of the Town of Alexandria, dec.[48], and guardian of Robert Kirk, son and heir-at-law, to Andrew Jamieson, for 11 years 7½ months, for £50 annual rent; Jamieson to repair bake house and ovens, costs to be deducted from rent due (Alex. D:413, this deed for that part of Lot 85 <u>east</u> of Union Street).
1792, MAY 8	John Murray & Co., merchants and partners, to Thomas Patten & Co., merchants and partners, same parcel, 30'x123' (FDB U:130; see also FDB X:506).
1792, DEC 11	Joseph Caverley to Andrew Jamieson, lease for $28 (Spanish milled). Deed mentions A. Jamieson's woodyard "as it is now enclosed" (Alex. D:469, 473).
1795, SEP 8	Robert Hamilton, lease to Robert Henderson, for 7 years at £36, in quarterly payments, at "SE corner of that two story framed dwelling house lately built by Joseph Caverly upon..." Kirk's wharf (Alex. F:309).

LOT 86
Wolfe, Between Water St. & Union

1763, MAY 9	Trustees to John Hunter, for £40 (TM:50).
1765, OCT 21	Trustees to Thomas Fleming, Lots 85 and 86, for £90.10 (Prince William Co. Land Causes, 1789-1793, p. 23).
1785, FEB 21	John Hunter to Michael Madden, lease for £50 annually, part of Lot 86 (Alex. A:176).
1788, MAR 19	John C. Hunter to Risden B. Harwood, of Md., for £150, part of Lot 86, 10 poles 17 links by 3 poles 18½ links. Michael Madden also claimed this piece (FDB R:205).
1788, JUL 30	Risden B. Harwood, City of Annapolis, to James Williams, same, for £400 Md., part 17½ links by 18½ links; Risden Harwood's wife Rachel to be examined (Alex. D:87).
1794, DEC 3	Abraham Morehouse, of Alexandria, and Robert Smock, late of Philadelphia, to Baldwin Dade, an annuity on several lots conveyed by Daniel Roberdeau

---

[48] <u>Virginia Journal and Alexandria Advertiser</u>, 6 JUL 1786, James Kirk, Esq., late mayor of Alexandria, died.

and John Fitzgerald to Abraham Morehouse, on Water St., Wolfe and Union streets, deeds of record in Alexandria Hustings Court (FDB X:505).

LOT 87
Wolfe & Water St.

1763, MAY 9	Trustees to Philip Alexander, for £38.10. (TM:50).
1792, MAR 26	Bridget Kirk to John Gill, lease for 10 years 5 months, 120'x30' (Alex. D:418, deed mentions "John Gill's garden fence").

(See also FDB X:505 for later transactions concerning Lot 87).

LOT 88
Wolfe & Water St.

1763, MAY 9	Trustees to Robert Adam (TM:50).
1768, MAR 11	Trustees to Joseph Watson (FDB H:1 msg; unrecorded deed in Circuit Court Archives, Drawer X).
c.1769	Joseph Watson to William Templeman (FDB H:140 msg).
c.1771	William Templeman to Jonathan Hall (FDB J:310 msg).
1784, SEP 29	"...now in the seizen of the heirs of Jonathan Hall" (FDB P:188).

LOT 89
Wolfe & Fairfax

1763, MAY 9	Trustees to William Ramsay in the name of Anne Ramsay (TM:50; see FDB P:188).
1784, MAY 1	Robert and Ann Allison, merchant, to James Holliday, cordwainer, for £120, 20'x100', to 10' Allison's Alley (Alex. A:66; see Alex. B:413).
1784, JUN 7	Robert and Ann Allison to John Harper, for £300, 60'x100' to 10' Allison's Alley; "lot originally conveyed by the Trustees to the said Anne by the name of Ann Ramsay Junior, daughter of William Ramsay" (Alex. A:60).
1784, JUL 28	Robert Allison, merchant, and wife Ann to Charles Lee, attorney at law, for £140, 23'x100', adjoining John Harper's parcel and a 10' alley laid out by Robert and Ann Allison, called "Allison's Alley" (FDB O:445).
1784, SEP 29	Robert and Ann Allison to John Elton, for £120, 20'x100' to Allison's Alley (FDB P:188).
1785, AUG 19	Robert and Ann Allison, merchant, to Robert McCrea and Robert Mease, for £375, part of lot, 123'5"x66' to a 10' alley (Alex. B:183).
1787, FEB 21	James Halladay, shoemaker, to Joseph Greenway, store keeper, for £112, 20'x100' to Allison's Alley (Alex. B:413).
1787, JUL 7	Joseph and Rebecca Greenway to William Hunter, Sr., for £112, 20'x100' (see Alex. C:163).
1787, AUG 24	John Harper to his son William Harper, for "natural love & affection," 100'x20' (Alex. E:110).
1789, AUG 10	John Harper to Samuel Harper, son of John, for £150, 40'x100' (Alex. D:1).

1789, AUG 31	Samuel and Sarah Harper to John Robert Wheaton (see FDB Y:386; see Alex. H:111).
1790, DEC 22	Robert McCrea, merchant, and wife Nancy and Robert Mease, merchant, to Samuel Johnston, of Baltimore, Md., for £356.8., 66'x123'5" with use of 10' alley (FDB T:170).
1796, SEP 14	William Summers and wife Isabella, the former Isabella Elton, widow of John Elton, dec.[49], lease to Joseph Carey, 100'x20', for $20 silver annual rent (Alex. G:477).
1796, OCT 5	John Robert Wheaton and wife Elizabeth, of New York City, to James McClenachan, for £500, 100'x40', conveyed by Samuel and Sarah Harper to Wheaton on 31 AUG 1789 (Alex. H:111).
1796, OCT 17	James McClenachan and wife Ann to Joseph Cary, 40'x100' to a 10' alley, for £400 (unrecorded deed, McClenachan to Cary, in Circuit Court Archives, Drawer X).
1797, MAY 27	William Elton, one of the brothers and devisee of John Elton, to Joseph Young, of Charles Co., Md. (Alex. I:347).[50]

(See also Alex. H:258, 262, 266; Alex. L:196).

LOT 90
Wolfe & Fairfax

1763, MAY 9	Trustees to George Johnston, Lots 90 and 91, for £15 (TM:50).
1766, FEB 23	George Johnston's will, probated 19 JUN 1767 (FWB B:432), provides for sale of lots by executors Daniel McCarty and Lee Massey.
1773, JUL 12	Richard Arell and wife Eleanor to Rev. William Thom, for purpose of a Presbyterian Church, on half of Lots 90 and 91, 88'3½"x246'10" (FDB L:215).
1783, JUN 18	Description of Lots 82 and 83 as being bounded on the south (Lots 90 and 91) by the Presbyterian burying ground (FDB O:55; see also FDB Y₂:5).

LOT 91
Wolfe & Fairfax

1763, MAY 9	Trustees to George Johnston (see information for Lot 90).

---

[49] Virginia Journal and Alexandria Advertiser, 14 OCT 1784, John Elton, house carpenter of Alexandria, dec'd., Isabella Elton is his executrix and his executors are Robert Allison and John Saunders.

[50] Whereas John Elton died owning two parcels... the estate of wife Isabella until daughter Mary's marriage or 21st birthday (on Mary's marriage or 21st birthday half the estate each to widow and daughter)... if Mary died before either event, and/or without issue, then the whole estate to Isabella... on Isabella's death the estate to be equally divided among John's brothers and sisters: Thomas, Anthony, William, Samuel, Joseph, Martha, Beersheba, Susannah and Mary... now daughter Mary has died under age and without issue. Isabella Shaw Elton Summers died 20 JAN 1821.

LOT 92
Wolfe & Royal

1763, MAY 9	Trustees to John Kirkpatrick, for £5.5. (TM:50).
1796, SEP 27	Wilson, Coltart, and others [heirs of Kirkpatrick] to Joseph Carey (see Alex. L:428).

(See also Alex. I:376).

LOTS 93, 94 and 95
Wolfe & Union; Wolfe, Between Union & Water St.; and Wolfe & Water St.

1763, MAY 9	Trustees to John Hughes, Lots 93 and 94, for £60.10. (TM:50). Later deed (FDB L:282) recites that Lots 93, 94 and 95 were conveyed by the Trustees to John Hughes, although the Proceedings show John Potts receiving Lot 95 (TM:50), and no deed seems to be recorded or indexed.
1774, MAR 18	Sarah Hughes, widow, and Stephen Paschall, executors of John Hughes, dec., late of Lower Merion, Philadelphia Co., Pa., who was a son of John Hughes, Esq., late collector of His Majesty's customs at Charleston, S.C., and Isaac Hughes, of Upper Merian, yeoman, another son of John Hughes, dec., to Daniel Roberdeau, of Philadelphia, Lots 93, 94 and 95, for £400 Pa. currency (FDB L:282).
1774, DEC 20	John Alexander, of Stafford Co., to Andrew Stewart and William Herbert, joint merchants and partners, and John Fitzgerald and Valentine Peers, merchants, all of Alexandria, Lots 94 and 95, lease for £39.10. annual rent (FDB M:127).
1784, DEC 1	William Herbert, John Potts, Jr. (of Philadelphia), and John Fitzgerald and William Lyles, Jr., division of Lots 94 and 95 (FDB P:305).
1785, MAY 7	Daniel and Jane Roberdeau lease to John Fitzgerald and William Lyles, Jr. as tenants in common, part of Lots 93, 94 and 95, 62'6"x115" (Alex. C:297; FDB W_2:100).
1794, APR 22	John Fitzgerald to Abraham Morehouse, lease part of Lot 93, 115'x62'2", and "also on the ground the 'Distillery and all the Houses and Buildings... and the several Stills, worms, tubbs, Cesterns, casks, pumps, and every piece of machinery and other articles and things now in and about the said Distillery'"; conveyed by Roberdeau to Fitzgerald and Lyles, for 10 years at $1000/year, and use of two slaves 'Jack' and 'Matt' for 2 years (Alex. F:20).
1794, JUL 4	Daniel Roberdeau to Archibald McClean [McLean], 24' front on Water Street east to the Potomac river; Roberdeau leased to John Fitzgerald who built a distillery[51] (FDB X:592; see Alex. F:27).
1794, JUL 4	Daniel and Jane Roberdeau to Archibald McClean [McLean], for £120,

---

[51] See Virginia Gazette, 24 NOV 1774, p. 2, description of distillery for lease, including buildings, wharf, and a horse-driven pump; notice details dimensions, furnishings, operations and layout.

	25'x125' (Alex. G:277).
1794, JUL 19	Daniel Roberdeau to Abraham Morehouse & Co., lease for 10 years, 176'7"x50", includes stone warehouse, for £120 annual rent. Morehouse & Co. to build another warehouse of stone or brick (Alex. E:279).
1794, JUL 22	Fitzgerald sold his interest to Abraham Morehouse, for £131.18. annual rent, payable to Roberdeau, and £168.2. to himself. Morehouse and Baldwin Dade erected "divers buildings on the aforesaid lots of ground." Morehouse and Dade agreed to a settlement (FDB X:593).
1794, JUL 29	Daniel Roberdeau and wife Jane to Abraham Morehouse, lease for parts of Lots 93, 94 and 95, and wharf adjacent to Lot 93, rent from Fitzgerald, Lyles, and Abraham Morehouse & Co. for 10 years, for £430 annual rent in quarterly payments (Alex. F:27).
1794, DEC 13	Morehouse to Robert Smock, of Philadelphia, and Daniel Ketcham, of New Jersey, for $40,633.33, the tenement, distillery and brewery on Lots 93, 94 and 95, being 176' on Water Street, extending to the Potomac channel (FDB X:593).
1795, AUG 19	Daniel Ketcham to Robert Smock, his moiety in the lots and buildings, for £1300 Pa. money (FDB Y:189).

(See also FDB Y:165; Alex. K:203, 333).

LOT 96
Wolfe & Water St.

1763, MAY 9	Trustees to Patrice C. Rowan, for £21 (TM:50; FDB F:225 msg).
c.1763	Rowan to George Johnston (FDB F:234 msg).
c.1765	George Johnston and wife to Joseph Thompson (FDB F:514 msg).
1769, DEC 18	Joseph Thompson and wife Ann to James Kirk (FDB H:313 msg; copy of this deed has been found and is filed in Drawer X). Deed indicates that lot was purchased by Joseph Thompson from George Johnston and sold to Kirk for £21.
c.1769	James Kirk to Thomas Fleming (FDB H:340 msg).
1783, DEC 16	Thomas Fleming and wife Betty to Samuel Montgomery Brown, merchant, lease for part of Lot 96, 76'x80', for £34.4. annual rent (FDB O:145).
1783, DEC 16	Thomas Fleming and wife Betty lease to Michael Maddin, 60'x80', for £30 annual rent (FDB O:149).
1784, MAY 10	Samuel Montgomery Brown and wife Mary to John Ehrmin, of York Co., Pa., lease for 25'x80' and use of 12' alley (FDB O:304, 309).
1784, JUN 1	Michael Madden to Paltzer Spangler, of York Co., Pa., lease for £24 annual rent, 30'x80' (FDB P:138).
1784, JUN 1	Michael Madden to Michael Swoope, of York Co., Pa., lease for £30 annual rent, 30'x80' (FDB P:141).
1784, JUL 16	Samuel Montgomery Brown and wife Mary to Zacharian Shugart, of York Co., Pa., lease for £19.7.6 annual rent, 25'x80' and use of 12' alley (FDB P:230).
1784, SEP 17	Thomas Fleming and wife to John Harper, for £165, 31'5"x150' and use of

	12' alley laid out by Fleming (FDB P:70).
1785, JAN 15	John Ehrmin and wife Elizabeth to Samuel Montgomery Brown, for £10, 25'x80' and use of 12' alley, same piece Brown and wife rented to Erhmin (FDB P:234).
1785, MAR 18	Thomas and Betty Fleming to John Muir, rents due from Michael Madden (Alex. B:221).
1786, NOV 15	Samuel Montgomery Brown and wife Mary to Baldwin Dade, for £81.5., and annual rent of £19.7.6, for 76'x80' (same parcel rented by Brown from Fleming), and 25'x80' (same parcel rented by Brown to Shugart) (FDB Q:329).
1787, FEB 19	Samuel Montgomery Brown and wife Mary to John Challoner, of Philadelphia, 51'7"x80' and use of 12' alley, for £77.5. and £23.3.6 annual rent, part of Brown's lease from Fleming (FDB Q:342).
1792, OCT 26	John Harper to William Harper, for £180, 150'x31'5", "to line between #96 & #97... to ground lately property of Samuel Montgomery Brown" (Alex. E:213).
1794, APR 9	Betty [Fleming] Valette inherited part of Lot 96. Eli and Betty Valette to John Lockwood one fifth (see Alex. H:49).
1794, JUN 11	John Lockwood to John Bass Dabney (see Alex. H:49).
1796, JUN 8	John Bass Dabney and wife Roxa to Thomas Patten, parts of Lots 77 and 96 (Alex. H:49).
1797, APR 29	Thomas and Mary Patten to William Millnor, for £96, 20'x80' (Alex. I:290).

(See also FDB X:429; FDB Z:486; Alex. I:419, 466; Alex. K:360, 430; Alex. M:192 power of attorney).

LOT 97
Wolfe & Fairfax

1763, MAY 9	Trustees to William Ramsay, for £12 (TM:50).
1789, SEP 21	Betty [Ramsay] Stewart to Philip Conn, for £150, 20'x103'5" and use of two alleys laid out by Betty (FDB S:456; see also information for Lots 46 and 47).
1795, OCT 7	Philip and Catharine Conn to John Hunter, for £150, 103'5"x20' (Alex. I:344).

(See also Alex. K:376, 397, 456 bond).

LOTS 98 and 99
Wolfe & Fairfax, Wolfe & Royal

1763, MAY 9	Trustees to John Orr, for £15, Lots 98 and 99 (TM:50).
c.1763	John Orr to French & Carlyle (FDB F:203 msg).
1785, MAY 14	Hannah Hartshorne's executors to Sarah and Rachel Hartshorne, part of Lot 98 (see Alex. N:160).
1799, JUN 4	Sarah and Rachel Hartshorne to William Shropshire, lease for $38 (silver)

LOT 100
Wolfe & Royal

1765, JUL 15	Trustees to John [Thomas?] Kirkpatrick, for £5.10 (TM:50; see also FDB O:226).
1796, MAR 21	By his will[52] Thomas Kirkpatrick provided for his real estate to be disposed for the benefit of his sisters who gave power attorney on 28 SEP 1791 to William Wilson and Roger Coltart to handle their real estate matters. Convey part of Lot 100 to Samuel Simmons (Alex. H:308).
1796, MAY 13	Kirkpatrick's heirs to William Wright, for £68., part of Lot 100 (Alex. L:441).
1796, SEP 27	Kirkpatrick's heirs to Alexander Perry, for £51., parts of Lot 100 (Alex. L:435).
1797, SEP 26	Alexander and Jane Perry to William Wright, for £51., 22'x110'6½" (Alex. L:475).
1798, APR 27	Kirkpatrick's heirs to John Hull, for £70., 24'x110'6½" (Alex. L:447).
1798, SEP 1	William and Ann Wright to John Turpin Brooks, lease part of Lot 100, for $66.66 silver, same conveyed by William Wilson and others to Alexander Perry and by Perry to Wright (Alex. K:226).
1800, JUL 9	William and Ann Wright to John Turpin Brooks, lease at $83.33 silver per annum, part of parcel William Wilson and others sold to Wright on 13 MAY 1796 (Alex. N:240).

(See also Alex. L:122).

LOT 101
Wolfe & Pitt

1765, JUL 15	Trustees to John Kirkpatrick, for £7.10.? (TM:50; see also FDB O:226).
1783, SEP 25	Thomas Kirkpatrick, merchant, to Charles Simms, attorney at law, for £430 (FDB O:226).

LOT 102
Wolfe & Pitt

1763, MAY 9	Trustees to Francis Lightfoot Lee, for £6.5 (TM:50; see Alex. I:341).
1765, JAN 15	John Muir and Harry Piper, Alexandria Trustees, to Francis L. Lee; conveyed to Bushrod Washington by Francis L. Lee (see Alex. G:229).
1795, DEC 23	Bushrod Washington and wife Ann, of Henrico Co., to Robert Hamilton, for 5 shillings, a lot or half acre purchased by Bushrod from Ludwell Lee (Alex.

---

[52] FWB E:36, dated 12 JAN 1785, probated 17 JAN 1785.

	G:229).
1797, JUN 28	Robert and Esther Hamilton to James Fletcher, for $300, 88'7"x22'7", "adjoining a Lot now in the tenure of Charles Simms" (Alex. I:341).

(See also Alex. H:457; Alex. N:404).

LOT 103
Wolfe & Pitt

1763, MAY 9	Trustees to Sarah Potter, for £7.10? (TM:50). She married Whiting Cook (Fairfax Court Orders, Bk. 1855, pp. 6, 7).
1784, SEP 27	[14 DEC 1784] Thomas Conway's will[53], and by his heirs and executors, to Charles Lee.
1786, JUN 5	Charles Lee to Dennis Ramsay, lease from 5 JUN 1787, for $47-2/9 (silver), 32'3"x94'6" (Alex. C:79).

LOT 104
Wolfe & Pitt

1763, MAY 9	Trustees to John Graham, for £18.15. (TM:51).
1798, OCT 19	Notley and Mary Young, City of Washington, to John Dunlap, for £540 (Alex. K:599).

LOTS 105, 106, 107 and 108
Duke & Pitt

1763, MAY 9	Trustees to John Muir, Lot 105 for £10.5., and Lot 107 for £10 (TM:51; FDB F:461 msg).
1763, MAY 9	Trustees to Henry Rozer [Rozier][54], Lot 106 for £11, and to Peter Wise, Lot 108 for £12 (TM:51). Deed for Lot 108 executed 2 DEC 1778 (FDB D$_4$:255).
1778, DEC 8	Peter Wise to Josiah Watson, 47'x123'5" of Lot 108 (FDB N:124 msg), "...a certain James Parsons... being then suposed to have some claim in equity of & in the said... part of the said lot... did by deed bearing date the ninth day of December one thousand seven hundred and seventy eight... relinquish all claim of, in, and to the same..." to Watson (see FDB Q:222).
1783, APR 29	Peter Wise to Josiah Watson, 24'x123'5" (FDB N:678 msg). James Parsons also relinquished claim to this parcel (see FDB Q:222).
1784, AUG 10	Peter Wise to Gerrard Trammell Conn, for £90, 24'x100', part of Lot 108 already sold by Conn to Charles Simms, for £400 (FDB P:301).
1785, JUN 14	Peter Wise, tanner, to Thomas Mitchum, bricklayer, for £90, 24'x100',

---

[53] Northumberland Co. Wills, Record Bk. 12, 1783-1785, p. 286, dated 27 SEP 1784, probated 8 NOV 1784.
[54] Henry Rozier was from Prince Georges Co., Md. No further transactions for his Lot 106 appear in Fairfax Co. records.

	adjoining Watson (FDB P:522).
1785, JUN 23	Peter Wise to Gerrard Trammell Conn, for £175, a parcel adjoining the lot on which Col. Charles Simms' house stands on Pitt Street and the house of Capt. John Hawkins built by Peter Wise on Lot 108 (FDB Q:32).
1785, JUN 23	Peter Wise to John Hawkins, for £325, 25'9-3/4"x84'4", adjoining Conn's parcels (FDB Q:126).
1788, MAR 17	Gerrard Trammell Conn, of Washington Co., Md., mortgage to Josiah Watson, for £79.1.5 and in satisfaction of a judgment against Conn by Joseph Janney & Co., "beginning at the south side of the lott where Charles Simms now lives on Pitt Street thence along the said street to the lott & house of John Hawkins thence westwardly parallel with Duke Street to J. Minchin's lott thence northwardly parallel with Pitt Street to Charles Simms lott thence binding with said lott to the beginning..." (FDB R:269, recorded 19 NOV 1788, probably part of Lot 108).
1788, MAR 20	John Hawkins and wife Alice to William H. Powell, for £300, part of lot sold to Hawkins by Wise (FDB R:51).
1789, DEC	John Muir's will, probated 19 APR 1791, provides for the inheritance of all his property by his sister Elizabeth Muir (FWB F:17). Elizabeth married Robert Donaldson (see Alex. G:93; see Alex. H:13).
1790, OCT 18	Transaction refers to part of a lot on Pitt and Duke, sold by William H. Powell to William Hunter, Jr., and by Hunter, Jr. to John Hopkins, 18 OCT 1790 (see FDB T:201).
1791, JUN 21	William Hunter, Jr. to George Augustine Washington, for £350, part of Lot 108, 76'7"x30±' (Alex. D:263).
1794, FEB 10	Josiah Watson to Gerrard Trammell Conn, to secure £79.1.5, the amount of an execution by Joseph Janney & Co. against G.T. Conn, which Watson engaged to pay (Alex. E:249). Conn paid and Watson conveyed to Conn, part of Lot 108.
1794, FEB 11	Gerrard Trammell Conn and wife Amelia Thame Conn, of Washington Co. [Md.], to James Kennedy, for £300, part of Lot 108 (Alex. E:245).
1794, FEB 14	Charles Simms gives consent to Gerrard Trammell Conn to "adjoin my wall in building..." (Alex. E:248).
1794, NOV 29	Josiah Watson and wife Jane to Gurdin Chapin, for £800, the two parcels of Lot 108 that were sold by Peter Wise to Watson, and that were relinquished by James Parsons, now deceased[55]; 71' on Pitt and 123'5" in depth (FDB X:424).
1796, JUN 22	Elisha Cullen Dick and wife Hannah convey part of Lot 105 to William Hartshorne (Alex. G:420; see Alex. G:443).

(See also: Lot 105-FDB U$_2$:188; Alex. H:489; Alex. K:475; Alex. L:201, 410; Alex. M:141. Lot 107-Alex. L:318; Alex. M:154. Lot 108-Alex. N:348; FDB Y$_2$:5).

---

[55] Virginia Journal and Alexandria Advertiser, 3 FEB 1785, Capt. James Parsons, of Alexandria, died.

LOT 109
Prince & Pitt

1763, MAY 9	Trustees to James McLeod[56], for £13.10. (TM:51; FDB F:308 msg).
1783, NOV 7	Robert McLeod, of Frederick Co., Md., heir of James McLeod, mortgage to James Kirk, of Loudoun Co. (FDB O:91).
1783, DEC 20	Robert McLeod, of Frederick Co., Md., son and heir of James McLeod, formerly of Alexandria, to James Kirk, for £180 (Alex. A:49).
1784, SEP 15	Robert McLeod, of Frederick Co., Md. to Richard Arell, for £400, all of Lot 109 (FDB P:48).
1784, SEP 15	Robert McLeod, of Frederick Co., Md. to Richard Arell, for £600, bond indicates McLeod sold to Arell but earlier conveyed to James Kirk; bond void if Kirk has title. If Kirk has title, will pay McLeod £300 in 3 years (Alex. F:521).
1786, JAN 17	Robert McLeod, of Frederick Co., Md. assigns right to bond to Samuel S. Thomas (Alex. F:523).

(See also Alex. H:431).

LOT 110
Prince & Pitt
(See also Lot 156)

1763, MAY 9	Trustees to James Laurie, for £17.5. (TM:51; FDB F:293 msg). Laurie died intestate and without issue. The lot descended to an heir in Great Britain, was escheated as British property, and conveyed to Thomas Conway, of Northumberland Co., Va., in 1780 (see FDB Q:291).[57]

---

[56] Benjamin Watkins Leigh [1781-1849], Virginia Reports, 31 Va. 4 Leigh, Vol. 4, pp. 325-26, Court of Appeals of Virginia, "Marsteller and wife and others v. Coryell," February 1833, complaint of trespass. "That the title of the lot in question was originally vested in the trustees of the Town of *Alexandria*, and that they, by deed dated the 13th May 1765, conveyed the same to *James M'Leod*. That *James M'Leod*, by verbal contract, sold the lot to one *Joseph Watson*, and put him in possession, but made no conveyance thereof. That *Watson*, by verbal contract likewise, sold it to *Edward Rigdon* and put him in possession; *Rigdon* died in 1772, having by his will devised this lot to his widow *Elizabeth Rigdon*; who sold it, by verbal contract, and delivery of possession, to *Richard Arell*. That, in the meantime, *James M'Leod* had died, leaving *Robert M'Leod* his son and heir at law; and that *Robert M'Leod*, by deed dated the 15th September 1784, conveyed to lot to *Arell*. That *Arell* continued to hold possession during his life, and died in actual possession, leaving the plaintiffs his heirs at law. And that the defendant entered upon the lot about a year after *Arell's* death. This was the trespass complained of. There was no evidence to shew, that *Arell's* heirs ever actually entered upon the premises after his death; nor any evidence to shew in whom the actual possession was, or that any one was in actual possession, during the interval between the death of *Arell*, and the taking of possession by the defendant. Verdict for the plaintiffs for 1230 dollars, subject to the opinion of the court, on the demurrer to evidence, whether the plaintiffs were entitled to recover in this action? The court held that they were not, and gave judgment for the defendant; from which the plaintiffs appealed to this court."

[57] The will of Thomas Conway, dated 27 SEP 1784, probated 8 NOV 1784 in Northumberland Co., indicates "The land I hold in Northumberland County should be equally divided between my brothers John Conway, Robert Conway, and Joseph Conway, and their heirs." The remainder of the estate both real and personal was to be divided equally between [his children] Mary Elleston, John Conway, Hannah Webb, Robert Conway, and Joseph Conway. The wills for the Hustings Court of Alexandria, 1782-1786 have not been located, so it is not clear

Alexandria, Virginia Town Lots, 1749-1801

[1782, DEC 19]	William McKnight to John Saunders and John Elton (see FDB P:144; see FWB E:27).
1784, DEC 11	Heirs of Thomas Conway, dec., to John Saunders, for £180, 24'x100' to 9' alley (Alex. A:119).
1784, DEC 11	Heirs of Thomas Conway, dec., for £180, to George Richards, 24'x100' and use of 9' alley (see FDB Q:291).
1784, DEC 11	Heirs of Thomas Conway, dec., to John B. Murray (for Murray, Obediah Bowen and John P. Mumford) and Thomas Porter, 123'5"x45', the portion south of the alley. Obediah Bowen, of New York, devised all of his estate to Jabez Bowen, of Providence, Rhode Island (FDB Z:54).
1784, DEC 11	Robert Conway and other devisees, heirs of Thomas Conway, dec., to James Rattle, for £511, [the corner portion] 51'5"x100' and use of a 9' alley (see FDB R:200).
1784, DEC 11	John Spann Conway to Joseph Conway, of Northumberland Co., for £120, 123'5"x22'6" (Alex. A:158).
1784, DEC 14	Heirs of Thomas Conway, dec.,[58] to Charles Lee, for £676, 24'x100' (Alex. A:133).
1785, OCT 15	Thomas [Lee] received a land office patent for Lot 110 (Patents H:558).
1786, JUN 5	Charles Lee lease to John McClanachan, 24'x100' for $56 (silver) annual rent, adjoining a 9' alley; provides that within two years McClanachan to build a good strong substantial dwelling house, 20 feet square at least, filled in with lime and sand and having a brick stone chimney (FDB Q:226[59]; see Alex. E:332).
1786, AUG 7	George Richards to David Wilson Scott, for £110, 24'x100' and use of a 9' alley (FDB Q:291).
1787, MAR 19	Joseph Conway and wife Lucy to Richard Conway, for £150, 22'6"x123'5" (Alex. C:7).
1787, APR 2	Thomas Conway's heirs to Joseph Conway, their interest in 22'6"x123'5" (Alex. C:7).
1788, APR 10	James Rattle and wife Anne to John Murray and Thomas Porter, for £170, [the corner portion] 51'5"x100' and use of 9' alley (FDB R:200; FDB Z:54).
1789, FEB 24	David Wilson Scott, of Dumfries, Prince William Co., to Richard M. Scott, for £40, 24'x100' and use of a 9' alley (FDB R:410).
1794, MAR 13	John and Ann McClanachan, of Prince William Co., to Thomas Patton and Joseph May, of Boston, Mass., for £604 and $56 (silver) rent to Charles Lee[60] (Alex. E:332).

---

whether a copy was filed in Alexandria.

[58] John and Susannah Conway, of Somerset Co., Md., Joseph Conway, Northumberland Co., Robert and Mary Conway, Cuthbert and Mary Ellison, and Hannah Webb.

[59] Refers to the Last Will and Testament of Thomas Conway of Northumberland Co., dec., which specifies "part of the aforesaid lot and half acre of land was sold and conveyed by the said Robert Conway and Susanna his wife, John Conway & Mary his wife, Joseph Conway and Cuthbert Elliston and the said Mary Conway by the name of Mary Elliston his wife and the said Hanah Conway [sic] by the name of Hannah Webb widow and relict of a certain John Webb deceased to the said Charles Lee by Indenture of bargain and sale bearing date the fourteenth day of December one Thousand Seven hundred and eighty four.

[60] Judge Charles Lee died 24 JUN 1815, at his home near Warrenton, Fauquier Co.

(See also information for Lot 156; see also FDB P:144; FDB X:520; FDB Z:52; Alex. H:247, 270).

LOT 111
Prince & Pitt

1763, MAY 9	Trustees to Jacob Hite, for £22.10. (TM:51).
prior to 1770	Jacob Hite to William Carlin (FDB H:31 msg; see FDB P:290).
1779, MAR 22	William Carlin and wife Sarah to John Reynell, of Philadelphia, 94'x24'. Reynell devised to Samuel Coates in his will (FDB N:143 msg; see FDB P:290).
1779, MAR 22	William Carlin and wife Sarah to John McAlister, 94'x49' (FDB D_4:308).
1779, MAR 22	William Carlin and wife Sarah to William Hartshorne, 94'x24'5" (see Alex. A:18; FDB N:140 msg).
c.1780	William Carlin [and wife Sarah] to Abraham Faw (FDB N:256 msg; see Alex. G:271).
1780, SEP 15	William Carlin and wife Sarah to George Duncan, 24'6"x94' (FDB N:373 msg; see FDB D_4:290).
1781, MAR 28	George Duncan and wife Elizabeth to Jesse Taylor, for £7000, 24'6"x94' (FDB D_4:290).
1781, APR 10	William Carlin and wife Sarah to Jesse Taylor, for £8000, part of Lot 111, 25'x97'x58'x25½'x113'x123½' (FDB D_4:297).
1781, JUN 27	John McAlister and wife Elizabeth to Josiah Watson, for £500, 94'x49' (FDB D_4:308).
1782, AUG 20	John Hendricks to Jacob Mattart, two parcels (see Alex. F:12).
1783, JAN 18	Abraham Faw to John Saunders, 20'x99' (FDB N:652 msg; see FDB P:157).
1784, JAN 22	William Hartshorne and wife Susanna to Christian Slimmer, for 5 shillings, part of Lot 111, 94'x24'5" (Alex. A:18).
1784, JUL 19	John Saunders and wife Mary to Philip Conn, lease for $25-1/3 (Spanish milled) annual rent, 12'8"x99'. Conn to build house within 1 year (FDB P:388).
1784, JUL 19	John Saunders and wife Mary lease to Lewis Cooke, 99'x12'8" (see Alex. G:86).
1784, AUG 25	Joseph Wilson, Jr. and wife Chloe, mortgage to Joseph Watson, 49'x94' (FDB P:282). This may be the same parcel conveyed by Watson to Wilson c.1782 (FDB N:471 msg).
1784, SEP 30	John Saunders and wife Mary to Robert Allison, 20'x99', for £120 (FDB P:157).
1784, DEC 24	Samuel Coates and wife Lydia, of Philadelphia, to Benjamin Shreeve, for £150, 94'x24', the same parcel devised to Coates by the will of John Reynell (FDB P:290).
1785, APR 1	Benjamin Shreeve and wife lease to Thomas Barclay, £20 (silver) or Half-Joes annually (Alex. A:184; see FDB R:1).
1785, MAY 20	John Saunders and wife Mary to Susanna Hamilton, of Georgetown, Md., lease for $25-1/3 (silver) annual rent, 12'8"x99' (FDB Q:10).
1786, SEP 11	Joseph Wilson and wife Chloe to Josiah Watson, for £600, 49'x94' (FDB

	Q:279).
1787, OCT 26	Benjamin Shreeve and wife Susannah to Isaac Nickels, of Loudoun Co., for £200, the rent on part of Lot 111 which Shreve and wife had leased to Thomas Barclay for £20 annual rent in 1785 (FDB R:1).
1789, APR 12	Jacob Mattart, of Frederick Town, Frederick Co., Md., butcher, to Thomas Price, of the same place, for £340, two parcels in Lot 111 (Alex. F:12).
1790, SEP 3	Uriah Forest, of Montgomery Co., Md., to Peter Casanave, part of Lots 111 (100'x20') and 113, for £1125 (Alex. D:355).
1791, SEP 15	William Miller to Thomas White, shop keeper, for £18, 99'x12'8" and $25-1/3 (silver) rent. Deed recites that Susanna Hamilton conveyed to William Miller on 6 AUG 1790 (Alex. D:409).
1791, SEP 26	Peter Casanove, of Montgomery Co., Md., to William Hodgson, for £930, 20'x100', all that part "on which a Brick house of... Peter Casanave standeth" (Alex. D:363).
1794, OCT 31	Thomas Price and wife Mary, of Frederick Co., Md., to Samuel Craig, for £250, two parcels conveyed by [John] Hendricks to [Jacob] Mattart and by Mattart to Price (Alex. F:16).
1794, NOV 14	William Hodgson to John Crips Vowell and Thomas Vowell, Jr., 20'x100' (Alex. E:469).
1795, APR 2	Thomas and Ann Barclay, Town of Georgetown, Md., to Samuel Craig, 94'x24'6" for £120. Craig to pay [Isaac] Nickolls, £20 annual rent (Alex. F:122).
1795, APR 30	Lewis Cooke and wife Elizabeth to Thomas Tresize and Richard May, for £85, 99'12'8", for $25-1/3 (Spanish milled) annual rent to John Saunders (Alex. G:86).
1796, JUL 16	Abraham and Mary Ann Faw to William Hartshorne, John Butcher and Mary Wanton, executors of John Saunders[61], for £400, part of Lot 111, 99'x58', free of rent (Alex. G:271).

(See also L:113, 274; Alex. M:13, 36, 98; Alex. O:69).

LOT 112
Prince & Pitt

1763, MAY 9	Trustees to George Washington, for £38 (TM:51).
1799, JUL 9	Will of General George Washington, probated 20 JAN 1800, indicates he had refused $3500 for the lot "though unimproved has been divided into proper sized lots for building on... forever... at three dollars a foot on the

---

[61] John Saunders was one of the members of the Society of Friends who in APR 1785 obtained a lot for Society use on the west side of St. Asaph Street from Benjamin Shreve. Saunders died 18 MAY 1790 [Virginia Gazette and Alexandria Advertiser, 20 MAY 1790]. His will, dated 13 MAY 1790, probated 24 AUG 1790, is to be found in Complete Records, Liber A, 1786-1800, pp. 24-30, at the Library of Virginia, Archives Division. Saunders' widow Mary, daughter of David Pancoast, married 31 MAY 1792 at Fairfax Monthly Meeting to Philip Wanton [Hinshaw, Vol. VI, p. 775]. Mary Pancoast Saunders Wanton, died 26 NOV 1846 in her 84th year, and was buried in the Quaker cemetery on Queen Street in Alexandria [tombstone].

street... and this price is asked for both fronts on Pitt & Prince Streets" (FWB H:17, 22, will notes he valued the lot at $4000).

(See also FDB B$_2$:276, 281).

LOT 113
King & Pitt

1763, MAY 9	Trustees to Philip Alexander, for £39 (TM:51). Deed from the Trustees is missing (FDB F:482, 3 msg), and is indexed under Robert Alexander rather than Philip.
1766, DEC 15	Robert Alexander and wife Mariamne [sic] to Charles Turner, for £9.13.4, quarter part of Lot 113, "conveyed to him by the Trustees of Alexandria" (FDB G:105). Turner died intestate, parcel escheated to Thomas Lord Fairfax. Fairfax granted parcel to Robert Muir, 6 FEB 1777. Muir died intestate, the parcel passed to his brother John Muir (see Alex. H:130).
1777, JUN 23	Robert Alexander and wife Mariamne to James Kirk, merchant, for £30, quarter part of Lot 113, 176'6"x30'10-1/5" (the ground of James Kirk referred to in FDB Q:112 for Lot 55) (FDB M:326).
1784, AUG 4	Robert Alexander died intestate. Part of Lot 113 descended to Henry McCabe[62] and to his son Henry McCabe, of Leesburg, Loudoun Co. (FDB P:51). Henry McCabe and wife Jane to William Hepburn, for £1000, 30'10¼"x176'6" adjoining Robert Allison.
1786, JUN 21	William Hepburn and wife Agnes to daughter Agnes Dundas, wife of John Dundas, 30'10¼"x176'6", same parcel as was conveyed by McCabe to Hepburn (FDB Q:231).
1789, JAN 27	Robert Allison and wife Ann to Uriah Forest, of George Town, Md., merchant, for £925, 31'6"x176'6" (FDB R:466; see Alex. H:73).
1790, SEP 3	Uriah Forest[63], of Montgomery Co., Md. [and Stoddart (see Alex. H:73)] to Peter Casanave, of same, for £1125, 176'6"x31½", and part of Lot 111 (Alex. D:355).
1791, SEP 26	Peter Casanave to William Hodgson, for £930, part of lot on which a brick house stands, 176'6"x31'6" (Alex. D:363; see FDB U:421).
1792, JUL 17	William Hodgson to John Dundas, for £32.8., 34'x6½", adjoining parcel sold by Henry McCabe to William Hepburn and by Hepburn to daughter Agnes Dundas, "...and also the right & privilege of joining the walls of the house which he the said John Dundas is now building, to the walls of the house standing upon the lott of ground sold by the said Peter Casanove unto the said William Hodgson till the same shall reach the square of the said

---

[62] See also Hening, Vol. X, p. 488, "An act to enable Henry McCabe to dispose of certain lands." Indicates that McCabe, some time in 1780 departed this life intestate, leaving several tracts of land in the county of Loudoun, and a lot and houses in the town of Alexandria, and a very small personal estate: That Henry McCabe, his only son in this county, has administered upon and sold the personal estate, which is not sufficient to pay the debts...

[63] Maryland Gazette, 18 JUL 1805, Gen. Uriah Forrest, died Sat. [July 6] at his seat near Georgetown. On the next day his remains were interred in the Protestant Episcopal Burying Ground of that place...

	Hodgson's house, and also the right liberty & privilege to take down the gavel end of the said Hodgson's house from the top of the square, and raise upon the said wall from the square, another wall the full thickness of the said gavel wall to the height he the said John Dundas shall carry the other brick work of his house, and thirty four feet long to serve as a common wall of Partition, between the said houses..." (FDB U:419).
1794, NOV 14	William Hodgson to John Crips Vowell and Thomas Vowell, Jr., that part of Lot 113 bought by Hodgson of Casanove, excluding the part Hodgson sold to Dundas, and half of the partition wall (Alex. E:469).
1796, MAY 21	John Crips Vowell and wife Margaret and Thomas Vowell, Jr. and wife Mary to Alexander Smith, for £1345, two parcels (Alex. H:73).
1796, JUL 4	Elizabeth Donaldson, sister and heir to John Muir, dec., to Mordecai Miller, for £415, quarter of Lot 113 (Alex. H:130).
1797, APR 7	William Hartshorne and Mordecai Miller, to James Kidd, a 5-year lease, paying in quarterly installments £40 per annum, for part lot (Alex. I:242).

(See also Alex. M:323).

LOT 114
King & Pitt

1763, MAY 9	Trustees to John Alexander, Jr. (TM:51).
1774, DEC 20	John Alexander, of Stafford Co., to Charles Jones, for £60, all of Lot 114 (FDB M:37, 39).
prior to 1780	John Goodrick, a British subject, lost Lot 114 when it was escheated as British property (see FDB Q:306).
1780, AUG 28	Baldwin Dade purchased the western half of escheated lot (see FDB Q:306). Dade obtained patent 22 JUL 1782.
1780, OCT 19	Jesse Taylor obtained by grant the eastern half of lot, bounded on the north by King Street, east by Pitt Street, south by Lot 112 (property of General Washington), and west by Baldwin Dade's half of Lot 114 (Patents E:458, 679).
1782, OCT 28	Baldwin Dade and wife Catherine to William Bird, 176'6"x61'8½" (FDB N:892 msg; see FDB Q:306).
1786, DEC 4	William Bird and wife Catharine to Patrick Allison, of Baltimore, clerk, for £600, 176'6"x61'8½" (FDB Q:306).

(See also Alex. L:430; Alex. M:87, 267).

LOT 115
King & Pitt

1763, MAY 9	Trustees to Michael Gretter, for £50.10. (TM:51).
1774, JUL 4	Michael Gretter and wife Elizabeth to Thomas Armat, for £300, part of Lots 50 and 115, 246'10"x46' (FDB M:12).
1774, SEP 9	Michael Gretter to William Hepburn, for £150, subject to wife Elizabeth's

	dower, 36'x100' part of Lot 115 (FDB M:34).
1775, FEB 13	Michael Gretter to daughter Elizabeth Simpson, wife of William Simpson, "for natural love and affection which the said Michael Gretter beareth unto the said Elizabeth his Daughter," for £50, part of Lot 115 (FDB M:136).
1775, APR 30	Thomas Armat and wife Sarah to Robert McCrea and Robert Mease, merchants, for £360, part of Lots 50 and 115, 246'10"x46' (FDB M:159).
1775, DEC 15	Michael Gretter to Thomas Armat, for £150, 36'x100', part of Lot 115 (FDB M:223).
1789, SEP 23	Michael Gretter mortgage to William Hepburn, part of Lot 115, 72'x30', "upon which the said William Hepburn's store house now stands and also joins to that piece of Ground upon which the said William Hepburn hath erected two three-stories brick Houses" (Alex. C:310).
1791, JUL 18/21	Michael and Elizabeth Gretter to Lawrence Hooff, for £150, part of Lot 115 and 50 (Alex. D:311, 317). Michael Gretter had given this parcel to daughter Elizabeth Simpson, wife of William. They conveyed to Lawrence Hooff. Sale confirmed 21 JUL 1791. Deed mentions a house "now occupied by John Gretter."

LOT 116
King & Pitt

1763, MAY 30	Trustees to Robert Rutherford, for £27 (TM:51; FDB F:455 msg; see also FDB L:277). Transaction may have been dated 13 MAY 1763 (see FDB R:321).
1774, APR 7/8	Robert Rutherford, of Co. of Berkeley and Parish of Norborn, and Mary his wife, to James Hendricks, merchant, for £155 (FDB L:277, 279).
1789, JAN 25	James Hendricks and wife Kitty to Richard Parker, of Philadelphia, merchant, for £2665.5.6 (FDB R:321).
1794, APR 1	Richard Parker to Thomas Richards, for £1500, all of Lot 116 (Alex. E:269).
1795, JUN 1	Thomas Richards and wife Nancy to Peter Wise, for £42, 176'7"x4' (Alex. G:90).
1796, APR 11	Thomas Richards leased to John McIver for a 5-year term, for £90 per annum, a house fronting 24' on King Street, and on east side of an alley, with kitchen, smoke house, necessary, and yard "to the fence," "being a part of the house built by James Hendricks... and which Thomas Richards lately occupied himself" (see Alex. H:433).
1796, JUL 23	Thomas and Nancy Richards to Samuel Craig, for £2150, 119'x23'9" with a brick house (Alex. H:134).
1796, SEP 30	Thomas Richards and wife Anne to Charles Lee, of Philadelphia, assign McIver's indenture, including the £90 annual rent, for $1000 (Alex. H:433).

(See also Alex. I:353; Alex. K:170, 174; Alex. M:173; Alex. O:242).

LOT 117
Cameron & Pitt

1763, MAY 9	Trustees to Thomas Kirkpatrick (TM:51).
c.1778	Thomas Kirkpatrick conveys something to Thomas Hughes, but the deed is missing (FDB N:23 msg).
1785, JAN 12	Will of Thomas Kirkpatrick, probated 17 JAN 1785, conveys all the residue of his estate to his sisters Katherine Coltart and Elizabeth Cutler (FWB E:36).
1796, SEP 27	Tripartite deed from William Wilson, of Alexandria, Roger Coltart, of Town of Fredericksburg, Elizabeth [Kirkpatrick] Cutler, widow, Katherine [Kirkpatrick] Coltart, widow, and Henrietta Kirkpatrick, all three sisters and co-heiresses of Thomas Kirkpatrick, dec.[64], to Joseph Maria Perin, for £61, part of Lot 117 (Alex. L:463).

(See also Alex. I:406; 477).

LOT 118
Cameron & Pitt

1763, MAY 9	Trustees to George Washington, for £10.10. (TM:51).
1800, SEP 22	Martha Washington, in her will probated 21 JUN 1802, conveys to her nephew Bartholomew Dandridge "and his heirs my lot in the town of Alexandria situate on Pitt and Cameron streets devised to me by my late husband George Washington deceased"[65] (FWB I:134). George's will describes the lot as being improved (FWB H:1).

LOTS 119 and 120
Prince & Pitt

1763, MAY 9	Trustees to Anthony Ramsay, for £6.5., for Lots 119 and 120 (TM:51). John Alexander retained 2/7 of the two lots.
1765, OCT 21	Trustees to Hannah Ramsay, Lot 120 (FDB A$_2$:45; FDB F:405 msg; see Fairfax Court Orders, Bk. 1765, p. 64).
1784, DEC 20	William Ramsay, Gent. to his daughters Sarah and Amelia Ramsay, part of Lots 40 and 119, 88'x246'10" as tenants in common, charging however a rent of £50 annually, payable to John Dalyell, with use of a 10' alley (FDB P:372).
1795, AUG 20	Dennis Ramsay, Robert Allison and Michael Madden, executors of William Ramsay, Sr., dec., to John Gill, 116'x72'6", for £104.10. (Alex. G:146).
1796, APR 13	Michael and Hannah Madden to William Pomery, for £80, 100'7"x24' part

---

[64] Virginia Journal and Alexandria Advertiser, 20 JAN and 3 MAR 1785, Thomas Kirkpatrick, merchant of Alexandria, dec'd., estate accounts with his executor Robert Adam, Robert McCrea, John Gibson, and William Hunter, Jr.

[65] The Times and District of Columbia Daily Advertiser, 16 and 20 DEC 1799, General George Washington died in Alexandria on Saturday evening, the 14th, about 11 o'clock.

	of Lot 120 (Alex. H:90).
1796, APR 13	Michael and Hannah Madden to John White, for £80, 101'7"x24' part of Lot 120 (Alex. H:93).
1796, APR 13	Michael and Hannah Madden to Thomas Richards, for £73, 101'7"x24', part of Lot 120 (Alex. H:97).
1797, APR 26	Michael Madden and wife Hannah [Ramsay] to Daniel McLean, for £140, 27'5"x100'6½", Madden to lay off 10' alley, parcel out of Lot 120 (FDB A$_2$:45).

(See also FDB Y$_2$:262 (#120); Alex. H:318 (#120), 341 (#120); Alex. L:98 (#120); Alex. N:104 (#119), 337 (#119 or #40)).

LOT 121
Queen & Pitt

1763, MAY 9	Trustees to James Connelly, for £2.10. (TM:51).
1777, MAY 17	James Connell's [sic] will, probated 16 JUN 1777 (FWB D:9), provides "that my house & tenements be given to John Sutton, watchmaker in Carlyle."[66]
1789, OCT 12	John Sutton mortgage to son John Davison Sutton, for £100 Sterling, 130'x166' of Lots 35 and 121. In 1778, John Sutton had conveyed to his mother Ann Sutton and children in trust (FDB S:146).
1790, JUL 13	John Sutton to William Bird, same parcel as mortgaged to John Davison Sutton, as security for Bird who is special bail for Sutton in suit by Wilsons & Co. of Kilmarnock and by John Black in District Court of Dumfries (FDB S:520).
1790, JUL 16	John Sutton to John Mandeville in trust, 130'x166', of Lots 35 and 121, "for the discharge & payment of all debts legally due from the said John Sutton or from John Mandeville or from the house of John Sutton & Co. or Sutton, Mandeville & Co." (FDB S:523).
1793, FEB 11	John Mandeville to Jonathan Mandeville, for £285, 130'x166' of Lots 35 and 121, held by John Mandeville for John Sutton in trust (FDB W:117).

LOT 122
Queen & Pitt

1763, MAY 9	Trustees to Richard Arell (TM:51).

LOT 123
Queen & Pitt

1771, NOV 6	Trustees to John Carlyle, for £5 (TM:68; FDB J:374 msg).

---

[66] Also see Hening, Vol. X, pp. 372-73, "An act to vest certain houses and tenements in the town of Alexandria in John Sutton and his heirs, in fee simple."

c.1771	Trustees to Charles Little (FDB J:375 msg).
1775, MAR 17	Charles Little to Samuel McLean, of Newcastle Co., Pa., tanner, lease of Lot 123 for £5.7.6 annual rent (FDB M:178).

LOT 124
Queen & Pitt

1771, NOV 6	Trustees to Thomas Carson, for £8.5. (TM:68).
1772, JUL 24	Thomas Carson, merchant, to William Hubburn [sic], ropemaker, for £20 (FDB K:113, 115).
1773, JAN 16	William Hepburn, rope maker, and wife Agnes to Robert McCrea, of Cumberland Co., Pa., merchant, for £20, the western half of Lot 124 (FDB K:260).
c.1783	William Hepburn and wife to Andrew Judge (FDB N:635 msg).
1782, AUG 8	William Hepburn and wife Agnes to William Anderson, 40'x90', for $20 (silver) annual rent, adjoining Andrew Judge (FDB P:32). Deed recorded 19 AUG 1784 (see Alex. B:389).
1783, AUG 8	William Hepburn and wife Agnes to John Gabard, 90'x43'5" (FDB N:638 msg; see Drawer X in Circuit Court Archives, John Gabard to Thomas Reed, 1783).
1783, SEP 24	John Gabard to Thomas Reed, 90'x43'5" for £36 (Drawer X).
1784, DEC 22	[Recording date] Andrew Judge and wife Rebecca to Michael Gretter, for $9 (silver) annual rent payable to William Hepburn (FDB P:215, first part missing).
1786, AUG 13	William Anderson and wife Elizabeth to Thomas Reed, part of Lot 124 (see Alex. B:389; see Alex. C:74).
1786, AUG 18	Thomas and Elizabeth Reed to Michael Gretter, for £50, 90'x24'. Gretter to pay Hepburn $12 (silver) annually (Alex. B:389).

LOT 125
Princess & Pitt

1771, NOV 6	Trustees to John Carlyle, for £11 (TM:68).

LOT 126
Princess & Pitt

1771, NOV 6	Trustees to John Carlyle, for £20 (TM:68).
1775, OCT 19	Col. John Carlyle to John Jolly, bricklayer, for £7.10.6 annual rent (FDB M:199).
1787, JUN 28	John and Rachel Jolly to Thomas Williams and Joseph Cary, mortgage to secure £180 owed Williams and Cary, part of Lot 126, 123'5"x36'3½" (Alex. C:118).
1787, AUG 13	John Jolly and wife Rachel to William Lowry and Company, merchants and partners, mortgage for debt of £91.16.9, 44'x70', part of Lot 126 (FDB R:17).

1788, MAY 7	William Newton to Thomas Williams and Joseph Cary, for £35, 123'5"x36'3½" (Alex. C:223).
1788, MAY 7	Thomas Williams and Joseph Cary to William Newton, for £35, 123'5"x36'3½" lost by Jolly through default (Alex. E:141).
1789, JUL 26	John Jolly to Dennis Whalin, for £150.10., all of lot, "except the house & benefit of a four feet alley thereupon purchased by Williams & Cary, merchants of the Town aforesaid" (FDB S:4).
1790, DEC 13	Dennis Whalin to William Summers, for £30, 93'x123'5" (Alex. D:179).
1793, MAR 11	Dennis Whalin to William Summers, for £3.10., remainder of Lot 126, to Williams and Cary's line, 123'5"x47' (Alex. E:98).
1794, APR 13	William Lowrey & Co. [sic], late of Alexandria but now of Baltimore, to Baldwin Dade, for £15 (Dade as the highest bidder), 70'x44', it being a parcel mortgaged by John and Rachel Jolly to William Lowry & Co., 13 AUG 1787. Jolly failed to pay. Sale at public auction to Dade (Alex. F:345).
1794, APR 14	Baldwin Dade and wife Catherine to William Lowry & Co., for £15, same parcel as above (Alex. F:355).
1794, APR 15	William Lowry & Co. and Olivia, wife of William, Baltimore, Md., to William Summers, for £10, same parcel as above (Alex. F:362).

(See also Alex. H:255).

LOT 127
Princess & Pitt

1763, MAY 9	Trustees to John Potts, for £12.5., "ex. Hugh Hughes" (TM:51).

LOT 128
Princess & Pitt

1763, MAY 9	Trustees to Henry Roser [Rozier], for £11 (TM:51).[67]

LOT 129
Oronoco & Pitt

1763, MAY 9	Trustees to John Carlyle, for £6.5. (TM:51).
c.1763	Trustees to John Ramsay (FDB F:277 msg).
1786, SEP 23	Thomas Ramsay to Thomas Hedrick, lease for £8, 63'5"x40' (Alex. B:346).
1788, SEP 10	Thomas Ramsay, heir at law and eldest son of John Ramsay, and wife Susannah to William Wright, for £115, part of Lot 129, 60'x176'7". Ramsay's widow Elizabeth, now Elizabeth Downey, releases her dower interest to Wright for 5 shillings (FDB R:242).

---

[67] Deeds from Rozier for other property state that he was from Prince Georges Co., Md. The surname is also spelled Rozer and Roser (FDB P:18).

1792, DEC 13	William and Ann Wright to Charles Lee, for £250, 176'7"x60' (Alex. D:474; examination of Anne Wright, at p. 477; see also FDB B₂:158).

LOT 130
Oronoco & Pitt

1763, MAY 9	Trustees to John and Ann Tarbuck, for £8.12. (TM:51).
1785, JAN 1	John Tarbuck, alias Scott, mariner, sells all of Lot 130 to William Patterson for £75 (Alex. B:188).
1786, FEB 24	Thomas Patterson to Mary Burnett and sons George and Charles, for £10, part of Lot 130, 40'123'5" (Alex. B:218).
1786, JUL 24	William Patterson, of Beaufort Co., N.C., to Susanna Patterson, for £1000, all of lot (FDB Q:315).
1789, OCT 27	Susanna Patterson to Charles Simms, for £300 (Alex. D:92).

(See also FDB Y:469; FWB G:441).

LOT 131
Between Oronoco & Pendleton, West of Pitt

1763, MAY 9	Trustees to John Carlyle, for £4.10. (TM:51).
1765, MAY 13	Trustees to James Adam (see Alex. L:271).
1785, AUG 2	James Adam and wife Elizabeth[68] to William Hunter, for £500, all of lot (FDB Q:53).
1798, AUG 2	William and Kitty Hunter to Jesse Simms, for $1000, Lots 131 and 132 (Alex. M:150; see Alex. L:271).
1799, FEB 18	Jesse Simms to Walter Story Chandler, of George Town, Montgomery Co., Md., for $1560, two parcels Lots 131 and 132 (Alex. L:271).

LOT 132
Between Oronoco & Pendleton, West of Pitt

1763, MAY 9	Trustees to James Adam, for £4.10. (TM:51).
1786, MAY 2	Robert Adam to William Hunter (see Alex. L:271).
1798, AUG 2	William and Kitty Hunter to Jesse Simms (see Alex. L:271; M:150).
1799, FEB 18	Jesse Simms to Walter Story Chandler, of George Town, Montgomery Co., Md., for $1560, two parcels, Lots 131 and 132 (Alex. L:271).

LOT 133
Between Oronoco & Pendleton, East of Pitt

1763, MAY 9	Trustees to James Adam, for £6.15. (TM:51).
1786, JUL 27	Robert Adam and wife Anne to Charles Lee, for £800, two acres which

---

[68] Alex. L:271, gives wife of James Adam as Jane.

1786, JUL 28   include Lots 133, 134, 135 and 136 (FDB Q:266). Charles Lee, attorney at law, to Robert Adam, merchant, mortgage for same property (FDB Q:268).

LOT 134
Between Oronoco & Pendleton, East of Pitt

1763, MAY 9   Trustees to Robert Adam, for £8.5. (TM:51).

(See information for Lot 133 for later transactions).

LOT 135
Between Oronoco & Pendleton, West of Royal

1763, MAY 9   Trustees to John Dalton, for £16.5. (TM:51).

(See information for Lot 133 for later transactions).

LOT 136
Between Oronoco & Pendleton, West of Royal

1763, MAY 9   Trustees to Robert Jones, for £12.5. (TM:52).

(See information for Lot 133 for later transactions).

LOT 137
Between Oronoco & Pendleton, East of Royal

1763, MAY 9   Trustees to John Hughes, Jr., for £3.10. (TM:52).

LOT 138
Between Oronoco & Pendleton, East of Royal

1763, MAY 9   Trustees to John Hughes, Jr., for £2.10. (TM:52).

LOT 139
Between Oronoco & Pendleton, West of Fairfax

1763, MAY 9   Trustees to Isaac Hughes, for £2 (TM:52).

LOT 140
Between Oronoco & Pendleton, West of Fairfax
1763, MAY 9   Trustees to Ruth Huges [Hughes], for £3 (TM:52).

LOT 141
Fairfax & Pendleton
1763, MAY 9   Trustees to Catharine Huges [Hughes], for £1.10. (TM:52).

LOT 142
Pendleton & Water St.
No record found.

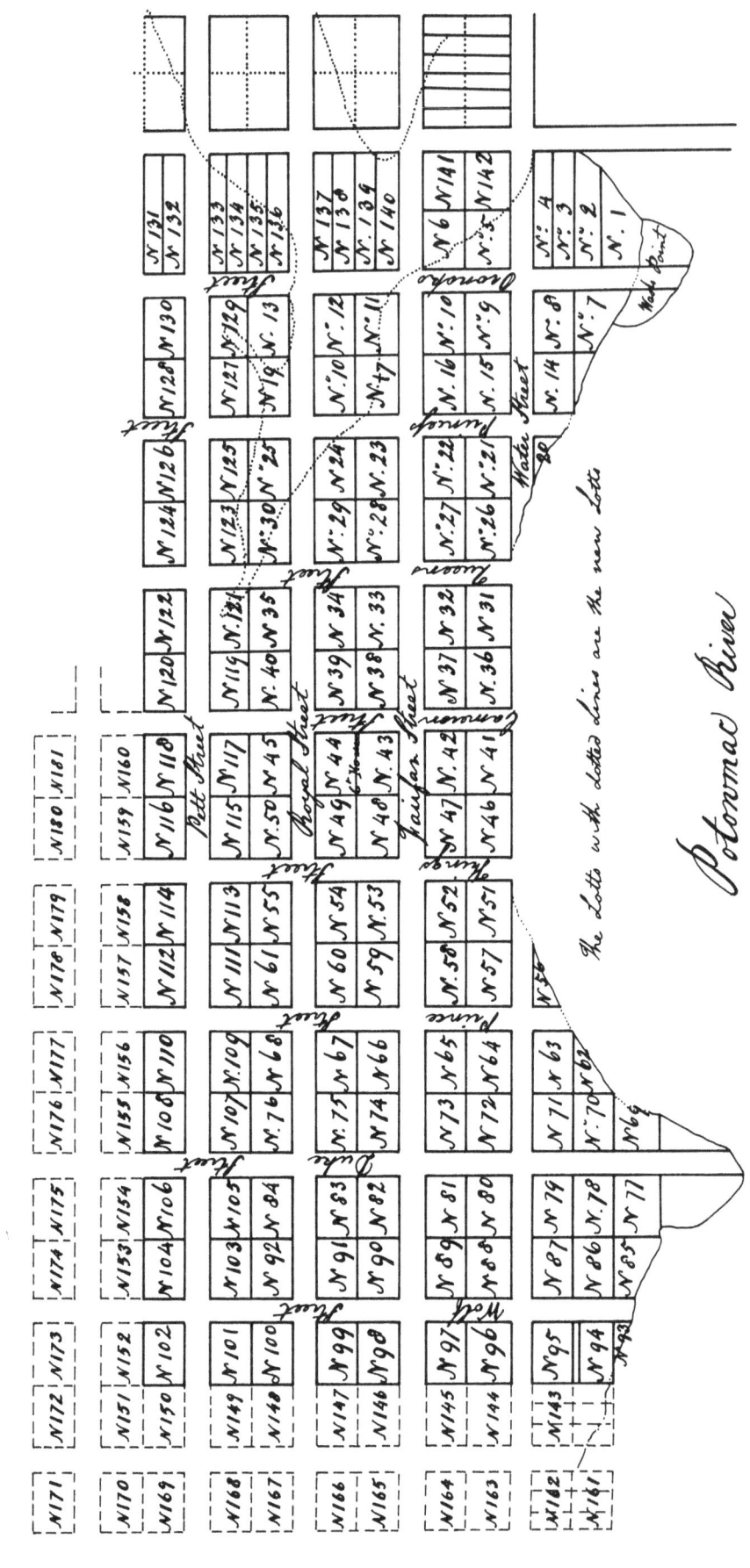

Figure 8 - Drawing of Extended Lot Sequence. [Constance K. Ring, Redrawn by Bill Sprouse]

Alexandria, Virginia Town Lots, 1749-1801

The following lots were added by John Alexander to the earlier series. The numbers marked with an asterisk (*) are assumed by the compiler.

LOT 143*
Water St., Union & Wilkes[69]

1774, DEC 20	John Alexander, of Stafford Co., to Andrew Stewart and William Herbert, joint merchants and partners, John Fitzgerald and Valentine Peers, merchants, for £39.10. annual rent. Grantees to build within 5 years a 20'x20' house on each lot (FDB M:127).
1784, JAN 19	Valentine Peers and wife Margaret to William Lyles, Jr., for £100, "one equal undivided fourth part of the said two pieces of ground" (FDB O:440).
1784, DEC 1	William Herbert, of Alexandria, and John Potts, Jr., of Philadelphia, to John Fitzgerald and William Lyles, Jr. Deed makes partition of the two parcels (FDB P:305). Andrew Steuart willed his property of the children of his brother Charles Steuart, Esq., in Ireland (FWB D:47). Will was dated 18 JUN 1775 and probated 21 APR 1778. Andrew's undivided fourth part was sold to John Potts, Jr., 20 APR 1784 (see Alex. B:158).
1784, DEC 22	John Potts, Jr. sells 1/4 interest to William Herbert for £401 (Alex. B:158).

LOT 144*
Wilkes & Water St. (Northwest Corner)

1774, DEC 19	John Alexander, of Stafford Co., to Jacob Cox, tobacconist, for £10.10. annual rent; Cox to build within 2 years a 20'x20' house (FDB M:89).
1781, JAN 19	Jacob Cox to John Sandford, for £4.8.3 annual rent, part of lot conveyed to Cox by Alexander (FDB N:405 msg; see FDB O:58).
1783, JUL 24	John Sandford and wife Betty to James Keith, for £370, 123'5"x50' (FDB O:58).
1784, NOV 8	John Sandford and wife Betty to John Saunders, for £120, 24'x123'5" (FDB P:134).
1792, DEC 19	Jacob Cox to William Wright, 74'x50'2", lease from 20 JUN 1793 for $41-1/12 (silver) annual rent, part of lot John Alexander leased to Jacob Cox (Alex. F:146).
1795, SEP 16	Jacob Cox to William Thornton Alexander, of King George Co., annual rent of $40-1/12 (silver) from Wright; Alexander remits annual rent of £10.10. from Wright (Alex. G:107).
1795, SEP 16	William [T.] Alexander and wife Lucy, of King George Co., to Jacob Cox, release from annual £10.10. rent in return for $41-1/12 annual rent Cox receives from Wright (Alex. H:11).
1796, APR 22	Jacob Cox to James Keith, for £43; remits annual rent of £4.8.3 (Alex. G:110).
1796, MAY 2	Jacob Cox to John Crips Vowell, for £400, part of lot (Alex. G:251).

---

[69] Contains two lots, the western lot of a half acre, the eastern lot less.

(See also Alex. N:58, 172; Alex. O:24).

LOT 145*
Wilkes & Fairfax (Northeast Corner)

1774, DEC 19	John Alexander, of Stafford Co., to Thomas Davis, of Alexandria, lease all of that lot described as adjoining the south side of Lot 97, for £7 annual rent. Davis to build house within 2 years and Wilkes Street, 66' wide, shall be kept open from the Potomac River to the west side of St. Asaph Street (FDB M:118).
1779, NOV 17	Thomas Davis to William Hunter and David Arell as joint tenants (FDB N:297 msg; see FDB O:22).
1783, SEP 5	William Hunter and David Arell divide lots they own as joint tenants (FDB O:22).
1783, SEP 8	David Arell to George Mason, cooper, 22'x98'5", for $25-2/3 (silver) annual rent (FDB O:45).
1784, JAN 12	David Arell to David Jones, 25'x116' for $20-5/6 (silver) annual rent (FDB O:290).
1784, JUL 8	William Hunter and wife Christiana to Gabriel Slacum, of Dorset [Dorchester] Co., Md., for £3.10. annual rent, 88'3½"x98'5" (FDB O:370).
1784, AUG 9	Gabriel Slacum and wife Catherine to Samuel Davis, of Philadelphia, for £101.15., 41'8"x98' part of the parcel conveyed to Slacum by Hunter (FDB Q:67).
1784, AUG 17	David Jones to Jesse Weatherly, same parcel conveyed to Jones by Arell (FDB P:14).
1785, MAR 15	David Arell to James Grimes, part of lot for $72 (silver) (FDB P:298).
1788, JUN 23	David Arell and wife Phebe to James Grimes, part of above parcel, reconveyed by Grimes and wife Sarah to Arell for $32 (silver) annual rent (FDB R:246).
1796, FEB 22	Peter Caverly, guardian of Richard Arell (son and devisee of David Arell, dec.), to James Grimes, lease 98'5"x22', sold by George Mason to William Bromley who defaulted on rent (Alex. G:470).

LOT 146*
Wilkes & Fairfax (Northwest Corner)

1774, DEC 19	John Alexander, of Stafford Co., Gent., to William Hartshorne, merchant, parts of Lots 146 and 147, for £4.3.4 annual rent (FDB M:112).
1774, DEC 19	John Alexander, of Stafford Co., Gent., to John Saunders, joiner, two thirds of a lot adjoining the parcel conveyed to Hartshorne, for £4.15. annual rent (FDB M:96).
1784, MAR 12	John Saunders, joiner, and wife Mary to John Yost, gunsmith, 36'x123'5" for £5.2. annual rent in Spanish milled dollars (FDB P:153).
1798, JUN 26	John and Rebecca Yost to Josias Milburne Speake, of Md., lease for £350 plus rents (Alex. L:342).

(See also FDB Z:379, 444).

LOT 147*
Wilkes & Royal (Northeast Corner)

1774, DEC 19	John Alexander, of Stafford Co., to William Hartshorne, merchant, 246'10"x58'10-1/3" of Lots 146 and 147, for £4.3.4 annual rent (FDB M:112).
1774, DEC 19	John Alexander, of Stafford Co., Gent., to Edward Mitchell Ramsay, joiner, 123'5"x117'8-2/3", for £3.11.8 annual rent (FDB M:93).
1784, DEC 15	David Arell to George Goodes [sic], for $54 (Spanish milled silver) annual rent, 36'x117'8-2/3" (FDB P:198).
1786, JAN 30	George Goodes assigns to George Herbert, for £200; Herbert to pay David Arell $54 (Spanish milled) per year (Alex. B:353).
1789, AUG 15	David Arell's will, probated 17 APR 1792, indicates that he gives to Christiana Arell the house "whereon I lately lived, 'including the garden on Wilkes St.' to the ground rented to Shakespeare... so as to include the tenement formerly occupied by Doyle" (FWB F:79).

LOT 148*
Wilkes & Royal (Northwest Corner)

1774, DEC 19	John Alexander, of Stafford Co., Gent., to Andrew Wales, brewer, for £4.10. annual rent, 123'5"x176'7" (FDB M:105).
1779, FEB 15	Andrew and Margaret Wales to William Hunter, Sr. (see Alex. C:175).
1787, SEP 29	William Hunter, Sr. and wife Christiana to Peter Bohrer, 123'5"x88' (Alex. C:175).

(See also Alex. K:220, 279).

LOT 149*
Wilkes & Pitt (Northeast Corner)

No record found.

LOT 150*
Wilkes & Pitt (Northwest Corner)

1774, DEC 19	John Alexander, of Stafford Co., Gent. to William Munday, joiner, for £3 annual rent; Munday to build 20' square house (FDB M:82).
1782, MAR 2	William Munday's will, probated 20 MAY 1782, states "...I give to my beloved wife [Elizabeth] a lott which I possess on ground rent in the lotts adjoining the Town of Alexandria numbered in the plan thereof one hundred & fifty, with all the improvements thereon..." for the lifetime of his wife (FWB D:422).
1785, APR 21	William Alexander and William Gibbons Stuart, surviving executors of John

Alexander, of Stafford Co., Gent., late dec.[70], and William Thornton Alexander, son and devisee of John Alexander, repossessed the lot for nonpayment of ground rent, and rented to Charles Simms, attorney at law, for £3 (FDB P:407).

LOT 151*
Wilkes & St. Asaph (Northeast Corner)

1774, DEC 20	John Alexander to Adam Lynn, for £3.15. annual rent (see FDB O:12; FDB N:898? msg).
1783, SEP 1	Adam Lynn and wife Catherine to Samuel Arell, 61'8"x176'6"x50'x123'5", for £3.15. (FDB O:12).
1784, JUL 5	Adam Lynn and wife Catherine to Barton Warren Baker, 40'x61'8½" for £7 annual rent (FDB P:185).
1785, MAR 1	Samuel Arell to William Hunter, Jr. (see Alex. D:99).
1785, MAR 22	Adam Lynn and wife Catharine to granddaughter Catharine Elizabeth, daughter of Elizabeth and Philip Webster, for 5 shillings, 61'8½"x20' (FDB P:304).
1789, SEP 29	Samuel Arell to William Hunter, Jr., for £200, same parcel as from Lynn to Arell (Alex. D:68).
1792, JAN 19	William Hunter, Jr. to John Hunter, for £1683, 126'7"x35'3½" (FDB U:233).

LOT 152
Wolfe & St. Asaph (Southeast Corner)

1774, DEC 19	John Alexander, of Stafford Co., Gent., to William Carlin, taylor, for £6.6. annual rent. Carlin to build a house. Alexander to lay off a street 66' feet wide "binding on the west side of the hereby granted lot... by the name of Saint Asaph Street" (FDB M:100).
1781, MAY 22	William Carlin and wife Sarah to Jesse Taylor, for £9000. Taylor to continue to pay rent, "...numbered in the plann of lotts adjoining said town, 152 adjoining the west side of a lott... represented... by the figures 102" (FDB D_4:300).
[no date]	Jesse Taylor and wife to John Mills, half of lot (see Alex. H:303).
[no date]	John Mills to Robert Hamilton, half (see Alex. H:303).
1795, DEC 23	Bushrod Washington and wife Ann, of Henrico Co., to Robert Hamilton, for 5 shillings, 176'7"x61'8½", purchased by Bushrod from John Chew and wife Margaret, having annual ground rent due Jesse Taylor of £3.3" (Alex. G:229).

(See also FDB B_2:493; Alex. M:237, Alex. N:404).

---

[70] Virginia Journal and Alexandria Advertiser, 4 NOV 1784 and 4 AUG 1785, John Alexander, of Stafford, dec'd., executors Seymour Hooe, Lucy Alexander, William Alexander, and William Gibbons Stuart of Alexandria, they will sell 100 lots of ground contiguous to the town of Alexandria.

LOT 153*
Wolfe & St. Asaph (Northeast Corner)

1774, DEC 19	John Alexander, of Stafford Co., Gent., to John Garner Hamilton, joyner, for £6.10. Hamilton to build house (FDB M:102).
c.1779	John Garner Hamilton to John Finley (FDB N:296 msg; see FDB P:170).
1784, OCT 2	John Finley to Benjamin Shreeve, for £50, 20'x113'5" (FDB P:170).
1785, JUN 20	[11 JUN 1784] John Finley died intestate[71], lot descended to Hugh Finley. Hugh Finley and Susanna Finley, of Orange Co., N.C., to John Hickman, for £50, 20'x113'5" (Alex. A:74, 79).
1785, JUL 16	Hugh Finley to Joseph Janney, Samuel Pleasants and John Field as tenants in common, for £4 rent, 80'x106'5" (see Alex. I:232).
1792, JAN 10	John Reynolds and wife Sarah mortgage to Andrew Wagener and Colbert Anderson, of Berkeley Co., 106'5"x23'5" (Alex. D:389). Reynolds had received from Hugh Finley on 10 JUN 1785. Mortgaged by Reynolds to Nathan Littler on 15 OCT 1791.
1792, JUN 19	John and Sarah Reynolds with Nathan Littler, of Frederick Co., to Andrew Wagener and Colbert Anderson, of Berkeley Co., for £44; Littler for 5 shillings quit claims (Alex. E:47).
1794, SEP 8	Benjamin and Susannah Shreve to George Clementson, 20'x113'5", for $20 a year (Alex. E:434; see Alex. H:162).
1794, SEP 11	Benjamin and Susannah Shreve to Francis Peyton, annual rent of £50 on above property (Alex. E:438).
1795, MAR 7	Samuel and Mary Pleasants, City of Philadelphia, Pa., to John Field, one third of Hugh Finley parcel (Alex. I:232; see Alex. I:237).
1795, MAR 28	John Hickman and wife Mary, of Frederick Co., to William Hickman, for £200, 113'5"x20', same parcel conveyed by John Garner Hamilton to John Finley, then Hugh Finley to John Hickman (Alex. F:375).
1795, NOV 17	William Hickman and wife Rebecca to Israel Wheeler and Joseph Miller, merchants of the City of Philadelphia, for £500, 113'5"x20' (Alex. F:528).
1796, SEP 20	Francis and Sarah Peyton to George Clementson, for £60, annual rent of £50 ($20) (Alex. H:162).

(See also Alex. A:84, 89; Alex. D:350; Alex. I:381; Alex. L:89; Alex. O:233).

LOT 154*
Duke & St. Asaph (Southeast Corner)

1774, DEC 19	John Alexander, of Stafford Co., to Windsor Brown and John Finley, joint merchants and partners, for £6.5. annual rent. Brown and Finley to build house (FDB M:78).
1785, JUN 22	Hugh Finley, brother and heir-at-law of John Finley, dec., and Robert Dougherty, nephew and heir-at-law of Windsor Brown, dec. (FWB E:98),

---

[71] Virginia Journal and Alexandria Advertiser, 13 JAN 1795, merchant of Alexandria, died.

	partition lot, except for a portion retained as tenants in common. Each had received an undivided moiety of lot (FDB P:516).
1785, JUN 22	Hugh Finley, brother and heir-at-law of John Finley, late of the Town of Alexandria, dec., and Susannah Finley [Hugh's wife] and Robert Dougherty, nephew and heir-at-law of Windsor Brown, dec.[72], to David Pancoast, 20'7"x100' (Alex. B:176; see Alex. B:180).
1786, FEB 23	Robert Dougherty to James and Alice Lawrason and Samuel Arell (see Alex. B:180).
1787, APR 24	James and Alice Lawrason and Samuel Arell to Peter Wagener and George Deneale, lease for £50, 78'x20' and 4' alley (Alex. D:323).
1788, SEP 22	James Lawrason and wife Alice and Samuel Arell to David Marshall Scott, lease 40'x78' (Alex. D:137).
1796, APR 20	Peter and Sinah Wagener agree to sell his share of lease to George Deneale, for £345.18., Deneale to pay annual ground rent of $1.04 to Lawrason and Arell (Alex. G:105).

(See also Alex. I:123; Alex. M:54).

LOT 155*
Duke & St. Asaph (Northeast Corner)

1774, DEC 19	John Alexander to James Parsons, for £9.15. annual rent; Parsons to build house (FDB M:115).
1778, DEC 9	James Parsons and wife Elizabeth to Josiah Watson (FDB N:123 msg; see FDB Q:120).
1786, JAN 3	Josiah Watson, merchant, and wife Jane to Arthur Lee, of Richmond Co., for £800, 100'5"x176'7" (FDB Q:221).
1786, JAN 4	Josiah Watson to Arthur Lee, of Richmond Co., 23'x176'7", for 5 shillings for release of Parson's rent agreements (FDB Q:120).
1786, JUN 5	Arthur Lee, of Richmond Co., to Lawrence Hooff, 24'x100', for $36 (silver) annual rent (FDB R:175).
1786, JUN 5	Arthur Lee, of Richmond Co., to Thomas Fitzpatrick, for $32 (silver) annual rent, 24'x100' (FDB R:374).
1788, JAN 5	Arthur Lee, of Richmond Co., to John Sullivan, 22'2"x100' for $23-1/12 (silver) annual rent. Lee to lay off 10' alley (FDB R:25).
1788, FEB 21	Arthur Lee, of Richmond Co., to Maurice Hurlihy, lease for $60 (silver) per year, 100'x28' (Alex. C:244).
1793, JUN 11	Maurice Hurlihy and wife Jane to Dennis Foley, for £140 and $60 (silver) annual rent to Lucinda Lee, representative of Arthur Lee, dec.[73], 28'x100'

---

[72] Virginia Journal and Alexandria Advertiser, 9 JUN 1785, Major Windsor Brown, died in Alexandria. His administrator, John Lomax of Alexandria, advertises for some Treasury land warrants belonging to the estate (14 SEP 1786).

[73] Middlesex Co. Wills, Bk. G, 1787-1793, p. 280, will probated 24 DEC 1792, devises lots in Alexandria to neices Hannah Washington, Ann Lee, Hariot Lee, Sally Lee, and Lucinda Lee; Virginia Gazette and Richmond (Daily) Advertiser, 21 DEC 1792, announces death of Arthur Lee, Esq., former diplomat, died at Urbanna, Middlesex Co.

	(FDB W:272).
1794, NOV 29	Josiah Watson and wife Jane to Gurdin Chapin, for £9.15., all the remaining part of lot not sold to Arthur Lee (FDB X:418; see also FDB B_2:37, 118; FDB Y_2:5).
1795, FEB 11	John D. Orr and wife Lucinda [heir of Arthur Lee] to James Keating, lease for £9 annual rent, 22'2"x100' (Alex. F:265; Alex. I:366).
1796, MAR 24	Dennis Foley mortgage to Cavan Boa to secure £20 to Boa for separate support of Foley's wife Elizabeth, 100'x28' (Alex. G:308).
1796, MAY 5	Thomas Fitzpatrick and wife Mary agree to live "asunder,"[74] Mary to have for her lifetime, house and premises on Duke St., each to pay half the paving; penal bond of £800 (Alex. G:283).
1796, JUN 17	John Sullivan and wife Honora decide to live separately. Honora and children to live in house fronting 16 feet on St. Asaph St. and 24' deep. Honora to have no claim on house, to pay paving costs "whenever said street should be paved"; elect Lanty Crowe as a good and trusty Citizen of this Town as guardian and trustee for the children and the property (Alex. G:276).

(See also Alex. H:292, 323; Alex. N:38, 366, 396).

LOT 156*

Prince & St. Asaph (Southeast Corner)
(See also Lot 110)

1774, DEC 19	John Alexander, of Stafford Co., Gent. to William McKnight, cabinet maker, for £9.5. annual rent; McKnight to build house, Alexander to keep street open (FDB M:109).
c.1780	William McKnight to Neil Mooney (FDB N:362 msg).
1782, DEC 19	McKnight lease to John Saunders and John Elton,[75] 50'x136' (see FDB P:145).
1783, OCT 13	William McKnight, cabinet maker, to William Ownbread, baker, for £115, "free & clear of all rent & encumbrances," 38'5"x126', "beginning at the west corner of a house on said lott now occupied by Neil Mooney" (FDB O:52).
1784, SEP 30	Saunders and Elton partition, Elton to have 16'3"x136' "with all Houses and Buildings thereupon...and...The free use of a three foot alley...", and of a four foot alley, and £200; Saunders to retain the larger parcel (FDB P:145).
1789, JUL 1	William Eichenbrade [Ownbread] mortgage to John Corn [Korn][76] and

---

[74] Oddly enough, only a short time passed until The Columbian Mirror and Alexandria Gazette included a notice by Thomas Fitzpatrick that his wife, Mary Fitzpatrick, had ill-treated and absconded from him (11 AUG 1796).
[75] John Elton is dead by OCT 1784; will dated 1 OCT 1784, probated 16 NOV 1784, leaves real estate to wife Isabella Elton and daughter Mary (FWB E:27). Isabella Elton, daughter of William Shaw, married c.1 NOV 1787 to William Summers. Isabella Shaw Elton Summers died 20 JAN 1821.
[76] John Korn, baker, died 5 AUG 1817 in his 59th year, buried Christ Episcopal Church cemetery.

	Jacob Wisemiller[77] as tenants in common (Alex. D:82).
1790, JUL 9	William and Magdalena Eichenbrade, baker, to Korn and Wisemiller, biscuit bakers, 38'5"x46' (Alex. D:145, 154).
1791, AUG 9	John Korn and Jacob Wisemiller to Job Green, for £108.10., 80'x18'5" (Alex. D:282).
1791, AUG 10	Job and Lydia Green, mariner, to John Korn and Jacob Wisemiller, for £120 (Alex. D:287).
1792, APR 22	William Ownbread, of Port Tobacco, Md., release to John Korn and Jacob Wisemiller, for £106.17.6 (Alex. D:421).
1794, JAN 20	Job Green to Stephen Cooke, whereas Job Green rented to Lemuel Bent a parcel "with a warehouse thereupon erected," now for $775, Green assigns rent to Cooke, should the warehouse be destroyed, Green will pay Cooke £75 annually (Alex. F:109).
1794, MAR 20	Charles Cartlish to John Baptist Bading, lease for £15, quarterly payments, the same parcel conveyed by Thomas West to Cartlish (Alex. E:375).
1797, MAY 27	William Elton, a brother and devisee of John Elton, to John Young, of Charles Co., Md., William's interest in John's estate (Alex. I:347).

(See also FWB E:27; Alex. L:416; Alex. M:258, 302).

LOT 157*
Prince & St. Asaph (Northeast Corner)

1774, DEC 20	John Alexander to Patrick Murray, for £13.5. annual rent; Murray to build (FDB M:121).
1775, AUG 22	Patrick Murray to Samuel Inglis, of Philadelphia, mortgage for £348 and interest (see FDB W:208).
1786, SEP 7	Patrick Murray and wife Margaret to Ann Inglish and William McKinzey, executors of Samuel Inglish [Inglis], dec., to secure debt of £348 owed by Murray and Hugh Neilson since 22 AUG 1775 (Alex. B:336).
1792, NOV 2	Charles Little, sheriff, to executors of Samuel Inglis, late of the City of Philadelphia, dec. Murray failed to satisfy note (FDB W:208).
1794, APR 15	William McKinzey, Ann [Inglis] Currie, and husband James Currie, to Elisha Cullen Dick, for annual rent to [John] Alexander's heirs (see Alex. G:39).
1795, NOV 14	Elisha Cullen Dick and wife Hannah to John Thomas Ricketts and William Newton, for £1000, all of lot; Dick to pay the annual rent to William Thornton Alexander (Alex. G:39).
1796, MAR 28	John Thomas Ricketts and wife Mary, and William Newton and wife Jane, to John Woodrow, lease, 123'5"x42½", for £21.5. annually (Alex. G:284).
1796, APR 20	John and Mary Woodrow to William Halley, for £12, that conveyed to Woodrows on 28 MAR 1796 by John Thomas Ricketts and William Newton as part of a larger parcel, for annual rent of £21 (Alex. H:337).

---

[77] Jacob Wisemiller, born in Germany in 1754, died 5 FEB 1820, aged 66 years, buried Trinity United Methodist Church cemetery.

(See also Alex. N:126).

LOT 158*
King & St. Asaph (Southeast Corner)

1774, DEC 20	John Alexander, of Stafford Co., Gent. to Charles Jones, for £60 (FDB M:39).
c.1778	Charles Jones to Adam Lynn (FDB N:162 msg; see FDB M:39 and FDB P:26).
1784, AUG 19	Adam Lynn and wife Catherine to Elizabeth [Lynn], wife of Philip Webster, "for natural love & affection" and 5 shillings, 20'x92' (FDB P:26).
1792, DEC 11	John Stone Webster and wife Mary [Lynn], of Prince Georges Co., Md., to William Irvin, for £80, 92'x20' (Alex. E:26).

(See also Alex. K:114; Alex. M:91).

LOT 159*
King & St. Asaph (Northeast Corner)

1774, DEC 19	John Alexander, of Stafford Co., to John Cannon, for £20 (FDB M:137).
1774, DEC 21	John Cannon to Peter Wise, for £10, part of lot (FDB M:139).
1786, AUG 5	John Cannon, of Prince William Co., and wife Sarah to Peter Wise, for £640, 61'x8½"x176'6" (FDB Q:403).

LOT 160*
Cameron & St. Asaph (Southeast Corner)

1774, DEC 19	John Alexander, of Stafford Co., Gent. to Peter Wise, for £6.5. annual rent; Wise to build (FDB M:86).

(See also Alex. K:607, could be Lot 160).

LOT 161
Wilkes, Between Water St. & Union (South Side)

1779, AUG 5	Heirs of John Alexander conveyed to Josiah Watson and William Hartshorne, two lots numbered 161 and 162 (see Alex. F:104).
1784, DEC 30	William Thornton Alexander and wife Lucy, of King George Co., to Josiah Watson and William Hartshorne, for £800, remit rent payments (Alex. F:104).

(See also Alex. L.422, 426; FDB Y:40; FDB O$_2$:183).

LOT 162
Wilkes & Water St. (Southeast Corner)

1779, AUG 5 — Heirs of John Alexander conveyed to Josiah Watson and William Hartshorne, two lots numbered 161 and 162 (see Alex. F:104).

1784, DEC 30 — William Thornton Alexander and wife Lucy, of King George Co., to Josiah Watson and William Hartshorne, for £800, remit rent payments (Alex. F:104).

(See also Alex. L:422, 426; FDB Y:40; FDB O_2:183).

LOT 163
Wilkes & Water St. (Southwest Corner)

1779, AUG 5 — John Alexander's executors to Robert Adam, for £25 annual rent (FDB N:314 msg; see FDB P:1, 455). Transaction was later found to have been improperly executed.

1784, JUL 1 — Robert Adam and wife Ann to William Hunter, for £25 annual rent, "...numbered in the plan of the lots adjoining the Town of Alexandria, 163" (FDB P:1).

1784, JUL 7 — William Hunter and wife Christiana to John Hawkins, of Prince Georges Co., Md., for £20.5. annual rent, 30'x70' (FDB P:261).

1784, JUL 16 — William Hunter and wife Christiana to Thomas Barclay, for £13 annual rent, 26'x75' (FDB P:161).

1785, APR 20 — William Alexander, one of the executors of John Alexander, late of Stafford Co., dec., to William Hunter, confirming the earlier deed to Robert Adam, improperly executed (FDB P:455).

1786, FEB 15 — William Hunter and wife Christiana to George Slacum, for £120, 102'x24' (FDB Q:246).

1787, SEP 29 — William Hunter, Sr. and wife Christiana to Peter Bohrer, for £349.2.6, 123'5"x49'3" (Alex. C:172).

1790, SEP 21 — John Hawkins and wife Alice to William Hunter, for 5 shillings, the same parcel rented to Hawkins by Hunter on 7 JUL 1784, 30'x70' (FDB S:537).

(See also Alex. K:12, 15, 18, 212, 351; Alex. L:199).

LOT 164
Wilkes & Fairfax (Southeast Corner)

1779, AUG 5 — Lucy Alexander, widow and relict of John Alexander, late of Stafford Co., Seymour Hooe and William Gibbons Steuart [Stewart] of the same county, and William Alexander, executors of John Alexander of the first part, to Henry Rozier, of Prince Georges Co., Md., for £20.10.; Rozier to build (FDB P:18).

1784, NOV 1 — Henry Rozer [Rozier] and wife Eleanor to Samuel Montgomery Brown (see FDB Q:339; see Alex. B:382).

1785, APR 20 — William Alexander, one of the executors of John Alexander, late of Stafford

	Co., dec., to Samuel Montgomery Brown, for £20.10, confirming Rozier's sale to Brown (FDB P:409).[78]
1785, SEP 1	Samuel Montgomery Brown and wife Mary to Philip France, for $50 (Spanish milled), 25'x123'5" (see FDB Q:333).
1786, OCT 14	Samuel Montgomery Brown and wife Mary to William Patterson, of Baltimore, Md., 76'7"x32' (Alex. B:382).
1786, NOV 15	Samuel Montgomery Brown and wife Mary to Baldwin Dade, for £125, the rent of $50 (Spanish milled) paid annually by Philip France; Dade to pay £2.10. annual rent to William Thornton Alexander (FDB Q:333).
1787, FEB 19	Samuel Montgomery Brown and wife Mary to John Challoner, of Philadelphia, 50'x123'5" and 25'x123'5", for £260.10. and £7.0.7½ annual rent to William Thornton Alexander (FDB Q:338).
1787, JUL 2	Baldwin Dade, farmer, and wife Catherine to Charles Lee, counselor-at-law, the rent of $50 (Spanish milled) due annually from Philip France (FDB Q:520).
1788, OCT 24	Samuel Montgomery Brown and wife Mary to Henry Sadler, of New York, for £320, 81'6"x75' (Alex. C:251).

(See also Alex. K:645; Alex. L:296).

LOT 165
Wilkes & Fairfax (Southwest Corner)

1779, AUG 5	John Alexander's executors to Samuel Arell, for £17.1. annual rent (FDB N:270 msg; see FDB O:77).
1780, FEB 17	Samuel Arell to James Adam, half of lot (FDB N:322 msg; see FDB O:77).
c.1780-1783	Samuel Arell and James Adam to Benjamin Dulany, all of lot (FDB N:397, 398 msg; see FDB O:77).
1783, SEP 6	Benjamin Dulany and wife Elizabeth to David Arell, for £50 (FDB O:77).
1785, MAY 25	David Arell and wife Phoebe to Charles Carroll, shoemaker, 20'x123'5", for $40 (silver) annual rent (FDB Q:129).

LOT 166
Wilkes & Royal (Southeast Corner)

1779, AUG 5	John Alexander's executors to Dennis Ramsay, for £16.10. annual rent to be paid to William Thornton Alexander (FDB D$_4$:279).
1798, JUN 11	William Thornton Alexander, King George Co., to Dennis Ramsay, for £99 plus £16.10. (silver) rent at 6 shillings each (Alex. K:449).

---

[78] FDB P:414, "...south side of Wilkes Street in said Town of Alexandria, and which in the plan of the said Town is described by the No. 164..."

LOT 167
Wilkes & Royal (Southwest Corner)

1779, AUG 5	John Alexander's executors to William Hepburn, for £10.3. annual rent to be paid to William Thornton Alexander, of Stafford Co. (FDB D_4:274).
1780, AUG 12	William Hepburn to William Hunter and David Arell, for same rent (FDB N:395 msg; see FDB O:22).
1783, SEP 5	William Hunter to David Arell, part of lot (FDB O:22).
1784, SEP 1	William Hunter and wife Christiana to James Fletcher and William Findley, for £100, as tenants in common, 21'x120' (FDB P:166).
1784, SEP 22	William Hunter and wife Christiana to Henry Beideman, 37'8½"x150', for £11.6.3 annual rent (FDB P:174).
1785, APR 22	William and Christiana Hunter to Godfrey Miller, butcher, lease, $37.50 (silver) annually, 25'x99'5"; Miller to build house; Hunter to keep open a 3' alley (Alex. A:208).
1785, NOV 1	James Fletcher and William Findley to Edward Edelin, of Prince Georges Co., Md., for £120, 21'x120' (FDB Q:229).

(See also Alex. N:100; Alex. O:1).

LOT 168*
Wilkes & Pitt (Southeast Corner)

1779, AUG 5	John Alexander's executors to James Parsons, for £10.5. annual rent payable to William Thornton Alexander. Fairfax, Royal, Pitt and St. Asaph streets to be lengthened; King, Prince, Duke, Wolfe and Wilkes streets to be continued (FDB D_4:256).

(See also Alex. D:258 [plat with text[79]]; Alex. M:116, 283, 395).

LOT 169*
Wilkes & Pitt (Southwest Corner)

1779, AUG 5	John Alexander's executors to David Arell, for £10 annual rent. Deed not recorded (see FDB O:175; see Alex. E:369).
1783, OCT 30	David Arell to William Hartshorne, for 5 shillings, releasing Arell of £10 annual rent, now to be paid by Hartshorne (FDB O:175).

---

[79] Agreeable to the Order of the Worshipful Court of Hustings for the Town of Alexandria, we the Subscribers appointed to divide the Estate of James Parsons deceased between John Parsons his son and Elizabeth Parsons his widow do make the Following report, Vizt. We allot to John Parsons as his proportion the lotts in the annexed Plot No. 1 & 4 on King Street, No. 5 on St. Asaph Street, No. 9 on Cameron Street and No. 2 and 3 on Wilkes Street. /s/ May 24, 1791, Wm. McKnight, Peter Wise, John Allison." Plat reproduced as Figure 9, page 117.

LOT 170*
Wilkes & St. Asaph (Southeast Corner)

No record found.

LOT 171*
Wilkes & St. Asaph (Southwest Corner)

1794, DEC 13　William Thornton Alexander, of King George Co., and wife Lucy to Michael Lutz[80], for £7 annual rent (FDB Y:100).

(See also Alex. K:645).

LOT 172
Wilkes & St. Asaph (Northwest Corner)

1779, AUG 5　John Alexander's executors to Cyrus Copper, for £6.5.0 annual rent, lease of Lot 172 (see Alex. L:176; FDB N:317 msg).

1785, JUN　Cyrus Copper, died intestate [FWB E:381], leaving widow Elizabeth[81] and daughters Elizabeth and Christiana, heirs (Fairfax Court Order Book, 1783-1788:156).

1798, OCT 15　Copper's daughter Elizabeth (wife of John Muncaster) and Christiana (wife of Philip G. Marsteller) divide estate; Lot 172 to Elizabeth (Alex. L:176).

LOT 173*
Wolfe & St. Asaph (Southwest Corner)

1780, OCT 9　John Alexander's executors to Johnson Smith, for £12.3. annual rent (FDB N:514 msg; see FDB O:243).

1782, JAN 2　Johnson Smith to William Ward,[82] for £50 and ground rent of £12.3. (FDB O:243).

1798, DEC 1　Deed recites that William Ward and his heirs were in arrears in ground rent in the amount of £255 by 5 AUG 1797; lot repossessed, resold by William Thornton Alexander and wife Lucy to William Hartshorne, Jr., Philip Wanton, and Elisha and John Janney, for $1,000 (Alex. K:640).

---

[80] Complete Records [Alexandria], Liber A, fols. 187-8, inventory for estate of Michael Lutz ordered 10 MAR 1796, returned 24 SEP 1796.

[81] Alexandria County Wills, in Complete Records, Liber A, 1786-1800, pp. 18-9, will of Elizabeth Copper, dated 20 APR 1789, probated 22 APR 1790; inventory, pp. 19-20; accounts, pp. 22-23, 143-4.

[82] Alex. K:640, gives different information on how Ward got lot.

Alexandria, Virginia Town Lots, 1749-1801

LOT 174
Wolfe & St. Asaph (Northwest Corner)

1779, AUG 5   John Alexander's executors to Valentine Peers and John Fitzgerald, as tenants in common, for £16.15. annual rent payable to William Thornton Alexander (FDB N:283 msg; see FDB O:432).

1784, MAR 15   Valentine Peers, merchant, and wife Peggy to John Fitzgerald, merchant, for 5 shillings Peer's moiety of lot, releasing Peers from payment of ground rent (FDB O:432).

1797, JUN 9   John Fitzgerald and wife Jane to Cleon Moore, 40'x123'5" for £15 annual rent (FDB A_2:40).

(See also Alex. N:73).

LOT 175*
Duke & St. Asaph (Southwest Corner)

1779, AUG 5   John Alexander's executors to Thomas Wilkinson, for £14.10. annual rent payable to William Thornton Alexander, Wilkinson to build (FDB N:234 msg; see FDB O:33).

1783, SEP 15   Thomas Wilkinson and wife Jane to Benjamin Shreeve and James Lawrason as tenants in common, for £30 (FDB O:33).

1785, JAN 12   Benjamin Shreeve, merchant, and James Lawrason partition lot; Lawrason to have northeast corner, 88'3½" on St. Asaph St. and 100' on Duke St.; Shreve to have 23'5" on Duke St. and 88'3½" on St. Asaph St., including the full width of the lot. Each to pay half the annual rent to William Thornton Alexander (FDB P:293).

1785, APR 8   Benjamin Shreeve to William Hartshorne, John Butcher, John Saunders, John Sutton and Aaron Hewes, of the Society of People called Quakers, for a meeting house, for 5 shillings, 63'x30' (FDB P:461).

1795, JUL 21   Benjamin Shreve and wife Susanna to James Lawrason, for £60, 20'x88'3½", "to equal the length of the line of Lawrason upon St. Asaph St.;" Shreeve to lay off 6'10" alley (Alex. G:382).

1795, SEP 14   William Thornton Alexander and wife Lucy, of King George Co., to Benjamin Shreve and James Lawrason, for £300; release of rent (Alex. G:358).

LOT 176*
Duke & St. Asaph (Northwest Corner)

1779, AUG 5   John Alexander's executors to David Arell, for £4.10. annual rent (see FDB D_4:312).

1781, JUN 30   David Arell to Adam Lynn, 123'5"x88'3½", for £7.5. annual rent (FDB D_4:312).

1783, SEP 6   David Arell to Benjamin Dulany, for £50, 123'5"x88'3½"; Dulany also to pay £7.5. annual ground rent (FDB O:75).

1784, OCT 21   Adam Lynn to Alexander Smith, 44'x123'5" for $44 (silver) annual rent

	(FDB P:182).
1785, OCT 18	Adam Lynn and wife Catherine to Richard Ratcliffe, for £50, 88'3½"x44'3½" and the $44 (silver) annual rent due from Smith (FDB Q:189; Alex. E:217 states 44'3½"x123'5").
1787, OCT 16	Richard Ratcliffe and wife Locian [Bolling[83]] to Samuel Hanson, for £730, 123'5"x44'3½" (FDB R:69).
1787, NOV 12	Samuel Hanson to Thomas Hanson, of Charles Co., Md., Overton Carr and Anthony Addison, of Prince Georges Co., Md., securities for Samuel Hanson, on bond to Richard Ratcliffe, for £1400. Transaction is for the parcel bought by Hanson from Ratcliffe, 16 OCT 1787 (see FDB S:131).
1788, APR 23	Richard Ratcliffe and wife Locian to Samuel Hanson, for £130, the rent of $44 (silver) paid by Alexander Smith to Adam Lynn (FDB R:73; Alex. E:217 states Lynn subsequently sold to Ratcliffe).
1791, FEB 21	Samuel Hanson to Alexander Smith, for £35, releasing Smith from payment of $44 (silver) annual rent (FDB T:97).
1793, NOV 1	Samuel and Mary Hanson to Isaac McPherson, for £381, parcel conveyed by Arell to Lynn, 88'3½"x123'5" (Alex. E:217).
1794, SEP 5	William Thornton Alexander and wife Lucy to Isaac McPherson, for £145; remission of £7.5. rent arranged by Arell with Lynn (Alex. E:361).
1799, APR 6	Isaac and Tacey McPherson to John Janney, for £1150, 89'x123'5" (Alex. L:325).

(See also Alex. O:41, 53).

LOT 177*
Prince & St. Asaph (Southwest Corner)

1779, AUG 5?	John Alexander's executors to Tobias Zimmerman, for £20 annual rent (FDB N:273 msg; see FDB O:138).
c.1780	Tobias Zimmerman to Hugh Gibboney, for £20 annual rent (FDB N:467 msg; see FDB O:138).
1783, NOV 24	Hugh Gibboney to David Stuart, for £115, 40'x123'5" (FDB O:138).
c.1783	Hugh Gibboney to James Wright, 55'6"x123'5" (FDB N:893 msg; see FDB O:153).
1783, DEC 15	James Wright and wife Sarah to Mathew Brown, 123'5"x27'9", for £4 annual rent (FDB O:153).
1791, JUN 18	David Steuart [Stuart] and wife Eleanor to James Patton and James Kennedy, 123'5"x50' (see Alex. G:301).
1796, MAR 8	James and Mary Ann Patton, and James and Letitia Kennedy to Mungo Dykes, for £200, 123'5"x50' (Alex. G:301).
1796, APR 16	John Taliaferro, Jr., of King George Co., to James Keith, on behalf of William Thornton Alexander, recovers rent in arrears due from property conveyed by Alexander's executors to Tobias Zimmerman, £20.18. due each

---

[83] FWB D:160, will of Gerrard Bowling [sic], dated 29 DEC 1779, probated 21 FEB 1780.

	5 AUG (Alex. G:430).
1796, JUL 12	William Thornton Alexander and wife Lucy, of King George Co. to Joseph Fullmer. Zimmerman and wife Elizabeth failed to pay £20.18. annual rent on property they leased out to others; owe Alexanders £239.14.8. Zimmerman had no property to be attached. Alexanders convey 123'5"x42' to Fullmer for £84 and £8.8 annually (Alex. H:115).
1797, NOV 1	William Thornton Alexander and wife Lucy, King George Co., to Elisha Bailey, for £12, lease 123'5"x32'; Bailey to pay $40 (silver) annually (Alex. I:320).
1799, SEP 3	Elisha Thomas Bailey and wife Jane to Joshua Doings, for £70, parcel; Doings to pay rent to William Thornton Alexander (Alex. M:296).

(See also Alex. K:484, 490; Alex. N:219).

LOT 178
Prince & St. Asaph (Northwest Corner)

1779, AUG 5	John Alexander's executors to Oliver Price, for £22.3. annual rent (FDB D₄:269).
1783, JUL 16	Oliver Price and wife Jane to Peter Wise, for £6.3. annual rent, 46'x123'5" (FDB P:342).
1783, JUL 21	Oliver Price to John Stewart, for £16 (FDB N:886 msg; see FDB P:241; see Alex. G:318).
1784, JAN 17	John Stewart and wife Elizabeth to William Hough, of Loudoun Co., for £90.4.4 and £5 annual rent, 30'x81' (FDB P:241).
1784, MAY 24	Peter Wise to Richard Ratcliffe, 46'x123'5", for £6.3. (FDB P:192).
1784, OCT 21	Oliver Price and wife Jane to John Hough, of Loudoun Co., for £160, 35'x70'6" and rent of £22.3. payable to William Thornton Alexander (FDB P:131).
1784, OCT 23	Oliver Price to John Hough (see Alex. D:94).
1786, NOV 24	Oliver Price to Samuel Smith, for £95.10., part of lot (Alex. B:398).
1787, MAR 19	Oliver and Jane Price to William Paton and John Butcher, for £24.10., 35'x7' (Alex. D:107).
1787, NOV 15	Samuel Smith and wife Mary to Oliver Price, for £150, part of lot (FDB R:303).
1790, JUN 21	John Hough and Sarah Hough, of Loudoun Co., to John Butcher and William Paton as tenants in common, for £160, 70'6"x35' (Alex. D:94).
1795, SEP 16	William Thornton Alexander assigned to Paton and Butcher, £16 annual rent due from Price's parcel not conveyed to Wise (see Alex. G:318; see Alex. G:353).
1795, SEP 17	Oliver Price and wife Jane, William and Mary Paton, and John and Ann Butcher, to Walter Pomery, Jr. and Jonah Isabel, Jr., part of lot (Alex. G:329).
1795, SEP 17	Oliver and Jane Price, William and Mary Paton, and John and Ann Butcher to Joseph Saul, 70'6"x25' (Alex. G:336).

1795, SEP 21	John Stewart and wife Cicily conveyed to [blank],[84] 100'7"x21' (Alex. G:318). William and Mary Patton [Paton] and John and Ann Butcher, for £120, release rent obligation, and Prices release Stewart (Alex. G:318).
1795, SEP 26	Walter Pomery, Jr. and wife Elizabeth, and Jonah Isabel to William Mendenhall[85], for £110, part of Lot 178 (Alex. G:399).
1795, NOV 7	William Patton [Paton] and wife Mary and John Butcher and wife Ann to Smith Keith, for £90, 100'7"x21', conveyed 21 SEP 1795 by John Stewart to William Paton and John Butcher (Alex. F:405).
1796, JUN 13	Joseph Saul and wife Mary, of Philadelphia, to William Mendenhall, for £90, 70'6"x25' (Alex. G:402).

LOT 179*
King & St. Asaph (Southwest Corner)

1796, JUL 21	Abraham Faw and wife Mary Ann to Lewis Tristler [Tressler], blacksmith, lease 80'x34', for $68 annually (Alex. G:266).
1796, JUL 21	Abraham and Mary Anne Faw lease to David Davey, merchant, 20' square, $10 annual rent (Alex. G:406).

(See also Alex. K:22).

LOT 180
King & St. Asaph (Northwest Corner)

1779, AUG 5	John Alexander's executors to James Parsons, for £10 annual rent (FDB D_4:260).
1784, NOV 8	James Parsons and wife Elizabeth to John Petit and Michael Simon Blondely as tenants in common, for £150, and £19.5.6 annual rent, 38'6"x34' (Alex. P:328).
1788, JUL 3	Michael Simon Blondely and wife Jane, lease to John Petit, 38½"x34'. Since 10 AUG 1787, Blondely occupied 34'x16', paying Parsons' heirs, £8.17.9 annual rent (Alex. D:111).
1791, NOV 2	John Baptist Petit to his wife Margaret Petit, all his real and personal estate (Alex. D:361).
1793, JUN 17	John Parsons, of King George Co., to William Summers, for £75, parcel #4. Deed recites, "Parsons willed to his son John, 1/3 of his estate, including Lot #180" [division in the Hustings Court record] (Alex. E:85, 91).
1793, NOV 23	John Baptist Petit mortgage to Henry Didier, of Baltimore, Md. (Alex. E:156).

---

[84] Alex. G:325, 21 SEP 1795, John Stewart and wife Cicily, for £60 to William Paton and John Butcher as tenants in common, 100'7"x21.'

[85] Complete Records [Alexandria], Liber A, fols. 351-58, accounts 360-1, inventory ordered for estate of William Mendenhall, dated 20 of 9th Mo. 1796 by Elisha Janney, Philip Wanton and Thomas Fisher, returned 7 OCT 1800.

1795, NOV 14	William Summers and wife Isabel[86] to William Jackson, of Baltimore. Summers erected a brick house on a parcel adjoining lot of Petit and Blondley, which abuts on a framed house erected by Joseph Jackson, which by a mistake of a former survey of the town lots, stands 4' more or less upon the parcel conveyed by Parsons to Summers. Now Jackson receives for £20, 4'x120' (Alex. F:471).
1796, MAY 12	Abraham Faw and Joseph M. Perrin, commissioners, sell property of John Baptist Petit by court order to Jesse Taylor. Petit died without paying off mortgage to Didier. Didier sued John James Neblon and his wife Margaret, daughter of Petit. Court appointed Faw and Perrin to sell for Didier, subject to widow Margaret Petit's dower right. Sale 5 MAY 1793. Taylor highest bidder (Alex. G:258).

(See also Alex. K:33; Alex. M:122)

LOT 181
Cameron & St. Asaph (Southwest Corner)

1779, AUG 5	John Alexander's executors to James Parsons, for £8.16. annual rent (FDB D$_4$:265).
1785, JAN	Will of James Parsons, probated 22 MAR 1785, instructed his executors to keep his estate together until his son John reached age 21 years (FWB E:63).
1795, APR 11	John Parsons, of King George Co., clerk, to John Mason, silversmith, power of attorney to sell to Joseph Saul, of Alexandria, two parcels allotted to John Parsons in a division of Lot 181 ordered by the Corporation Court of Alexandria. One parcel contains the brick house in which John Parsons' mother now lives. Lot 181 was divided by Peter Wise, William McKnight and John Allison. Sale to Saul to release Parsons of annual rent to William Thornton Alexander (Circuit Court Archives, Drawer X, unrecorded deed).
1800, FEB 20	John and Mary Washington Parsons to William Smith, for £90 and rents, 25'6"x113'5" (Alex. M:366).
1800, JUL 2	William and Sarah Smith, to James Kincaid, Charles Jones and Patrick Burns, for £60 in trust for the Grand Lodge of Virginia (Alex. N:180).

---

[86] Virginia Journal and Alexandria Advertiser, 1 NOV 1787, announces the recent marriage of William Summers and Mrs. Isabel Elton of Alexandria. The Times and Alexandria Advertiser, 28 OCT 1797, indicates that William Summers of Alexandria died yesterday.

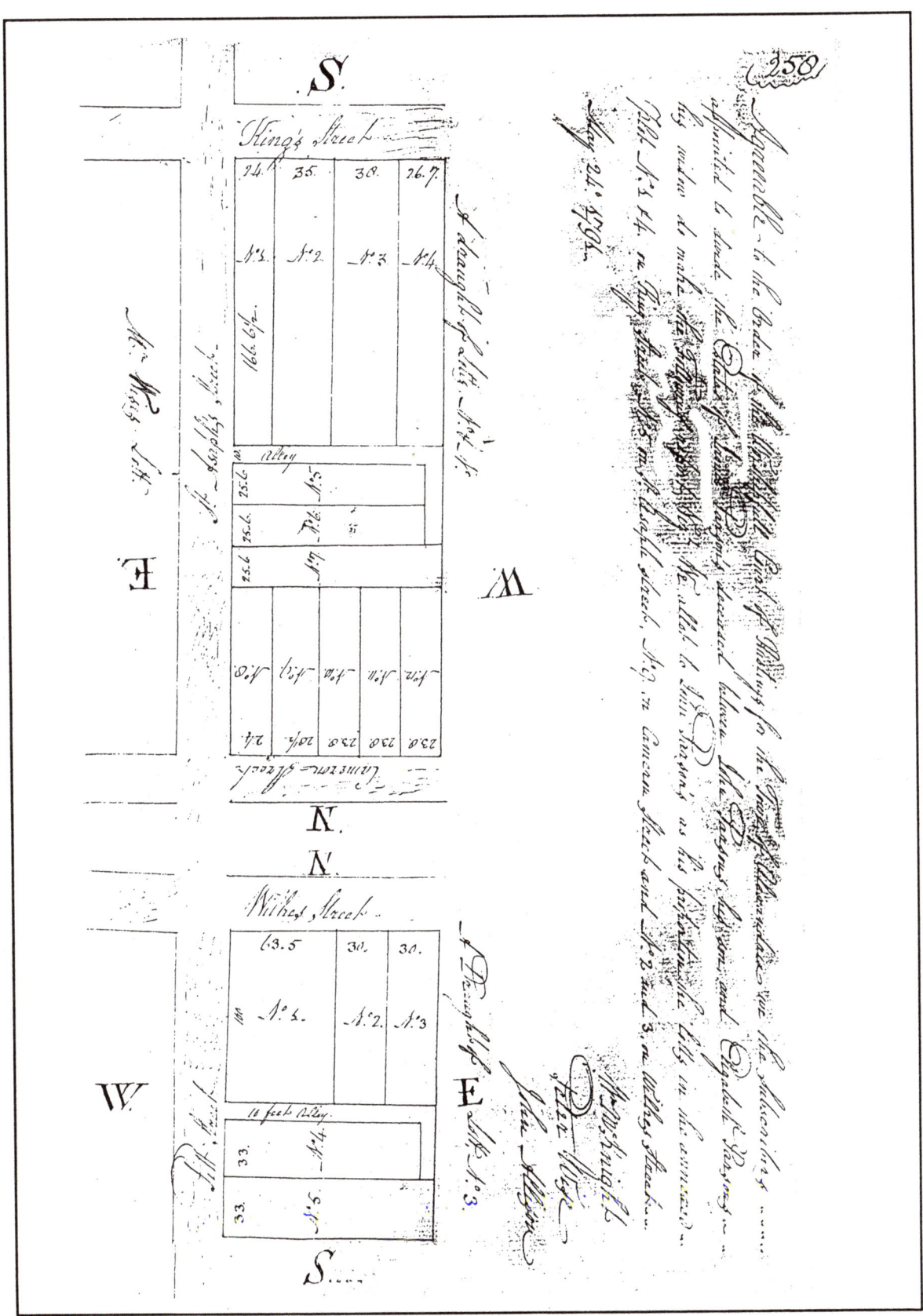

Figure 9 - Plat of Lots 168 and 181. [Alexandria Hustings Court Deeds, Bk. D, p. 258]

At a Meeting of the Majority of the Trustees of Alexandria Town July the 13th 1749

Present: Richard Osborn, John Pagan, William Ramsay, Gerard Alexander, John Carlyle, & Hugh West, Gent.

John West Junr. appointed Clerk of this Town in order to keep an account of the proceedings.

And appointed Cryer at the Sales of the Lotts.

It is agreed that the Lotts be sold at publick Vendue within [___] Months from the time that they are set to sale.

Then Proceeded to sell the Lotts as Followeth Vizt.

Lot No.	Purchaser	Pistoles
36	To John Dalton	19
31	Gerard Alexander	19½
26	Allan Macrae	22
21	John Carlyle	30
46	William Ramsay	30
51	Laurence Washington	31
20 & 21	Roger Lindon	45½
1	William Fitzhugh	26½
2	John Pagan	10½
56 & 57	Honble William Fairfax	35
62 & 63	Coll. George Fairfax	39
69 & 70	Coll. Nathaniel Harrison	46
77 & 78	Nathaniel Chapman	56½
32	Gerard Alexander	20
27	John Alexander	8
37	John Dalton	16
42	John Carlyle	16
52	Laurence Washington	16
47	William Ramsay	16

(1)

Figure 10 - Copy of First Page of the Proceedings, Board of Trustees, Town of Alexandria.

PROCEEDINGS
of the
Board of Trustees
Town of Alexandria
1749-1780

An old journal, inscribed "Proceedings of Board of Trustees, Town of Alexandria, 1749-1767," can be found preserved in the rare book collection of the Alexandria Library, Lloyd House. The record abruptly ends at page 59, which suggests that another volume was once extant. The record may have been started as the official Proceedings, but later used as a personal account book of either Samuel Arell or Samuel Arell Marsteller. Page references to this source are cited as "Page X." Inside the back cover is noted that it was presented to the Fairfax County Court in 1793 by Dennis Ramsay, Mayor of the Town of Alexandria.

The original Proceedings record which continues beyond page 59 of the first volume has not come to light but photostatic copies of the Proceedings from 1767 to 1780, made quite some years ago, are to be found in the collection of Lloyd House. Page references to this text, presumably once kept by Warwick P. Miller, are cited as "Miller Page X."

A typescript of the Proceedings, 1749-1780 was prepared for use in connection with the case of the United States of America versus Herbert Bryant, Inc., et al. (consolidated civil cases #73-2211 and 73-1903). Page references to this source are cited as "Bryant Page X." Copies of this work by Mrs. George Kirk and Ms. Gay Montague Moore can also be found at Lloyd House [Virginia Reference 975.5296 MIN]. Proceedings or minutes for the subsequent period to 1792 are not known to have survived.

Oftentimes in the historical community the record is referred to as the "Trustees' Minutes." References to it in the present work are coded "TM," followed by the applicable page number, e.g. "TM:35." The Proceedings provide an important chronicle of the early development of this seaport town. They are presented here with the intent of making the information more widely available and with the hope that researchers will discover and use this valuable resource.

I am indebted to Dr. James D. Munson, whose enthusiasm sparked the making of the following transcript.

Wesley E. Pippenger
Arlington, Virginia

Page 1

At a Meeting of the Majority of the Trustees of Alexandria Town, July the 13th 1749:

Present   Richard Osborn   John Pagan
               William Ramsay   Gerard Alexander
               John Carlyle   &   Roger West, Gent$^{n.}$

John West, Jun$^{r.}$ appointed Clerk of this Town in order to keep an account of the proceedings, And appointed Cryer at the sales of the Lotts.

It is agreed that the Lotts be sold at publick Vendue within five Minutes from the time that they are set to sale.

Then Proceeded to sell the Lotts as Followeth, Viz.

			Pistoles
No. 36	Sold	John Dalton	19
31		Gerard Alexander	19½
26		Allan Macrae	22
41		John Carlyle	30
46		William Ramsay	30
51		Laurence Washington	31
20 & 21		Roger Lindon	45½
1		William Fitzhugh	26½
2		John Pagan	10½
56 & 57	Honble	William Fairfax	35
62 & 63	Coll^o	George Fairfax	39
69 & 70	Coll^o	Nathaniel Harrison	46
77 & 78		Nathaniel Chapman	56½
32		Gerard Alexander	20
27		John Alexander	8
37		John Dalton	16
42		John Carlyle	16
52		Laurence Washington	16
47		William Ramsay	16

Page 2

		Pistoles
No. 71	Sold Maj^r. Henry Fitzhugh	16

        Richard Osburn
        William Ramsay
        John Carlyle
        John Pagan
        Gerard Alexander
        Hugh West

At a Meeting of the Majority of the Trustees, July 14th, 1749. Sold the Following Lotts, Viz.

			Pistoles
No. 33	Sold	Hugh West	8
38 & 39		Henry Salkeld	23
48		John Pagan	13½
49		John Alexander	15
79		Ralph Wormely, Esqr	10
45		Charles Mason	10½
50		Adam Stephen	11½
40		Harry Piper	6
55		George Mason	8
3		William Hicks, Esqr	10
4		Harry Piper	10
24		William Munday	11
54		William Strother	7
53		George Mason	7
59	Coll^o	William Fitzhugh	7
60		John Peyton	8

It is agreed that the Trustees adjourn till the 20th of September next, at which time the deeds are to be executed for the above Lotts and the remaining Lotts to be sold and that the Clerk prepare Blank Deeds for the same.

Page 3
NB The underwritten Lotts sold afterwards

Lott	Buyer	Pistoles	[signed]
No. 72 & 73	John West	15	Richard Osborn
64 & 65	Aug. Washington	15	William Ramsay
80 & 81	Anne West	12	John Carlyle
66 & 67	Wm. Henry Terrett	10	John Pagan
74 & 75	Pearson Terrett	10	Gerrard Alexander
58	John Champ	8	Hugh West
83 & 84	George West	8	
68 & 76	Hugh West, Junr	8	
82	William West, Junr	4	

The above P^r order of the Trustees,

        John West, Clerk

NB by Mr. Chapmans Order, the following Lott Sold to the Rev^d Mr. John Moncure, 5/9, N° 61.

Sepr 20th 1749
    Cash Dr. to Owin Winn for Collo. William Fitzhugh £17.9.2
    Do. Dr.   To Charles Mason 11.5.9

The following Lotts the Deeds were made out for on the 20th of Sepr 1749

Name	No.	£
John Dalton	No. 36	£20.8.6
Do.	37	17.4.0
Gerard Alexander	31	20.19.4
Do.	32	21.10.0
John Carlyle	41	32.5.0
Do.	42	17.4.0
John Dixon for William Hicks, Esq.	3	10.15.0
William Ramsay	46	32.5.0
Do.	47	17.4.0
Lawrence Washington	51	33.6.6
Do.	52	17.4.0

Page 4

Name	No.	£	paid
William Fitzhugh	No. 1	£28.9.9.	pd. £7.9.2
John Pagan	2	11.5.9	
Do.	48	14.10.3	
Henry Salkeld	38)	24.14.6	
Do.	39)		
John Alexander	27	8.12.8	
Do.	49	16.2.6	
Charles Mason	45	11.5.9	pd. J.W.
Harry Piper	40	6.9.0	

Do.	4	10.15.0
Wm. Henry Terrett, 66 Do.	67	10.15.0
Hugh West	33	8.12.0

At a Meeting of the Majority of the Trustees of the Town of Alexandria, December 14th 1749.
Present   The Hon$^{ble.}$ William Fairfax, Esqr·   John Carlyle
George Fairfax   Gerard Alexander
William Ramsay   Hugh West

Ordered that on the 28th Instant the Trustees do meet in order to sell the remaining Lotts in Alexandria Town, which now are unsold, and that Advertisements be sett up to that purpose, and every Trustee to have notice of the same and that they certifie whether they will act in the capacity of a Trustee or not.

William Fairfax   G. William Fairfax   John Carlyle
William Ramsay   Gerard Alexander
Hugh West

Page 5

At a Meeting of the Majority of the Trustees of Alexandria Town, December the 28th 1749, Viz.

Richard Osborn   William Ramsay   John Carlyle
John Pagan   Gerard Alexander & Hugh West

Ordered, as there was not proper notice given for the sale of the Lotts, that they be further Advertised for Sale on the 8th Day of January Next.

The Deeds were offered Hugh West for the Lotts No. 68 & 76, 84, 83 & 82, Which he refused to accept and says that as the persons for Whom he bought them are under Age that if Deeds be executed in their Names they cannot be re-conveyed Which reasons the Trustees think insufficient and therefore and therefore [sic] they have Ordered the Deeds to be made out. =

Ordered that Deeds be executed for all the Lotts that are already sold Which Deeds are to bear date from the 20th day of Sep^r· last agreeable to a former order for all the Purchasers to receive their Deeds that Day, Which Deeds were ready prepared but for want of the appearance of the said purchasers the Trustees apprehend they ought to be dated on that day. And have therefore ordered their Clerk to make out the same in order to be recorded at March Court Next.

Richard Osbourn   John Pagan
William Ramsay   Gerard Alexander
John Carlyle   Hugh West

Page 6

Feby. 27th 1749/50

At a Meeting of the Majority of the Trustees of the Town of Alexandria (Viz.) George William Fairfax, John Pagan, Gerard Alexander & Hugh West, Gent.

John Dalton is appointed a Trustee in the Room of Richard Osborn, Deceased.[87]

Ordered that the Trustees do meet on the third Thursday in March Next in order to sell the remaining Lotts that now are unsold to the highest bidder And that Advertisements be set up to that purpose and that all persons who have accounts against the Trustees are to bring them in order to have them adjusted on this third Thursday in March.
 G.W. Fairfax
 Lawrence Washington
 William Ramsay
 John Carlyle
 John Pagan
 Gerard Alexander
 Hugh West

Page 7
March 28th 1750

Deeds for the following Lotts were executed.======
(Viz.) No. 62 & 63 To Willoughby Newton, Gent. ... £41.18.6
    60 To John Peyton, Gent. .... 8.12.- pd. J.W.
March 29th 33 To Joseph Skelton (instead of H.W.) . 8.12.-

At a Meeting of the Majority of the Trustees of Alexandria Town the 7th Day of April 1750. Present. G. Willm. Fair^x., Lawrence Washington, William Ramsay, John Carlyle, Gerard Alexander, Hugh West & John Dalton, Gent.

Agreed to settle Mr. John Alexander's proportionable part sold before this Day.

---

[87] FWB A:329, the will of Richard Osborne, dated in OCT 1748, was probated 27 MAR 1750 in Fairfax Co.

	Sold For	his part		
No. 36)	£37.12.6	1/6	£6.5.5)	
37)			)	
			)	
38)	24.14.6	1/6	4.2.5)	£11.9.4
39)			)	
40	6.9.0	1/6	1.1.6)	
26)	23.13.0	1/4	5.18.3)	
27)	8.12.0	1/4	2.3.0)	£8.1.3
1	28.9.9	19/25	21.15.0)	
2	11.5.9	5/6	9.8.1)	
3	10.15.0	11/13	9.1.11)	49.6.11
4	10.15.0	11/13	9.1.11)	
31)	42.9.4			42.9.4
32)				
33	8.12.0			8.12.-
				£119.18.10

Page 8

Mr. John Alexander, Dr.

To	Cash paid you by Mr. Gerrard Alexander	£42.9.4
To	3/4 of Lott No. 27	6.9.-
To	Lott No. 49 you Bought	16.2.6
		£65.0.10

H Tobb°

To	Runing a Dividing Line 200	
To	your part in laying of the Lotts, 179-1/5	
To	your part of Charges	3.4.0
		379-1/5 & £69.1.2

H

To	379 Tob°, a 14/ P^r C^t	2.13.-
To	Cash paid Pr John West	28.9.0½
		£100.3.2½

Proceedings of Board of Trustees, Town of Alexandria, 1749-1780

Page 9
    Contra   **Cr.**

By Sundry Lotts Sold for £119.18.10

                The property of
                Samuell Arrell Marsteller

[This page is dominated by a bold inscription as an ornate monogram. The rest of the page is blank.]

Page 10 [Faces Page 11 below]

Trustees of Alexandria   **Dr.**

1749, Sep^r	To Mr. Hugh West for Francis Porter	£9.6.8
	To D^o for William Gladin	3.5.0
	To Maj^r John Carlyle for Thos Crafford	12.0
	To D^o for Gerard Boling	12.0
	To John West J^r, Sundry paid .... £1.14.10½)	
	To D^o for sale of the Lotts .... 2.3.0)	8.17.10½
	To D^o as Clerk .... 5.0.0)	
	(H Nett.	
	To Surveying the Town . 1344	
	To Runing 3 lines ..... 600)	
	1944	£22.13.6
1756, June 15	To Mr John West, Pr Clerk	5.0.0
	To Mr George West, P^r D^o	3.15.3
		£8.15.3

Page 11 [Faces Page 10 above]

    Contra   **Cr**

	H Nett	£ pd.
By Nathaniel Chapman & Co. for Philip)	784 &	13.14.6
Alexander part of Y^r Contract Charges)		
By Hugh West his part, D^o	380-4/5	6.8.8
By John Alexander, D^o	179-1/5	3.0.4
	1344	
Philip Alexanders line	200	
Hugh West	200	
John Alexander	200	
	1944 &	£22.13.6

1756, June 15 By P.A. part of the Contra 5.2.3
      By J.A. part 1.3.4.8
      By Hugh West, D⁰ 2.9.7-3/4
                    8.15.3-3/4

Page 12

Ordered, That the Trustees meet on Thursday the 19th Instant in order to sell the remaining Lotts which now are unsold and that Advertisements be set up for that purpose.

           Signed the Trustees,
           Lawrence Washington
           G.W. Fairfax
           William Ramsay
           Gerard Alexander
           Hugh West
           John Carlyle
           John Dalton

At a Meeting of the Majority of the Trustees of Alexandria Town, April 20th 1750
   Present Lawrence Washington, William Ramsay
   John Carlyle, John Pagan, Ger^d Alexander,
   and Hugh West, Gent^n

Proceeded to sell the following Lotts:

			Pistoles
No. 14	Sold	Hugh West	45
28	. . .	Anthony Ramsay	6½
29	. . .	Nathl Smith	6
34	. . .	Jonathan Ray [Rae]	6
23	. . .	William Monday	5½

Page 13

Ordered that Wm Ramsay, John Pagan, John Dalton & Hugh West, or any two of them do sign all the Deeds for the Lotts that now are sold and that they the said Wm Ramsay, John Pagan, John Dalton & Hugh West or any two of them do employ some proper person to carry the Deeds to the several Proprietors of such Lotts & Demand the pay for the same.

           Lawrence Washington
           William Ramsay
           John Carlyle
           John Pagan
           Gerrard Alexander
           Hugh West

At a Meeting of a Majority of the Trustees at Alexandria May 30th 1751
Present   William Ramsay
John Carlyle
John Dalton
John Pagan
Garr^d. Alexander
Hugh West

Ordered that the Clerk prepare the Deeds against the fourth Tuesday next Month being the 25th Day of the said Month & that the Clerk have them then at the Court House in Order to be there executed.

Page 14

It is thought ~~not~~ necefsary by the Trustees Present that there be a Meeting held in said Town on the second Saturday of every Month in order to propose & put in execution such Schemes as may be proposed for the benefit & Advancement of the Said Town also that the Clerk be ordered to Attend.

And further that Advertisements be put up in Fairfax County and others sent down the Country signifing that the several Deeds for the Lotts sold will be executed [at] Fairfax Court the 25th of Next Month.

William Ramsay
J^n. Carlyle
J^n. Dalton
J^n. Pagan
Garr^d. Alexander
Hugh West

At a Meeting of the Majority of the Trustees of Alexandria Town, June 15th 1751 (Viz.) The Hon. William Fairfax, Esqr., George William Fairfax, Lawrence Washington, W^m. Ramsay, John Carlyle, Hugh West & John Dalton, Gent^n.

Proceedings of Board of Trustees, Town of Alexandria, 1749-1780

Page 15

The aforementioned order made at the last meeting being read is hereby confirm'd.

Ordered that Advertisements be sett up signifying that the remaining Lotts in said Town be sold on the second Saturday in July next to the highest bidder Which shall be in the Forenoon & the absent Members have notice thereof.

      William Fairfax
      G. William Fairfax
      Lawrence Washington
      William Ramsay
      John Carlyle
      Hugh West
      John Dalton

Page 16

At a Meeting of the Major part of the Trustees of Alexandria Town, Augt the 3rd 1751

      Pres^t

The Honble William Fairfax, Esqr.	John Pagan
G. William Fairfax	Hugh West
Lawrence Washington	John Dalton, Gent^n
John Carlyle	

Maj^r John Carlyle is appointed to have a good road cleared down to point Lumley and to see the streets kept in repair.

As nothing else appears to be done this day tis agreed to adjourn till the second Saturday in Sepr next:

      William Fairfax.
      Lawrence Washington.
      John Carlyle.
      John Pagan.
      John Dalton.
      Hugh West.

Page 17

At a Meeting of the Majority of the Trustees of Alexandria, Feby 6th 1752 (Viz.) The Honble William Fairfax, Esqr, George William Fairfax, William Ramsay, John Carlyle, John Pagan, Hugh West & John Dalton, Gent^n.

Ordered that John West, Junr, Survey the Marsh adjoining this Town and annex it to a plan of the Town in order to be presented to the Aſsembly, and to obtain their Act to include in the Town bounds that part which is at this time without the same and that the whole may be disposed off [sic] to the highest bidder in order to improve it as a Common Pasturage &c.

  Sign'd the Trustees   William Fairfax.

G[o.] William Fairfax.
William Ramsay.
John Carlyle.
John Pagan.
Hugh West.
John Dalton.

Page 18

At a Meeting of the Major part of the Trustees of Alexandria Town, July the 18th 1752, (Viz.) George William Fairfax, William Ramsay, John Carlyle, John Pagan, Hugh West & John Dalton, Gent[n.]

George Johnston, Gent., appointed a Trustee in the Room of Lawrence Washington, Deceas'd.[88]

Agreeable to a former order to have a plan of the Marsh adjoining The Town annexed to a plan of said Town it was done accordingly & Presented to the Afsembly, which was receiv'd and pafsed but was afterwards rejected on account of the Kings having Afsented to the Act as before pafsed.

Ordered that the remaining Lotts in this Town which are at present unsold be sold on the third Tuesday in August next to the highest bidder and that Advertisements be sett up for that purpose.
Ordered that the Deeds be made out to all the persons who have bought Lotts & are not yet executed on the said third Tuesday in Augt. next.

Ordered that on Monday next the bounds of the Town be settled as many of the posts are lost. Ordered that on Col[o.] George Fairfaxes motion that all dwelling Houses from this day not begun or to be built hereafter shall be built on the front and be in a line with the Street as chief of the Houses are now, and that no Gable or end of such House be on or next to the street, except an Angle or where two streets ~~meet~~ Cross, otherwise to be puled [sic] down.

Hugh West	G. William Fairfax	John Pagan
John Dalton	William Ramsay	G[o.] Johnston
	John Carlyle	

---

[88] This entry for the July 18th meeting is puzzling, as Lawrence Washington did not die until July 26th. The contemporary manuscript copy is clear on the meeting's date of July 18th. The original document might have read July 28th, but we cannot know.

Page 19

At a Meeting of the Majority of the Trustees of Alexandria the 21st day of Feb[y]. 1753=

      Present
   The Hon[ble.] William Fairfax, Esq[r.]
    G[o.] William Fairfax, Esq[r.]
    William Ramsay)
    John Carlyle   )
    John Dalton   ) Gent[n.]
     &   )
    George Johnston)

John Pagan, Gent., formerly a Trustee being about to remove himself beyound Sea, Josias Clapham, Gent., is appointed to succeed him as a Trustee for the Town of Alexandria and present, M[r.] Pagan having resign's & refused to Act.

Ordered that on Tuesday ~~next~~ the first day of March next all the lotts in this Town that are unsold be sold to the highest bidder.

Ordered that the whole Town be resurvey'd & good white Oak Posts be provided for the Corners of each Lot, and M[r.] John Dalton & M[r.] Josias Clapham are hereby appointed to agree with some person to provide the said posts & to fix the same in the ground.

Ordered that Deeds be executed to the Justices of Fairfax County & their Succe∫sors for the Lotts No. 43 & 44 otherwise called the Market place for the use of the Court House & Prison.

   Josias Clapham
   John Dalton
   George Johnston
   William Ramsay
   John Carlyle
   William Fairfax
   G[o.] William Fairfax

Page 20

At a Meeting of the Major part of the Trustees of Alexandria Town, March 1st 1753=
     Present, William Ramsay
         John Carlyle
         Hugh West
         John Dalton
         George Johnston
         Josias Clapham

Proceedings of Board of Trustees, Town of Alexandria, 1749-1780

Proceeded to sell the Lotts:
    No. 5   Sold . . . . Samuel Mead, for . £1.3.0
       35   . . . . . . James Connell 5   Pistoles
       15   . . . . . . William Yates 12   D°.
       16   . . . . . . John West, Jr. 6   D°.
       22   . . . . . . Josias Clapham . . . . 12½ D°.
        8   . . . . . . Hugh West 50   D°.

No. 9, 10 are Ordered by the Trustees to be the Lotts which the Ware houses are to be fixed.

                    William Ramsay.
                    John Carlyle.
                    Hugh West.
                    John Dalton.
                    George Johnston.
                    Josias Clapham.

Page 21
At a Meeting of the Trustees of the Town of Alexandria the 18th day of June 1754
    Present   the Honble. William Fairfax   ) Esqr.
                      Go. William Fairfax   )

                      John Carlyle   )
                      William Ramsay   )
                      Hugh West   ) Gentn.
                      John Dalton   )
                      &   )
                      George Johnston   )

George Mason, Gentn., is appointed a Trustee in the Room of Philip Alexander, Deceased.[89]

John Hunter, Gentleman, is appointed a Trustee in the room of Josias Clapham, Gentn., who hath resign'd.
    Present   George Mason)
) Gentn.
               John Hunter   )

---

[89] As an inhabitant of Fairfax Co., Philip Alexander opposed a group that petitioned the Virginia legislature on 1 NOV 1748 to have a town established at Hunting Creek warehouse on the Potomac river. He favored placement at the head of Great Hunting Creek, as the former site was amidst his estate. Philip Alexander died 19 JUL 1753, one day after making a will which was probated in Stafford Co. on 14 AUG 1753. He was buried near his home "Salisbury" which is now a part of Cedar Grove Farm in St. Paul's Parish of King George Co.

Proceedings of Board of Trustees, Town of Alexandria, 1749-1780

Ordered that the Lott No. 20 & 21, Late the property of Roger Lyndon, Deceas'd; the Lott No. 50, the property of Adam Stevens; the Lott No. 54, Property of William Strother; the Lott No. 60, the Property of John Peyton; the Lott No. 61, the Property of John Moncure, Clerk; the Lotts No. 64 & 65, the Property of Agustine [sic] Washington; the Lott No. 67, the Property of W^m· Henry Terret: in the Town of Alexandria, be sold to the highest bidder at Publick Vendue the several Proprietors thereof haveing failed to build thereon according to the Directions of the Act of Afsembly in that case made & provided and it is further Ordered that the Clerk do give Publick notice that the sale of the said Lotts will be at the Town aforesaid on the first Day of August next.

Page 22

Ordered that George West be appointed Clerk in the Room of John West

William Fairfax — John Dalton
G^o· William Fairfax — George Johnston
William Ramsay — George Mason
John Carlyle — John Hunter
Hugh West

Sep^r· 9th 1754, Sold the following Lotts (Viz.)

No.		£ s d
20 & 21	Late the Lotts of Roger Lyndon to Mr. William Ramsay	£2.5.0
50	M^r· Adam Stevens former Lott	18.5.6
54	M^r· George Masons Lott	0.10.0
61	To William Sewel	5.7.6
67	To M^r· John Carlyle	5.7.0
64 & 65	To M^r· W^m· Ramsay, 36½ Pistoles	37.1.9
80	To M^r· George Mercer, 9½ Pistoles	9.13.6
81	To Daniel Wilson	10.10.0
60	To Thomas Harrison	4.13.0

Page 23

The following Lotts Deeds were made out for on the 9th of Sep^r· 1754:

William Sewel	No. 61	£5.7.6
George Mercer	80	9.13.6
Daniel Wilson	81	10.10.0
Adam Stephen	50	18.5.6
M^r· George Mason	54	0.10.0
M^r· John Carlyle	67	5.7.0
M^r· William Ramsay	64 & 65	37.1.9
M^r· William Ramsay	20 & 21	2.5.0
M^r· Thomas Harrison	60	4.13.0

Page 24

At a Meeting of the Major part of the Trustees, Decem.r 19th 1754:
    Present   G. William Fairfax   Esquire
                    John Carlyle.   )
                    Gerr.d Alexander.)
                    George Johnston.)
                    John Dalton.   ) Gent.n
                    John Hunter.   )
                    W.m Ramsay.   )

It is Ordered that Cap.n John West be called upon for the purchase Money of Lotts No. 72 & 73 being fifteen Pistoles.

It is Ordered that the Court House Lott be paled in with Posts & Rails in a Workman like Manner & that Advertisements be set up for Workmen to repair at Alexandria to undertake the same on Saturday the 28th Instant.

It is further Ordered that John Carlyle, John Dalton, George Johnston & W.m Ramsay view what is further necefsary to be done to the finishing of the Court house & report the same on Saturday the 28th Ins.t & That M.r John Dalton be appointed Overseer of the Town of Alexandria in the room of M.r John Carlyle who hath resign'd.

The Trustees agrees to meet in order to dispatch the above on Saturday on the 28th Instant.

G.o Wm. Fairfax.   John Dalton.
Wm. Ramsay.   George Johnston.
Jn. Carlyle.   John Hunter.
Gerr.d Alexander.

Page 25

At a Meeting of the Majority of the Town of Alexandria, Jan.y 11th 1755.
               Present   G. William Fairfax, Esqr.
                              William Ramsay.   )
                              John Carlyle.   )
                              John Dalton.   ) Gent.n
                              George Johnston.)
                              Gerr.d Alexander.   )

Ordered that Deeds be executed to Cap.t John West by M.r John Dalton & M.r George Johnston for the Lotts Number 72 & 73 not being executed before.

The persons appointed to view the insufficiency of the Court House being not ready further time is given them.
    G. Wm. Fairfax.

Wm. Ramsay.
John Carlyle.
John Dalton.
George Johnston.

January 22nd, 1755, Deeds were Executed for the following Lotts:

Captn. John West . . . .   No. 72 & 73 . . . . . .   £16.2.6

Page 26

At a Meeting of the Major part of the Trustees of the Town of Alexandria, June 18th 1755
     Present
   G. Wm. Fairfax, Esqr.
   John Carlyle)
   Wm. Ramsay)
   John Dalton.   ) Gent^{n.}
   George Johnston)
   George Mason)
   John Hunter.   )

Ordered that John Carlyle, Gent., do erect & build at Point Lumley in this Town a Warehouse of the following Dementions (Viz.) One hundred feet long twenty four feet wide thirteen feet Pitch'd. To be three Divisions double strided, the sills to be rais'd four feet from the ground & so compleatly finished; and that he lay his accounts of expence for the building thereof before the Trustees of the Town when the same is compleated, the the [sic] same may be examined by them & that he receive the Money now Due to the Trustees to enable him to carry on the work and that the residue of the Money by him to be advanced be repaid him out of the Rents arifing from the said Warehouse Together with Interest thereon after the Rate of five p^{r.} c^{t.} from the time that the house is finished. And it is further Ordered that he do Rent the said house, when compleated for the most advanced price that can be had & lay his accounts for Rents received from time to time before the Trustees and so continue to do untill the Trustees shall think it Necefsary to make some further order therein.

Page 27

Its further Ordered that Wm. Ramsay, John Dalton, George Johnston, Gent^{n.}, do overlook & Inspect the said Building. It is agreed that the Trustees adjourn till to Morrow Morning.
   G. Wm. Fairfax.   John Dalton.
   Wm. Ramsay.   George Mason.
   John Carlyle.   John Hunter.
   George Johnston.

Page 28

At a Meeting of the Majority of the Trustees of the Town of Alexandria, September 30, 1755
    Present the under written Trustees

It is agreed that the Ware house at point Lumley be fill'd in with Sand & Rubbish from the Point but in such a manner as not to prejudice the foundation of said house.

That Brick or Stone Chimneys be built to such houses or Smith Shops as at present have Wooden Ones by the first day of December next or Notice be given to the Sherriff to pull them down.

G°. Wm. Fairfax.	George Mason.
Wm. Ramsay.	John Hunter.
John Carlyle.	George Johnston.
Gerrd. Alexander.	
John Dalton.	

Page 29

At a Meeting of the Trustees of the Town of Alexandria, June 16th 1756.
    Present
        The Honble. William Fairfax.   )
            George William Fairfax.   )
                William Ramsay.   )
                John Carlyle.   )
                John Dalton.   ) Gentn.
                Gerrard Alexander   )
                George Johnston.   )

Ordered that whereas Mr. John Dalton has been for some time Overseer of the Town & being Desirous of being Acquited, It is Ordered that George Johnston, Gentn., be appointed Overseer in his Room.

Page 30

At a Meeting of the Majority of the Trustees of the Town of Alexandria, June 17th 1756
    Present   The Honble. William Fairfax.
            George William Fairfax.
                William Ramsay.
                John Carlyle.
                Gerrd. Alexander.
                John Dalton.
                George Johnston. Gentn.

Ordered that Five pounds be allowed to John West, Junr. for his attendance formerly as Clerk &c.

Proceedings of Board of Trustees, Town of Alexandria, 1749-1780

Ordered that George West be allowed £3.15.3 for his Trouble & Ordered that the Proprietors of the Town Lands pay as followeth to satisfy the above demands of £8.15.3 (Viz.)

    Philip Alexanders part £5.2.0
    Hugh Wests, Do. 2.9.7-3/4
    John Alexander, Do. 1.3.4-1/4
                                                      £8.15.3

By Order of the Trustees was sold on the 7th day of May To Mr John Muir, Lott No. 84 for the sum of £10.15.0

Elapsed formerly the property of George West and Ordered the Deeds be made out for the same.
                                             Wm Ramsay, Clk.

June 23rd 1757
                    Present the Honble W^m. Fairfax, Esqr
                                G. W^m. Fairfax, Esqr
                                Col^o John Carlyle.
                                Mr John Dalton.
                                Mr George Johnston.
                                Wm Ramsay.

It is agreed that Captn John Copithorn[90] pay for the use of the Warehouse in his pofsefsion twenty Shillings p^r Month & Ten Shillings p^r Month more if he use the remainder of the upper room.
                                Wm Ramsay, Clk.

Page 31
At a Meeting of the Majority of the Trustees of the Town of Alexandria, October 13th 1758
                Present   John Carlyle.
                                              William Ramsay.
                                              John Dalton.
                                              George Johnston.
                                              John Hunter.
                                              Gerr^d Alexander.

Agreed to=
Mr. Robert Adam is appointed a Trustee in the room of the Honble Wm Fairfax, Esqr, Deceased.[91]

---

[90] Maryland Gazette, 30 JUN 1757, John Copithorn, at his store in Alexandria, has various goods for sale. He intends to leave for England in the Ship he is now building.

[91] Kenton Kilmer and Donald Sweig, The Fairfax Family in Fairfax County, A Brief History (Fairfax: Office of Comprehensive Planning, 1975), p. 29. William Fairfax died at Belvoir, September 3, 1757, and was buried on the grounds of the mansion. Maryland Gazette, 15 SEP 1757, obituary notes he was also president of His Majesty's Council of Virginia and Collector of the Revenues for South Potomac.

Proceedings of Board of Trustees, Town of Alexandria, 1749-1780

M[r.] John Muir is appointed a Trustee in the room of Hugh West, Deceas'd.[92]

Ordered that some Effectual Methods be used to suppress the keeping & raising of Hoggs by the Inhabitants of this Town and that those already raised be either kept up in inclosure or killed by the last day of Nov[r.] next.[93]

       William Ramsay.
       John Carlyle.
       John Dalton.
       George Johnston.
       John Hunter.
       Robert Adam.

Page 32

At a Meeting of the Majority of the Trustees of the Town of Alexandria, the 18th Day of July 1759 Present G. Wm. Fairfax. George Mason.
          George Johnston. Robert Adam.
          John Hunter.   John Muir.
                  Gerr[d.] Alexander.

On the representation of John Carlyle & John Dalton that a good & convenient Landing at Cameron Street in the Town of Alexandria may be made of General Utility to the Town and that they will undertake to accomplish the same provided they and their Heirs in Consequence on the expence they will be at may have leave to apply to their use one half of the said Landing the same being Considered by the Trustees leave is granted to the said John Carlyle & John Dalton to execute the same & to appropriate one half thereof to their use as a landing.

       G[o.] W[m.] Fairfax
       G[o.] Mason
       G[o.] Johnston
       John Hunter
       Robert Adam
Agreed to   John Muir
       Gerr[d.] Alexander

---

[92] Hugh West died 21 NOV 1754, leaving a will dated 9 FEB 1754, which was probated in Fairfax Co. on 21 NOV 1754 [FWB B:74].

[93] Also see Waverly K. Winfree, comp., The Laws of Virginia; Being a Supplement to Hening's The Statutes at Large, 1700-1750 (Richmond: The Virginia State Library, 1971), pp. 443-446, October 27, 1748 to May 11, 1749, "An Act for erecting a Town at Hunting Creek Warehouse in the County of Fairfax." ...And Be it further Enacted by the Authority aforesaid That no Person whatsoever residing within the said Town shall keep any Swine running at large within the Bounds thereof, but that it shall and may be lawful for any Person whatsoever to kill or destroy the same and immediately give Notice to the Owner or Owners thereof. Provided always that nothing in this Act shall be construed to prohibit Persons driving Hogs for Sale in or through the said Town or to prohibit Persons residing near the said Town from letting their Hogs run at large.

Proceedings of Board of Trustees, Town of Alexandria, 1749-1780

Page 33

At a Meeting of the Trustees of the Town of Alexandria, Feby. 4th 1760

Present	
	John Hunter)
John Carlyle	Robert Adam) Gent[n.]
William Ramsay	John Muir)
John Dalton	
George Johnston	

Ordered that John Hunter & Robert Adam succeed George Johnston in the office of Overseer of the Streets and Landings[94] in the Town of Alexandria and that the said Hunters District shall be from the main Street Opposite M[r.] Carlyles Gate to the lower end of the Town and the said Adams from the said gate to the upper part of the Town.

John Hunter	W[m.] Ramsay
Robert Adam	John Carlyle
John Muir	John Dalton
	George Johnston

On Wednesday, the 20th Feb[y.] was sold to Thomas Brownley Lot No. 17 for Eight pounds Current money. And Deeds were made out to the said Brownly by John Carlyle & George Johnston bearing date the 21st Feb[y.]

                John Carlyle
                G[o.] Johnston

Page 34

At a Meeting of a Majority of Trustees for the Town of Alexandria the 1st Day of September 1760

Present	
George Johnston	William Ramsay
John Hunter	John Carlyle
&	Gerr[d.] Alexander
Robert Adam	John Dalton

On Examining the Records of the Town we find an Omi∫sion in not entering what was agreed on before the day of Sale of any of the said Lotts, that is, that evr'y purchaser of River side Lotts by the terms of the sale was to have the benefit of extending the said Lotts into the River as far as they shall think proper without any obstruction from the Street called Water Street.

It appears to us who were not Trustees at the time of the sale of Said Lotts by the proof of those

---

[94] Maryland Gazette, 3 APR 1760, "A lottery will be held in Alexandria for repairing the public wharf and erecting a grammar school. Managers are George William Fairfax, William Ramsay, John Carlyle, Gerard Alexander, John Dalton, George Johnston, George Mason, John Hunter, Robert Adam and John Muir. Buy tickets from Col. John Champe or Allan Macrae, merchant, at Dumfries; Hector Ross and Benjamin Greyson, merchants, at Colchester; Philip Richard Fendall or Charles County; Messrs. Symmers and John Weldon, merchants, at Upper Marlborough; or the printing office in Annapolis."

that were present, Alſo by Mr. John West, Junr. the Clerk at the same time that those who did purchase Lotts on the River side shou'd be intituled to the said priveledge that is that each owner of River side Lotts might build on or improve under his Bank as he should think proper Without any Moleſtation from the Street Called Water Street Intersecting.

Page 35
We have therefore caused this entry to be made in the Town Book to serve such purchasers of Water Lotts as were Originaly intended & to prevent disputes for the future.

      Given Under Our Hands
       William Ramsay
       John Carlyle
       Gerrd. Alexander
       John Dalton
       George Johnston
       John Hunter
       Robert Adam

Page 36
At a Meeting of the Trustees for the Town of Alexandria on Feby. the 2nd 1761, Present

William Ramsay	Robert Adam
John Carlyle	John Hunter
John Dalton	John Muir
George Johnston, Gentn.	

Charles Digges, Gent., is appointed a Trustee for the Town of Alexandria in the place of Gerrard Alexander, Gent., Deceased.[95]

John Carlyle & John Dalton, Gent., having produced their account for Building the Warehouse at Point Lumley together with the Rents received for the same it is ordered that Mr. William Ramsay, Mr. John Muir, and Mr. Robert Adam Examine the said account, settle the same & enter it fairly in the Town Books.

Ordered that the aforesaid gentlemen together with Mr. John Carlyle & Mr. John Dalton, Examine & State & Settle the Accounts relative to the sales of the Lotts & return a fair Copy thereof that the same may in like manner be entered in the Books.

Page 37
It Appearing to the Trustees that the Lott No. 60 sold to Thomas Harriſson in the Year 1754 remains unimproved to this Day notwithstanding the frequent declarations of the Trustees that the same should be sold if it was not built upon according to Law. It is therefore Ordered that

---

[95] Will of Gerard Alexander, dated 9 AUG 1760, probated 18 MAY 1762 in Fairfax Co., by the oath of Francis Dade [FWB B:327]. Division of his property is shown in Fairfax Co. Record of Surveys, 1787-1865, p. 61.

Advertisements be sett up at the door of the Court house of this County that the said Lot will be exposed to Sale to the highest bidder on the second day of the next Court the sale to be on the said Lott.

Ordered that the Money due from Col°· Adam Stevens to this Town for the first purchase of a Lott in the said Town be again demanded of him by M__r__· William Ramsay & in case of his refusal or delay of the payment that suit be immediately brought against him.

     William Ramsay
     John Carlyle
     John Dalton
     G°· Johnston
     John Hunter
     Robert Adam
     John Muir
     Charles Digges

Page 38

At a Meeting of the Trustees for the Town of Alexandria this 10th Day of Feb__y__· 1761. Present

  John Carlyle John Hunter &
  William Ramsay John Muir, Gent__n__·
  John Dalton
  George Johnston

The Gentlemen to whom the settlement of Accounts Exhibited by Meſsr__s__· Carlyle & Dalton respecting the Warehouse in the Town of Alexandria was referred having made a report that the same has been Carefully Settled & examined by them it is Ordered that the same be Recorded & it is Recorded as follow__h__· Viz.

Dr. The Town of Alexandria		By Sundy. Lotts sold)	
To the Amount of Charges &c)		& Rents received)	198.4.2
of buildg. a Warehouse let)	259.11.1½	Balance Due Carl__y__·)	
the Landing & Acct.)	_____	& Dalton)	61.6.11½
filled	£259.11.1½		259.11.1½

To the Contra Balance £61.6.11½
P__r__· the Oath of John Carlyle &
John Dalton before the Trustees

     W__m__· Ramsay
     John Carlyle
     John Dalton
     G°· Johnston
     John Hunter
     John Muir

Page 39

The Gentleman to Whom the account of the Sales of the Lotts in the Town of Alexandria was refered having Considered the same and made a slate thereof the same is Ordered to be Recorded & is Recorded as followeth

Dr.		John Alexander, Senr., Acct. Currnt. with the Trustees of Alexandria		Date		Cr.
Date			£ / D	Date		
1749		To H. West for part of Lotts) No. 1,2,3,4)	11.18.5		By Lotts No. 31, 32 Sold for..	42. 9.4
					By Do. 33...H. Westt..........	8.12.6
		To Cash received of G. Alexander	42. 9.4		By Do. 34...John Rea..........	6. 9.0
		To Lott No. 27.................	8.12.		By Do. 35...James Connell.....	5. 7.6
		To Ditto 29...................	16. 2.6		By Do. 1...Colo. Fitzhugh....	28. 9.9
		To Yr. Part Charges Acct. No. 1.	5.13.2		By Do. 3...Mr. Dixon..........	10.15.0
		To Cash pd. you pr. J. Westt....	28. 9.0½		By Do. 2...Mr. Pagan..........	11. 5.9
		To Ditto pr. J. Dalton..........	4. 5.5		By Do. 4...Saml. Mead........	1. 3.0
		To Mr. Ramsays Lot No. 4........	10.15.0		By yr. part of 26,27,28,29....	11. 8.5
1756		To J. Pagan............2......	11. 5.9		By Do. of 36,37,38,39.........	11. 9.4
July	10	To Mr. H.W. part of Lot 5.......	4.7½			
		To Yr. part of Charge No. 2.....	1. 3.9			
1757		To Cash in full pd. C&D.........	7. 5.0			
			£ 148. 4.1			£ 148. 4.1

Dr.		Mr. Hugh West, Deceased, Account Currt. with the Trustees of Alexandria				Cr.
1749		To John Alexander his part) of Lott No. 26, 27, 28, 29)	11. 8.5		By Lott No. 26, Allen Macrea..	23.13.0
					By Do. 27, sold Jn. Alexander.	8.12.0
		To Mr. Mcrea you received......	13.13.0		By Do. 28, Any. Ramsay........	6.19.9
		To No. 27, 28, J. West, Jur.....	13. 8.9		By Do. 29, Natt. Smith........	6. 9.0
		To 20 & 21, R. Lyndon you recd..	48.18.3		By 20 & 21, Roger Lyndon......	48.18.3
		To 22, Josias Clapham...........	13. 8.9		By 21 Do., Josias Clapham.....	13. 8.9
		To 23 & 24, Wm. Munday..........	17.14.9		By 23 & 24, Wm. Munday........	17.14.9
		To 14 yr. self..................	48.18.3		By 14 yr. self................	48.18.3
		To 15, Wm. Yates................	12.18.0		By Do. 15, Wm. Yates..........	12.18.8
		To 16, Jn. Carlyle..............	6. 9.0		By Do. 16, Jn. Carlyle........	6. 9.0
		To 8 yr. self...................	53.15.0		N. Sold 30,25,17,9,10,11,12, 13,18,19 247.15.9	247.15.9
		To Lotts 68,76,82,83,84.........	21.10.0			
		To Do. 33......................	8.12.0		By yr. share of Jn. Alexanders Lots No. 1,2,3,4,5...........	12.13.0
		To yr. proporn. Charges No. 1...	6. 8.8		By Jn. West Junr., 28,29......	13. 8.9
		To Do.................2.......	2. 9.7½		By Porter & Gladden for pd....	12.11.8
	NB	Mr. West has not Cr. for lott No. 8 which he is Charged with.......... 53.15. Contra Balance........ 3.13.				285.19.2
					Balance Settled Feby. 10th 1761	3.13.3
Jany.	13	1750 57. 8.3	289.12.5			£ 289.12.5

Page 40

Dr.	Me*fr*s· Chapman & Co. for P. Alexander's part of the Land		£	/	D
Date					
1749	To Yr. Proportion of Charges pr· Accot· No. 1		13	4	6
	To Ditto pr· Act 2		5	2	3
	To John Alexander his part of Lotts 36, 37, 38, 39, 40		11	9	4
	To Adam Stephen pr· Lott No. 50 not received		12	7	3
	To Nathaniel Chapman 1/4		143	3	2
	To Lawrence Washington 1/4		143	3	2
	To Wm· Ramsay 1/6		95	8	8
	To Carlyle & Dalton 1/6		190	17	5
			614	15	9
	Dr. Nathl. Chapman Current		Acct.		
1749	To Lotts No. 77 & 78 Cost	56½ Pist·	60	14	9
	To Ditto 69, 70 for Colo· H. Harrison	46 Pist·	49	9	
	To Ditto 71, Colo. H. Fitzhugh		17	4	
	To Ditto 74, 75, 66, 67, Mr· Terret	20 Pist·	21	10	
			148	17	9
	Dr. Lawrence Washingto[n], Esqr., deceased Dr.				
1749	To Lotts No. 51, 52, Yr· Self	43½ Pist·	46	15	3
	To Do. 48, John Pagan	13½	14	10	3
	To Do. 79, Ralph Wormley	10	10	15	0
	To Do. 64, 65, Augtn· Washington	15	16	2	6
	To Do. 53, 54, 55, 59, George Mason		31	3	6
	To Balance Due you		23	16	8
			143	3	2
	Dr. William Ramsay				
1749	To Henry Salkald Lotts, No. 36, 37		24	14	6
	To Harry Piper 40		6	9	0
	To your own 46, 47		49	9	0
	To Collo· West 80, 81		12	18	0
	To James Connell 35		5	7	6
	To Jona· Rea 34		6	9	0
			150	7	0
	Dr. Mefrs· Carlyle & Dalton				
	To John Dalton Lotts No. 36, 37		37	12	6
	To John Carlyle 41, 42		49	9	0
	To William Fairfax, Esqr· 56, 57		37	12	6
	To Collo. Champe 58		8	12	0
	To George Fairfax, Esqr· 62, 63		30	00	0
	To John Dixon 3		10	15	0
	To Collo· Fitzhugh Inpt·		11	0	7
	Balance Due C & D		1	3	8
			202	7	9

Page 41

Date	Account Curr^t with the Trustees of Alexandria		Contra Cr.		
1749	By Sales of Sundry Lotts, P.A. Land p^r Account		614	15	9
		£	614	15	9
	Contra	Cr.			
	By 1/4 of Contra N^t Sum		143	3	2
	By Balance		5	14	7
			148	17	9
	Contra	Cr.			
	By 1/4 of Contra N^t Sales, P.A. land		143	3	2
WR	to pay £9.18.4 23.16.8				
NC	5.14.7 1.3.8				
HW	3.13.3 25.0.4 due				
	Lott 28) Q^r				
	29)				
	Who received		143	3	2
	Contra	Cr.			
	By 1/6 part of the sale of the Lotts, P.A.		95	8	8
	Balance due from you		9	18	4
			105	7	0
	Contra	Cr.			
	By 2/6 of the Sale of the Lotts, P.A.		190	17	4
	By John Alexander		11	10	5
			202	7	9

Page 42

Sales of Jno. Alexanders part of the Town						
Date		To Whom Sold	Whom received	Lot	£	/	D
1749 July	13	Gerrard Alexander	Your Self	31, 32	42	9	4
		Hugh West		33	8	12	0
		Johnathan Rea	Wm. Ramsay	34	6	9	
		James Connell	Do.	35	5	7	6
		Colo. Wm. Fitzhugh		1	28	9	9
		John Dixon	C & D	3	10	5	
		John Pagan	Your Self	2	10	5	9
		Mr. Ramsay	Do.	4	10	15	
		S. Mead, Nt. pd.	Robert Adam	5	1	3	
			Nt. sold	6, 7	125	6	4
Sales of Mr. Hugh Wests part of the Town						
1749 July	13	Allen Macrea	H. West	26	23	13	0
		John Alexander	Do.	27	8	12	
		Anthony Ramsay	Do.	28	6	19	9
		Nath. Smith	Do.	29	6	9	
		Roger Lyndon	Do.	20, 21	48	18	3
		Josias Clapham	Do.	22	13	8	9
		Wm. Munday	Do.	23, 24	17	14	9
		H. West	Do.	14	48	18	3
		Wm. Yates	Do.	15	12	10	
		John Carlyle	Do.	16	6	9	
		H. West	Do.	8	53	5	
				£	247	15	9
			30, 25, 9, 11, 12, 13, 18, 19				
		Thomas Bromley	C & D	17	8		

Page 43
Sales of P. Alexanders part for Chapman & Co.

Date	To Whom Sold	No.	To Whom paid	£ / D
1759 13 July	John Dalton	36, 37	Carlyle & Dalton	37.12.6
	Henry Salkald	38, 39	Wm. Ramsay	24.14.6
	Harry Piper	40	Do.	6. 9.
	John Carlyle	41, 42	Carlyle & Dalton	49. 9.
	Market Place	43, 44		
	Charles Mason	45	John West, Junr.	11. 5.9
	Wm. Ramsay	46, 47	Mr. Ramsay	49. 9.
	John Pagan	48	Law^{r.} Washington	14.10.3
	John Alexander	49	In Account	16. 2.6
	Dr. Stephens	50	Out Standing	12. 7.3
	Law^{r.} Washington	51, 52	himself	50.10.6
	George Mason	53)		
	Wm. Strother	54)	Law^{r.} Washington	23.13.
	George Mason	55)		
	Wm. Fairfax, Esqr.	56, 57	Carlyle & Dalton	37.12.6
	John Champe	58	Do. . . . Do.	8.12.
	Col^{o.} Wm. Fitzhugh	59	Law^{r.} Washington	7.10.6
	John Payton	60	John West, Junr.	8.12.
	G. Wm. Fairfax	62, 63	Carlyle & Dalton	30. 0.
	John Moncure	61	Nill	
	Augt. Washington	64, 65	Law^{r.} Washington	16. 2.6
	Wm. Henry Terrett	66, 67	N. Chapman	10.15.
	H. West, Junr.	68	In acc^{t.} H. West	4. 6.
	Col^{o.} Harrison	69, 70	N. Chapman	49. 9.
	Henry Fitzhugh	71	Do.	17. 4.
	John West	72, 73	Carlyle & Dalton	16. 2.6
	Pearson Terrett	74, 75	N. Chapman	10.15.
	H. West, Junr.	76	In acc^{t.} N. West	4. 6.
	N. Chapman	77, 78	N. Chapman	60.14.6
	R. Wormley	79	Law. Washington	10.15.
	Ann West	80, 81	Wm. Ramsay	12.18.
	Wm. West	82)		
	George West	83, 84)	H. West in Acc^{t.}	12.18.

                 614.15.9
      Ded^{t.} John Alexander, p^{t.}
     of No. 36, 37, 38, 39, 40 11. 9.4
                 603. 6.5
            N^{t.} Sales

Page 44
At a Meeting of the Trustees for the Town of Alexandria Augt 17, 1764. Present

        Wm Ramsay   John Hunter
        John Carlyle   Robert Adam
        George Johnston John Muir

It is alowed & agreed to by the Trustees that Thomas Fleming have Liberty to Build a Ware house under the Bank of Point Lumley as near the Bank as is convenient of the following Dimentions, Viz. Forty foot by Twenty four foot at his own proper Cost and Charge he to have the sole use & Benifit of the said house for three lives such as he think proper to put into a lean to be granted him by the said Trustees he or his Succefsors paying the Trustees for the use and benefit of said Town Annualy the sum of five Shillings Current Money. This Indulgence is granted this Fleming in Consideration [illegible] ~~this Town~~ of his usefulnefs as a Ship Carpenter & his Inclination to serve this Town to the utmost of his Power.

Note it is further allowed the said Fleming to strike out any one of the Three Named persons during their existence or life & to insert any other persons Names he things proper.

Page 45
This Day the Trustees has agreed with Thomas Fleming to make an Addition to the Wharf at Point West agreeable to a Bond enter[ed] into by the said Fleming and Articles of agreement by the said Trustees in such manner as is mentioned in said agreement for the sum of One Hundred Pounds current Money the said Wharf to be fully compleated & finished in a Workman like Manner Twenty Six foot wide from the Outer end to the length of the Wharf in Shore & to be supported by the said Fleming in good repair during the space of Seven Years.

Augt 17th 1761
John Muir is appointed Overseer
of the Streets & Landings of the
Town for Twelve Months
Wm Ramsay agrees to Aid &
afsist the said John Muir

    Wm Ramsay
    John Carlyle
    G^o Johnston
    John Hunter
    Robert Adam
    John Muir

Page 46
At a Meeting of the Trustees, July 2nd 1762
        Present   Wm Ramsay   George Johnston
                     John Carlyle   John Hunter
                     John Dalton   John Muir

On the Application of John Kirkpatrick for Liberty to build a Vefsel on the upper Point call'd West Point it was granted him. Whereas it is apprehended that some disputes may hereafter arise toutching the Bounds of some Lotts in the Town of Alexandria and Particularly the Lotts purchas'd by N. Harrifon to prevent Which and to Afsertain the Bounds of the said Lotts its

Ordered that the Original Platt of the said Town[96] and by which all the Lotts were sold be Recorded in the Records of the County of Fairfax and that the Proper Bounds of these Lotts be Established and perpetuated by affixing strong and substantial posts at the Corners thereof.

       W^m. Ramsay
       John Carlyle
       John Dalton
       George Johnston
       John Hunter
       John Muir

Pages 47 and 48 are Blank

Page 49

At a Meeting of the Trustees, Feby 1st 1763
   Present W^m. Ramsay
       John Carlyle
       John Dalton
       George Johnston
       Robert Adam
       John Muir

Ordered that several Lotts lay'd off by Act of A*f*sembly be sold on Monday the 9th Day of May next and that John Carlyle have the Day of Sale advertised in the Virginia & Maryland & Pensylvania Gazettes & bring in his account for the same. Lott No. 60 which was ordered to be sold as appears by an order of the Trustees the 2nd Day of Feby 1761 still continues unimproved out of Indulgence to the Proprieter.

Its now Ordered that Advertisements be put up at the Court house Door the first Day of Next Court for the Sale of the said Lott on Wednesday the 16th Instant.

       Wm. Ramsay
       John Carlyle
       John Dalton
       George Johnston
       Robert Adam
       John Muir

---

[96] Fairfax Co. Record of Surveys, Bk. 1, p. 56, dated 18 JUL 1749; Alexandria Husting Court Deeds, Bk. H, 1795-1797, p. 332.

Proceedings of Board of Trustees, Town of Alexandria, 1749-1780

Page 50

At a Meeting of the Trustees of the Town of Alexandria the 9th Day of May 1763

Present   W^m· Ramsay   Robert Adam
          John Carlyle   John Muir
          John Dalton   John Hunter
          George Johnston   Gent^n·

Harry Piper, Gentleman, is appointed a Trustee for the said Town of Alexandria.
          Present   Harry Piper, Gentleman

Pursuant to the Act of Afsembly for this purpose lately made and agreeable to the Advertisements published in the Gazettes, the Trustees on this 9 day of May 1763 were proceeded to the Sales of the said Lotts annex'd by Law to the Town of Alexandria for ready Money but John Alexander, Junior, of Stafford C°·, Gent^n·, whose Lands were to be first sold being present and desiring that his Lotts might be sold for twelve Months Credit in order to enhance the the Value thereof the Trustees consented thereto & thereupon the following persons at twelve Months Credit at the Price set to each persons Name (Viz.)

No.	Name	£	No.	Name	£
85	Thomas Fleming	£50.10.	95	John Potts	32.0.
86	John Hunter	40.	96	Patk. Rowan	21.0.
87	Phil. Alexander	38.10.	97	W^m· Ramsay	12.0.
88	Robert Adam	21.	98) 99)	John Orr	15.0.
89	W^m· Ramsay	10.	100	J^n· Kirkpatrick	5.15.
90) 91)	George Johnston	15.	101	The same JK	7.10.
92	John Kirkpatrick	5.5.	102	Francis Lee	6.5.
93) 94)	John Hug[h]es JC	60.10.	103	Sarah Potter	7.10.
		£240.15.			£107.

Page 51

Sales Continued

No.	Name	£	
104	John Graham	18.15.	
105	John Muir	10.5.	
106	Henry Roser [Rozier]	11.	
107	John Muir	10.	
108	Peter Wise	12.	Note that Deed<u>s</u> were executed by John
109	James McLeod	13.10.	Carlyle & W^m· Ramsay, Dec^r· 2nd 1778
110	James Laurie	17.5.	
111	Jacob Hite	22.10.	
112	G°· Washington	38.	
113	Phillip Alexander	39.	
114	J^n· Alexander, Ju^r·	40.	
115	Michael Greater [Gretter]	50.10.	

116	Rob.t Rutherford	27.	
117	Tho.s Kirkpatrick	3.5.	√ ℰ
118	Geo. Washington	10.10.	
119)	Antho.y Ramsay	6.5.	John Alexander has 2/7 of the two
120)			Lotts
121	James Connelly	2.10.	John Alexander's property
122	Rich.d Arell	2.10.	
		334.15.	
123			
124			
125			
126			
127	John Potts	12.5.	Ex. Hugh Hughes
128	Henry Roser GW	11.	
129	John Carlyle	6.5.	
130	John & Ann Tarbuck	8.12.	
131	John Carlyle	4.10.	
132	James Adam	4.10.	
133	James Adam	6.15.	
134	Rob.t Adam	8.5.	
135	John Dalton	16.5.	
		78.7.	

Page 52

Sales of Lotts Continued

No. 136	Rob.t Jones	12.5.	
137)	John Hughes, J.r	3.10.	
138)		2.10.	
139)	[Isaac] Huges [Hughes]	2.	
137)		2.	
140	Ruth Huges [Hughes]	3.	
141	Catharine Huges [Hughes]	1.10.	
25	Hugh West	5.	
18	George West	5.	
11	John West	5.	
12	D.o	1.	
6	W.m West	1.	
13	John Bushby	14.10.	
19	Hugh Huges	16.10.	H. Huges [Hughes] E.
		74.15.	

Ordered that the Accounts of Charges on the Sales of the Lotts Surveying & staking the Town & every charge Whatsoever be brought in and charged in proportion to the respective proprieters and Deeds for each Lott be made out amediately & tendered to each Purchaser & that Peter Robinson be directed to make out the same & that five Shillings be allow'd him for each Deed.

    John Hunter W.m Ramsay

Proceedings of Board of Trustees, Town of Alexandria, 1749-1780

Robert Adam   John Carlyle
John Muir   John Dalton
Harry Piper   G°. Johnston

Page 53

At a meeting of the Trustees of the Town of Alexandria, May 30th 1763

Present
Wm. Ramsay   Robert Adam
John Carlyle   John Muir
John Dalton   Harry Piper
G°. Johnston   John Hunter

Ordered that John Muir & Harry Piper sign the Deeds & Execute the same bearing date this day to the several purchasers & that the same be recorded and afterwards Advertised in the Virginia & Maryland Gazettes.

Ordered that Robert Adam, Gent[n]., be overseer of the Main street from the upper part of M[rs]. Chews Lott to the lower part of her Lotts and that he make so much of the said Main street dry and fitt for traveling for Waggons & foot people by the first of Septem[r]. Next or pay for his failure twenty Shillings to the Trustees for the use of the Town.

And that George Johnston in like Manner & under the same penalty put the Main Street in Order from the ~~Said Dalton upper Corner~~ lower part of M[rs]. Chews Lotts to the Corner of M[r]. John Daltons Lott.

And That John Dalton in like Manner & under the same penalty put the Main Street in Order from the said Daltons upper Corner along his own front half way the street between him & John Carlyle, Gent[n].

And that the said John Carlyle in like Manner & under the same penalty put the main street in order from where the said John Dalton Leaves off to the lower end of his own Lott.

[Change in handwriting] And that Wm. Ramsay, Gent., in like manner and under the same penalty put the said main street in order from the upper part of his own Lott to the lower part thereof together with half the next street and that William Ramsay continue his district down to Col°. George Fairfaxes Lott.

And that John Carlyle in like manner and under the ƒame penalty put the main Street in order from the

Page 54

Corner of W. Fairfaxes Lott to the lower corner of the said Fairfax Lott and one half of the adjacent street. And that Doctor John Hunter in like manner and under the same penalty put the said Main street in order from the lower corner of the said Fairfaxes Lott to the lower corner of Going Langphir's Lott with the Street adjacent.

And that the said overseers Jointly keep the Publick landings in repair and divide the labouring tithably in Alexandria equally between them.

Robert Adam	Wm. Ramsay
John Muir	John Carlyle
Harry Piper	John Dalton
	Geo. Johnston
	Jn°· Hunter

At a meeting of a majority of the Trustees for the Town of Alexandria the 20th Sept. 1763

Present

John Carlyle	)	John Muir
John Dalton	)	Robert Adam
Geo. Johnston	)	& Harry Piper

John Kirkpatrick and Thomas Fleming, Gentlemen, are appointed Trustees for the Town of Alexa. in the room of Charles Diggs [Digges] who hath removed out [of] this Colony and John Hunter who is deceased.

Ordered that any three of the Trustees state and Settle the accounts of John Patterson and Rich.d Leek [Leake] together with an aud. of the Lottery and make report thereof to the trustees at their next meeting.

John Muir	Rob. Adam	John Carlyle
Harry Piper	Geo. Johnston	John Dalton

Page 55

At a meeting of a majority of the Trustees for the Town of Alexandria the 19th day of April 1766

Present

John Carlyle	John Muir
John Dalton	Harry Piper
Rob.t Adam	John Kirkpatrick
	Thomas Fleming

Pursuant to an order of the Trustees dated the 2nd July 1762 we have met and called upon John West, Jun.r, late surveyor of this County (who laid off this town originally) together with the Chain carriers Thomas Crafford and Gerrard Bowling to affix the boundaries of Lott number Sixty nine adjoining to the Publick landings which place

Proceedings of Board of Trustees, Town of Alexandria, 1749-1780

[they] have now shown to George West the present surveyor who is required to Record the same in his book of Surveys of this County.[97]

And further the said John West, Junior, Thomas Crafford and Gerrard Bowling having given a Certificate under their hands which they say they are at any time willing to swear to the same are ordered to be recorded. Mr. Thos. Fleming is appointed Surveyor of the Publick Landings and Streets in this Town.

Harry Piper	John Carlyle
John Kirkpatrick	John Dalton
Thos. Fleming	Robert Adam
	John Muir

Fairfax County, Alexandria, 19th April 1766. I, John West, Junr., late Surveyor of this County do hereby Certifie that the place now shewn to Geo. West, Surveyor, is at the corner of the Lott No. 69 adjoining to the Publick landing or within a very few feet thereof which Lott as well as all the others at the time of my laying off the said Town in July 1749 was Staked with Locust Posts at the corner of each Lott by Wm. Gladding.

Given under my hand this 19th April 1766.
Geo. Johnston, Gent.
Anty. Ramsay
Archibald Johnston

John West, Junr.
late Surveyor of Town

Page 56

We Thos. Crafford and Gerrard Bowling were the appointed Sworn Chain Carriers in the Surveying and laying out of the town of Alexandria in July 1749, and at the request of the Trustees met George West present Surveyor and John West, Junr., late Surveyor of Fairfax, and went with the said John and Geo. West and affixed posts to the corners of Lott numbered Sixty nine in or within a very few feet of the former and first corners a*f*scertained by the original platt and survey in 1749, this we Certify under our hands this 19th day of April 1766.

Tes.
Geo. Johnston, Junr.
Ant^{y.} Ramsay
Archibald Johnston

Thomas Crafford
his
Gerrard X Bowling
Mark

At a Meeting of a Majority of the Trustees for the Town of Alexandria, 16th December 1766
    Present
       absent   Geo. Wm. Fairfax
    Wm. Ramsay   Robert Adam
    Jno. Carlyle   Harry Piper
    Jno. Dalton   John Kirkpatrick

---

[97] No copy of the West survey has been discovered among the records of Fairfax County. However, a copy (which is presented here as Figure 7) is found at the Library of Congress, G3884.AE.1763.W4 vault.

Proceedings of Board of Trustees, Town of Alexandria, 1749-1780

Whereas deeds were granted by William Ramsay & John Pagan two of the trustees of the town of Alexandria bearing date the 28th day of March Anno Domini 1752 to the Hon. Geo. W^m. Fairfax, Esqr., for two Lotts of land in the same Town, No. 56 & 57, On the motion of Geo. W^m. Fairfax, Esqr., it appears to us the above mentioned Trustees that No. 56 should have been included in Lott No. 57 as one lott liable to the conditions of improvement by act of Afsembly-- And that he never having had a deed in his name or his fathers for Lott No. 58, It is now ordered that one Deed of conveyance be made out to the said Geo. W^m. Fairfax his Heirs and Afsigns and that M^r. W^m. Ramsay and Mr. John Carlyle be appointed and are hereby authorized

Page 57

authorized [sic] to make good the said deed of Conveyance for these Lotts being improved agreeable to the act of Afsembly for constituting and erecting the said Town.

    Robert Adam   W^m. Ramsay
    Harry Piper   John Carlyle
    John Kirkpatrick   John Dalton
    Geo. W^m. Fairfax, Esqr.
Present

The trustees proceeded to appoint a trustee in the room of Geo. Johnston, decd.[98], and have unanimously chosen George Washington, Esqr., as Trustee for the town aforesaid.
    absent John Kirkpatrick.

On the application of John and Thomas Kirkpatrick for leave to make what ground they see fit and build a Ware House or Warehouses on the east side of Water Street opposite to Lott No. 26 and to the North side of Queen Street not interfering with Lott No. 20, the present property of Mr. Jacob Hite. The Trustees on the application aforesaid to grant and give to the said John and Thos. Kirkpatrick their Heirs succefsors and Afsigns all the right and title they the said Trustees have with full power right and Liberty to make ground out of Potomack, to build Warehouses, Wharfs to occupy and enjoy in as full a manner to them the said Jno. & Thos. Kirkpatrick their Heirs and Afsigns for and during the space of Ninety nine years they paying Annually or when demanded for the use of the said town of Alexandria the Sum of five Shillings current money commencing the 25th of December 1768.

    Robert Adam   Geo. W^m. Fairfax
                      Wm. Ramsay
    Harry Piper   John Carlyle
                      John Dalton

---

[98] Loudoun Co. Wills, Bk. B, pp. 180-81, dated 27 NOV 1776, codicil 27 NOV 1776, probated 11 AUG 1777; Maryland Gazette, 4 SEP 1766, George Johnston, Esq., died Friday last [Aug. 31], at Alexandria, an eminent practitioner of the new law in Virginia and in this province.

Page 58

At a meeting of the Majority of the Trustees for the town of Alexandria, 2nd day of Feby. 1767

      Present

John Muir	John Carlyle
Harry Piper	John Dalton
John Kirkpatrick	Robert Adam
Thomas Fleming	

On examining the school House we find it in very bad repair and thinks it necefsary not only to put it in better [sic] but also to make some small additions in order to make the upper room usefull not only for meeting of the Trustees but for such other purposes as may be thought necefsary. Mr. Robert Adam and Mr. Thomas Fleming agrees to have the necefsary repairs done that is a new front door and remove the present door in the partition of the grammer school, to make an entry and a door to enter into the other room, a door in the upper room, the lower windows to have window shutters, the plaistering to be repaired and whitewashed the house to be painted the windows to be glazed and when finished to bring in their Charge for the same--

As it appears to us that the House has been very much injured by the negligence of the School Masters it is now determined that each Master give security to repair the any injury that the House may sustain during the time they have it.

Ordered that Mr. Rob. Adam and Mr. Thos. Fleming visit the school and examine the fame for twelve months.

Harry Piper	John Carlyle
John Kirkpatrick	John Dalton
	Rob. Adam
Thos. Fleming	John Muir

Page 59

At a meeting of the Majority of the Trustees for the Town of Alexandria to inspect and to adjust the accounts of the publick Warehouse and of the school House they took the same into consideration 4th April 1767.

      Present

Wm. Ramsay	John Muir
John Carlyle	Harry Piper
John Dalton	John Kirkpatrick
Robert Adam	Thos. Fleming

Mfrs. Carlyle and Dalton produced an account against the publick warehouse of Seventy three Pounds four fhillings and tenpence, £73.4.10, which was allowed, they also produced an

Proceedings of Board of Trustees, Town of Alexandria, 1749-1780

account of expences arising from the removal of the Court House[99] amounting to fifty two pounds ƒeven ƒhillings and five pence half penny. William Ramsay likewise produced an account arising from the removal of the Court house and for the ƒcheme of a Lottery to build a Church and Markett house in the said town amounting to Eleven Pounds twelve ƒhillings which amounts were refer'd to another meeting of the Trustees, there not being a sufficient number exclusive of the said Mƒrs. Carlyle & Dalton and the said Wm. Ramsay.

A Copy of John Hunter, dec., account was produced by which it appears that a Balance is due from the said John Hunters estate of eight pounds four ƒhillings. There also appears due from W^m. Ramsay an amount of a Lottery drawn for the benefit of the said town Eleven Pounds, there also appears a Balance due from John Dalton of Forty three pounds on the same account. Mr. Thomas Fleming also exhibited an account of Rent &c.

Note About Page Numbering. This point marks the end of the Marsteller record. The text continues without a break, but in a different transcript (kept by Warwick P. Miller) with different handwriting and different pagination. As a consequence, users will note that the Miller record jumps from Page 60 and continues here with Page 66. Again, the text content is unbroken and complete; only the page numbers of the two sources do not coincide. Pagination here is used from the Bryant suit transcription since it reflects no break in sequence.

Page 60
[Miller Page 66] account of rents &c. [sic] arising from the public Warehouse whereby it appear[s] that the sum of fifty pounds seven shillings is now in the hands of said Fleming.

It is ordered that Mr. Jno· Dalton pay to Mr. J. Carlyle, eighteen pounds sixteen shillings & three half pence a balance of Account exhibited by him against the said Town as Treasurer for the Lottery.

John Pattison account was exhibited, it appears that a balance of Thirty one pounds thirteen shillings & one penny is due to him. Richard Leake likewise exhibited an account by which it appears that the sum of fifty seven pounds twelve shillings & ten pence is due to him. In consideration of Mr. Leakes laying out of his money for want of a sufficient fund to pay the same the Trustees agree to pay the said Leake the sum of ten pounds, after finishing the above entries the following accounts were ordered to be stated--

---

[99] In 1752, the Fairfax County courthouse and prison were removed from Spring Field (near Tyson's Corner) to the Town of Alexandria [Fairfax Harrison, Landmarks of Old Prince William, A Study of Origins in Northern Virginia (Richmond: Old Dominion Press, 1924; reprint ed., Baltimore: Gateway Press, Inc., 1987), p. 321]. The First session of the court in the new location convened on May 3, 1752, situated on the north side of Market Square, nearly opposite Carlyle House [Virginia Gazette, April 30, 1752; Fairfax Co. Deeds, Bk. D, p. 360; TM:19]. In 1789, the General Assembly passed legislation for establishing a new county courthouse outside the town line, nearer the center of the county. The site was to be on William Fitzhugh's land (the "Ravensworth" tract) or in any case within one mile of the crossroads at Price's ordinary [Hening, Vol. XIII, p. 79].

Vizt. The Town Warehouse to Me*f*rs. Carlyle & Dalton   Dr.
carried forward, Dr.   Me*f*rs. Carlyle & Dalton, Contra   Cr.
To Robert Loxham for Rent, £2.5.   By balance due £61.6.11½
To Jno. Kirkpatrick for Do.   3.   By Interest 17.2.10½
            balance   73.4.10   . . . . 78.9.10
                       £78.9.10   By Balance £73.4.10

[Miller Page 67]

Dr.   Mr. John Hunter, deceas'd, his account   Cr.
To balance due to the Lotts, £44 By Cash per Jn°· Pattison . . . . £10.
                                  By 17 Tickets returnd . . . . 8.10.
                                  By Cash pd. Mr. Carlyle 8
                                  By Richard Leake . . . . 5.6.
                                  By Thom^s· Fleming . . . . 4.
                                  By balance . . . . 8.4.
                                                . . . . 44.0
To Balance   £8.4   By order to W. Templeman for £8.4

Dr.   William Ramsay   Cr.
To balance due the Lottery £11   By order of W. Templeman for £11

Dr.   Mr. John Dalton   Cr.
To balance due the Lottery £43   By John Carlyle £18.16.1½
                                   By W. Templeman 24.3.10½

Page 61

Dr. Mr. Thomas Fleming		Cr.	
To Robert Adam	£26	By building a Wharf	£100.
To John Hunter	4	By sundry repairs	8.17.6
To John Carlyle	20	By comifsions	6.
to Sundry rents from)		By interest	5.
Jan. 7, 1762 to Jan. 7, 1767			
	120.4.0	. . . . balance	50.7.
	£170.4.6	B. bal fro. W. Templeman	£170.4.6

[Miller Page 68]

1760, Dr. Mr. John Carlyle		Cr.	
To Cash from Geo. Johnston	£14.	By Col. Fairfax, bal^e· of)	
To Do. George Mason	35.	his Lottery account)	£64.
To Bal. of his Lottery Acct.	39.	By Jonas Green	23.11.1
To Mr. Jno. Muir	36.4.2	By Nathan Hughes	2.8.
To John Hunter	8.	By Thom^s· Fleming	20.
To John Dalton	18.16.12	By Rich^d· Leake	26.1.3½
		By John Pattison	10.3.1
		By Advertisem^t· &c.	2.16.9½
	£151.0.3½	. . . .	£151.-.3½

Dr. Richard Leake		Cr.	
To Cash from W. Johnston	£8.18.6	By brick Work at the	
To Carlyle & Dalton	14.	School House	90.
To John Carlyle	28.1.3½	By addition to Do.	10.
To John Muir	16.10.	By raising the wall)	
To over pd.	10	5½ ft. & building Chimney)	25.17.6
Balance due		By interest on do	10.
to Wm. Templeman	68.6.10½	. . . .	£135.17.6
	£135.17.6		
To Wm. Templeman	68.6.10½	By balance	£68.6.10½

Page 62

Dr.	John Pattinson		Cr.	
1760	To plank & scantlin	£25.16.7	By building school house	£99.18.7
	To John Muir	10.5.10	By Glafs charged	6.7.6
1762	To John Pattinson	10.3.1½		
	Carlyle			
Feb. 13	To Glafs	6.7.6		
	To W. Adam	12.		
	To John Hunter	10.		
	Bal^le. Wm. Templeman	31.13.1		
		£106.6.1		£106.6.1

| | To Wm. Templeman | 31.13.1 | By Balance due | £31.13.1 |

Continued

It is ordered that Col^o. John Carlyle give Mr. ^Wm. Templeman orders on the several persons indebted, to pay the sums due to Rich^d. Leake & John Pattinson.

John Muir	W^m. Ramsay
Harry Piper	John Carlyle
Jno. Kirkpatrick	John Dalton
Thomas Fleming	Robert Adam

Ordered that the Trustees meet again the Eleventh Inst. [at] the Town House.
                    W^m. Ramsay, Clk. for the day

Dr.	Mr. Wm. Templeman		Do. Cr.	
To an order on Dr. Hunter, Esqr.		8.4	By R. Leake bill,	£68.6.10½
To an order on Mr. Fleming		50.7	By Jno. Pattinson, do	31.13.1
		58.11		£100.
To Do. Mr. Ramsay		11.		
To John Dalton		24.3.10½		
		£93.14.10½		

Page 63

[Miller Page 70] At a meeting of the Trustees to settle the length of Lott number twenty the property of Jacob Hite or to affix the length it shall go down the river opposite to Lott number twenty six, the property of Mefrs. John & Thomas Kirkpatrick; after taking the same into consideration, do say, that the said Lott number twenty shall extend down the river opposite to Lott number twenty six, fifty nine feet and * terminate, as being agreeable to the plan by * the said Lotts was sold, or near to the same. * Trustees did in the presence of and at the * of the parties to prevent any dispute that might arise concerning the bounds of the said Lotts and this they say shall be binding on the parties forever. February the eight day one Thousand & sixty eight. Present

Memorandum deeds [Present:] W^m. Ramsay
are to made out John Carlyle
to Me*f*rs. John & John Dalton
Thomas Kirkpatrick John Muir
agreeable to the entry. Harry Piper
  Thomas Fleming

(**** parts torn out in old book, W.P. Miller[100]).

Page 64

[Miller Page 71] At a meeting of the Trustees they took under consideration the following accounts which appear as below they are stated, vizt.

Mr. Thomas Fleming Dr.	
To warehouse rent recd. from Tho. Kirkpatrick	0.15.0
To do do Harry Piper	1.0.0
To Ramsay & Fleming	3.0.0
To Robert Adam	1.0.0
To Harry Piper	0.10.0
To Capt. Orney	9.0.0
	£15.5.0

The above sum to be paid to Me*f*rs. Carlyle & Dalton outstanding debts to be collected & paid to the same Gentlemen amounting to £32.6.6. Me*f*rs. Carlyle & Dalton exhibited an account agt. the Town amounting to £52.7.5½ which could not be adjusted for want of a sufficient number of Trustees, also William Ramsay an account of £11.12. under the same circumstances. The Trustees also agreed to meet on Saturday the 31st inst. in order to rent out the Town Warehouses to the highest bidder.

Present December 24th 1768
[Miller Page 72]
William Ramsay Robert Adam
John Carlyle John Muir
John Dalton Harry Piper
  Thomas Fleming

Agreeable to the above entry the following Trusteees, vizt. Wm. Ramsay, John Carlyle, Jno. Dalton, Robt. Adam, John Muir, Harry Piper & Thomas Fleming met & proceeded to rent out the Town Warehouse & at public & open sale did rent out the same warehouse for five years on the following conditions, vizt., Robert Adams for Andrew Wells [Wales], did agree to take the same for five years at thirty five pounds p. annum the trustees are to put the same in such repair

---

[100] Presumably Warwick Price Miller, from Sandy Spring Monthly Meeting, Montgomery Co., Md., married 20 APR 1848 to Mary Moore Stabler [Hinshaw, Vol. VI, p. 766]. He is the presumed copyist of this different transcript with different handwriting and discontinuous pagination as noted above.

Page 65

as W^m. Ramsay, Harry Piper & Thomas Fleming shall on viewing the same think necefsary. The rent to commence from the first day of Jany. last past & those that have any of the Rooms now in pofsefsion to remain till the expiration of the time they took them for at the expiration of the said five years, the house to be returned in good condition & order allowing for all reasonable & natural decays, [Miller Page 73] and that no repairs naturally belonging [to] the house shall be done by him without consulting & with the approbation of the Trustees or such persons as they shall appoint.

The rent to be paid annually to the Trustees or such person as they shall appoint to receive the same.

Jany. 7th 1769	William Ramsay	Robert Adam
	John Carlyle	John Muir
	John Dalton	Harry Piper
		Thomas Fleming

At a meeting of the Trustees it is agreed on & order'd to be entered on record that John Carlyle & William Ramsay be appointed overseers of the Streets in Town for six months & that they be supported in the execution of their office agreeable to the act of afsembly relating to the Town. And that Andrew Wells be allowed to build a shed to the Town warhouse at his own expence & to leave the same at the expiration of his term.

October 19th 1769
John Muir	William Ramsay
Harry Piper	John Carlyle
Thomas Fleming	John Dalton

[Miller Page 74] At a meeting of the Trustees this 30th December 1769 from the large Increase of the flour & grain trade there seems a necefsity to make buildings under the Bank at the Point known by the name of West's Point, and in order to induce those that

Page 66

incline to advance money for building a Warehouse of sixty feet long, & forty feet wide, they are content that the rents for the said warehouse, shall go to discharge the principal & interest, till fully pay'd, and also, that the Interest to be allowed to the said adventurers shall be after the rate of Six p'Cent.

An order was made the 17th day of August 1761, giving a grant of a Lease, for three Lives to Thomas Fleming to build a warehouse forty feet by twenty four on Point Lumley. As Mr. Fleming has not built the said Warehouse and is at present supplied with a water lot, he declines the said Lease & Building.

William Ramsay	Robert Adam
John Carlyle	John Muir
John Dalton	Harry Piper

Thomas Fleming

[Miller Page 75] At a meeting of the Trustees of the 7th day of February 1770

The Marsh lots continuing unimproved it is ordered the Clerk give notice to the owners of the Lots in the said marsh, that that they determine that in case the said owners does not, begin to drain the said marsh in twelve months, that it must be done by the Trustees Agreeable to the act of Afsembly and in case they the said owners will not reimburse the said expence, that they will conform to the Act of Afsembly by a sale of the same.

Mr. John Orr is appointed Clerk for which he is to be allowed Five pounds p. Annum.

In order to fix the bounds of Point West as well as Point Lumley, Application be made to the County Surveyor to meet on some certain day, that the Trustees may attend and have the Bounds properly fixed and when completed, that a plan of the Town laying down the said points with precision, having large

Page 67

freestones fixed at particular places, be recorded in the Clerks office of the County.

[Miller Page 76] As the subscription is completed for building a warehouse on Point West agreeable to an order of the 30th December, Mr. Robert Adam undertakes to carry on said building and keep a regular account of the same to settle with the Trustees when called upon also to receive from the subscribing parties such proportions necefsary for carrying on the said work.

Mr. Jonathan Hall is appointed a Trustee in room of Mr. John Kirkpatrick. Ordered that the Clerk make application to those that stand indebted for rents, for their balances and make report of their answers that on their non-payment suits may be brought for the recovery of the said balances.

    W^m· Ramsay   Robert Adam
    John Carlyle   John Muir
    John Dalton   Thomas Fleming

At a meeting of the majority of the Trustees of the Town of Alexandria this sixteenth day of February 1770.

Ordered that whereas by a former order the Owners of the Lots in the Marsh adjoining the Town in case [Miller Page 77] they did not begin to drain the said Marsh in Twelve Months that is must be done by the Trustees agreeable to the Act of Afsembly &c. & upon revising the former order it is agreed that only three months notice be given to the Respective owners of the sd. Lotts.

Ordered, that Mr. Dalton make application to William Munday or Benjamin Sebastian that the chimney of the House now pofsefsed by sd. Monday is not finished according to law & make Report.

Page 68

Ordered that the several persons who have demands against the Town shall bring their accts. in on Saturday night next that they may be adjusted.

    John Carlyle   John Muir
    John Dalton   Harry Piper
    Robert Adam   Jona. Hall

At a meeting of a majority of the Trustees of the Town of Alexandria this first day of March 1771

The Trustees finding that there are five Lotts in the said Town yet unsold, vizt. No. 30, 123, 124, 125 & 126, it is therefore [Miller Page 78] ordered that advertisements be sett up at all publick places in the said County for the sale of the said Lotts at public vendue for ready money on monday the eighteenth instant.

Ordered that a remonstrance be drawn up to the Worshipful the Court of Fairfax representing the ruinous condition of the County Wharf, it is further ordered that Mr. John Dalton & Mr. Jonathan Hall draw up & present the said Remonstrance.

Ordered that Mr. John Dalton in the name of the Trustees sign an order empowering Jno. Orr to demand the outstanding Debts arising from the rents of the Town Warehouse at Lumley Point &c.

    John Carlyle   Harry Piper
    John Dalton   Thomas Fleming
    Robert Adam   Jona. Hall

At a meeting of the Trustees the 6th day of November 1771

Agreeable to an order of the 1st day of March last the lotts then ordered to be sold were so, as follows:

No. 30	Sold	Alexander Black	£16.3.
No. 123	Sold	John Carlyle	5.
No. 124	Sold	Thomas Carson	8.5.
No. 125	Sold	John Carlyle	11.

Page 69

        No. 126   Sold   John Carlyle . . . . 20.

[Miller Page 79] Conformable to an order directing John Dalton & Jonathan Hall to draw up & present a remonstrance to the worshipful Court of Fairfax representing the ruinous condition of the public wharf, they report that they did do so & the Court gave for answer, they thought that an application should be made to the general aſsembly for the power as we requested.

Ordered that a petition be drawn to be presented to the next aſsembly to empower the Trustees to repair the said wharf and to tax such veſsels as are not taking off Tob^a from the Warehouse and that William Ramsay & John Dalton draw up the same.

Ordered that John Dalton apply to the several debtors for Warehouse rent; and those that will not pay to bring suits for.

    William Ramsay   Harry Piper
    John Carlyle   Thomas Fleming
    John Dalton   Jona. Hall

At a meeting of the Trustees the 29th day of November 1771
[Miller Page 80]   present
    Harry Piper   John Carlyle
    John Muir   William Ramsay
    Tho. Fleming   John Dalton
    Jonathan Hall   Robt Adam

Ordered that those indebted to the Trustees for rent of the warehouse while under direction of Mr Thomas Fleming, that on a second application if they do not pay the same sums due, that suits be brought for the same.

Also that when any rents due the said Town and not paid within one month after the same is due that it be distrained for.

Mr Andrew Wales produced his acc^t against the Warehouse. Mr. Fleming & Mr Jonathan Hall are appointed to examine what work has been done, as the acc^t appears high.

Page 70

Mr Jonathan Hall is appointed Surveyor of the Streets & the roads to the Landings.

Ordered that Wm Ramsay & John Carlyle apply to Wm Munday to put his chimneys in safe order as they are too low & dangerous and in case he does not conform to their orders that they take such steps to enforce it as the laws allow.

Ordered that a meeting of the Trustees is to be on the first Monday in every month at ten o'clock P.M. [Miller Page 81]
    William Ramsay   John Muir

Proceedings of Board of Trustees, Town of Alexandria, 1749-1780

    John Carlyle   Harry Piper
    John Dalton   Thomas Fleming
    Robert Adam   Jona. Hall

At a meeting of the Trustees monday 5th day of Jany 1772. Present
    John Muir   John Carlyle
    Thomas Fleming   William Ramsay
    Jonathan Hall   John Dalton
                            Harry Piper

Mr Fleming & Mr Hall have examined the work done by Andrew Wales at the Warhouse and return for the answer that his acc^t amounting to seven pounds thirteen shillings & five pence is right and has placed it to his credit accordingly.
    Harry Piper   Wm Ramsay
    Thomas Fleming   John Carlyle
    Jona. Hall   John Dalton
                            John Muir

At a meeting of the Trustees the 27th day of November 1772
Present   William Ramsay   Robert Adam
               John Carlyle   Thomas Fleming
               John Muir   Jonathan Hall
               John Dalton

Page 71
[Miller Page 82] Ordered that distress be made upon the effects of Andrew Wales in the Town Warehouse on point Lumley for the arrears of rent due from him for the said warehouse, that Mr Hall, Mr Fleming & Mr Ramsay go with the officer that makes the distress.

Know all men whom it may concern that I, Jonathan Rae, Carpenter & Joiner for & in consideration of the sum of seventeen pounds four shillings current money to me in hand paid, have aliend bargained & sold and by these presents do alien bargain & sell unto Wm Ramsay, Merch^t one Lott No. 34 with a dwelling House thereon with all the appurtenances belong to the said house & lot as nowe the premises are exclusive of the rent to be paid me till November which house & lott and appurtenances I will warrant & defend to be the property of the said William Ramsay his heirs & assigns forever against the claim or claims of any person or persons Whatsoever. Witness my Hand this 25th day of March 1772.
    John West   Jonathan Rae
    Draper L. Wood

Whereas it appears that the above named Jonathan Rae bought & paid for the above named Lott but never had deeds for the same & that he conveyed the said Lott to William Ramsay [Miller Page 83] the day & year above mentioned by a bill of sale of which the above is a copy in order to secure the said William Ramsay more effectually in the said Lott it is ordered that deeds be made to the said Wm Ramsay by John Muir & Harry Piper, Gent^n for the Lott aforesaid.

It is also ordered that no person or persons inhabitants of the Town of Alexandria do on any pretence whatsoever raise or keep any hogs in the said Town unlefs the owner of such hogs keep the same in penns or inclosures so that they do not run at large & injure the inhabitants of the said Town. In the

---

Page 72

act of Afsembly which make & constitute the said Town it is enacted that no inhabitants of the said Town shall raise any Hogs & that any person may kill the same, notwithstanding this many persons in the said Town do raise & keep Hoggs it is ordered that Jonathan Hall & William Ramsay put up in conspicuous places advertisements that after the first day of January if any inhabitant of the said Town keep any Hoggs running at large that every [Miller Page 84] person or persons have a right to destroy the same as empowered by the Act of Afsembly.

    William Ramsay   Robert Adam
    John Carlyle   John Muir
    John Dalton   Thomas Fleming
                  Jona. Hall

At a meeting of the Trustees the 30th day of March 1773
present   Harry Piper   William Ramsay
           Robt. Adam   John Carlyle
           John Muir   John Dalton
           Jona. Hall

Carlyle & Dalton presented their acct. as settled April 4th 1767 with their sundry rents as follows from that time

Dr. The Town Warehouse to Carlyle & Dalton		**Cr.**	
1767		1770	
Apr^l 4 To the sum due as p. formr. acct,	£73.4.10	Feb 10 By Cash from [A] Wales	£ 6.
To Int. on do till Feb. 10 '70)		By Cash from do	13
2 yrs. lo m$^{o.}$ 6 days)	10.9	By do	6
1770			
March 12 To Int. on £73.4.10 1mo.	6.1	Ball due	£25
	84.19.11		59.19.11
1770 to Ballance	59.19.11	1771	84.19.11
March 12 To Int. on do till May 6, 71)		May 6 By cash	20.4
1 yr. 1 mo. 26 days)	3.9.3	Ball^e	43.5.2
	63.9.2		£63.9.2

Page 73
1771

May 6 to balance	43.5.2	By And^y Wales	34.17.8
To in or do till Jany 1, 1773		By Tho. Fleming	20.2.6
1 yer. 9 mo.	3.15.8		
	47.0.10		
Balance	7.19.4		
	£55.0.2	. . . .	£55.-.2

Ordered that advertisements be put up for Letting out to the lowest bidder the extending & carrying a breastwork & filling in the same from the south side of the warehouse wharf at point west so as to include the old wharf, on saturday the 15th day of may next.

Ordered that James Connell be Overseer of the Streets & Landings from King Street Northerly, and that Peter Wise be Overseer from the said Street & Landings Southerly, King Street to be done by both.

    William Ramsay   John Muir
    John Carlyle   Harry Piper
    John Dalton   Jona. Hall
    Robert Adam

July 17, 1773
In Compliance with an order made the 30th day of March 1773 for putting into execution an act of a*f*sembly for joining the public & County wharf together in a breastwork or platform, the The Trustees in compliance with the said order did avertise the same and no undertaker appearing to contract for the same Mr. Ramsay agrees to undertake the finishing & completeing the same in a workmanlike manner in the sum of one hundred & fifty Pounds out of the Town funds, so son as they can be collected for the performance of which the sd. Wm Ramsay will agre to enter into an engagement with Trustees specifing in what manner the sd. work shall be done. In the mean time, Mr. Wales is to be called on for the money that is in hands, the Trustees to meet again on Saturday the 24th inst.

    William Ramsay   John Muir
    John Carlyle   Harry Piper
    John Dalton   Jona. Hall
    Robert Adam

December 2nd 1773
The warehouse at Point Lumley rented to Andrew Wales expires on the first day of Jany. next it will be nece*f*sary to advertise the same it is therefore ordered that advertisements be put up that the same be rented on saturday the 18th inst. to the highest bidder for three years--in the mean time that application be made by Mr. Carlyle & Mr. Ramsey for the balance of rents due as well as to [illegible] [Miller Page 87] the present rents due on the first day of Jany. next and in case of nonpayment that they may levy the same by distre*f*s, and that they also apply to Mr Thomas Kirkpatrick for his ground rent as well as to every one for rent formerly due and to enforce the payment of suits.

    Harry Piper   John Carlyle

Proceedings of Board of Trustees, Town of Alexandria, 1749-1780

    Thomas Fleming   John Dalton
    Jona. Hall   Robert Adam
                         John Muir

Febry. 24, 1774
Rented a certain Lot of Ground on point West to Capt. Richard Conway for the term of sixty three years bounded on the south by Oronoko street & on the East by an alley of twenty feet containing Thirty Six feet square as by a plat & survey at present recorded. The conditions are that the said Richard Conway his heirs & a*f*signs pay annually for the first term or twenty one years thirty six shillings (the first rent payable the first day of Jany. 1775) also for the second term of twenty one years three Pounds twelve shillings p. annum and for the third term of twenty one years, seven pounds four shillings p. annum.

Page 74 [Miller Page 88]

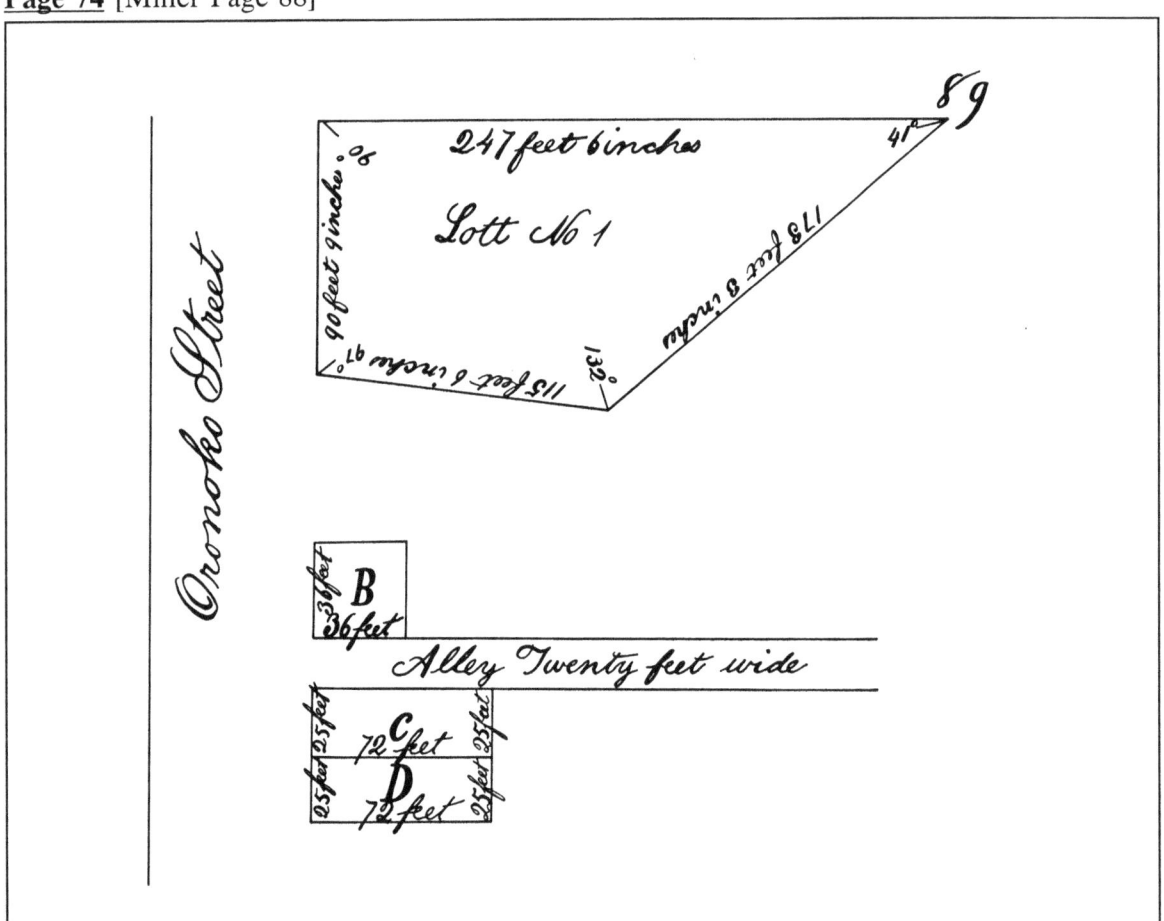

Figure 11 - Plat of Lots Rented to Messrs. Conway, Macrae, Mease and Adam, 24 FEB 1774. Scale by Jonathan Hall of 60 feet in an inch. [This copy not to scale.]

Proceedings of Board of Trustees, Town of Alexandria, 1749-1780

At a meeting of the Trustees this 8th day of March 1774
C a lot on point West 25 feet front on Oronoko Street on the south seventy two feet in depth running northerly and bound on the West by an [Miller Page 89] alley as by a plat dated the 24th of Feby. last, was rented to Robt. Macrae & Robt. Maez [Mease] for Sixty three years from the first day of January next following. The said Robt. Macrae & Robt. Maez to pay for the first term or twenty one years Two pounds sixteen shillings & three pence annually & every year, for the second term of twenty one years five

Page 75

pounds twelve shillings & six pence annually, & for the third or last term of twenty one years Eleven pounds five shillings p. annum.

Also rented D a lot on point west to Robert Adam twenty five feet in front of Oronoko Street on the South running with the line of C Seventy two feet, for Sixty three years the rent to commence from the first day of January next ensuing, the said Robert Adam to pay annually and every year for the first term or twenty one years four pounds seven shillings & six pence, for the second term of twenty one years eight pounds fifteen shillings p. annum and for the third or last term or twenty one years Seventeen pounds ten shillings p. annum, [Miller Page 90] and at the same time it is agreed by the Trustees that no buildings shall be erected on the eastward of the said lott D during the term of sixty three years.

Ordered that Mr. John Muir & Mr. Harry Piper sign the leases of the lots on point west.
    William Ramsay
    John Carlyle
    John Dalton
    Robert Adam
    John Muir
    Thomas Fleming
    Jonathan Hall

At a meeting of the Trustees the twenty ninth day of March one thousand seven hundred & Seventy four the Trustees then present rented to Thomas Fleming twenty five feet of Ground taken from Point Lumley the property of the town of Alexandria but invested in the Trustees for such uses & purposes as the sd. Trustees shall think proper for the benefit of the sd. Town that is to say the said twenty five feet of ground to adjoin to the ground

Page 76

of the sd. Thomas Fleming & to extend from thence Northerly on the following terms for the first twenty one years, six pence per foot ground rents in fronts for [Miller Page 91] the next twenty one years, seven shillings per foot in front & for the next twenty one years fourteen shillings p. foot in front, in the whole sixty three years to himself his heirs & afsigns the same ground to extend to the river Potomack as per lease to be granted to the said Thomas Fleming & agreeable to a plat hereto annexed, the rent to commence from 1st day of Jany. next.

Wm. Ramsay
John Carlyle
John Dalton
Robert Adam
John Muir
Harry Piper
Jonathan Hall

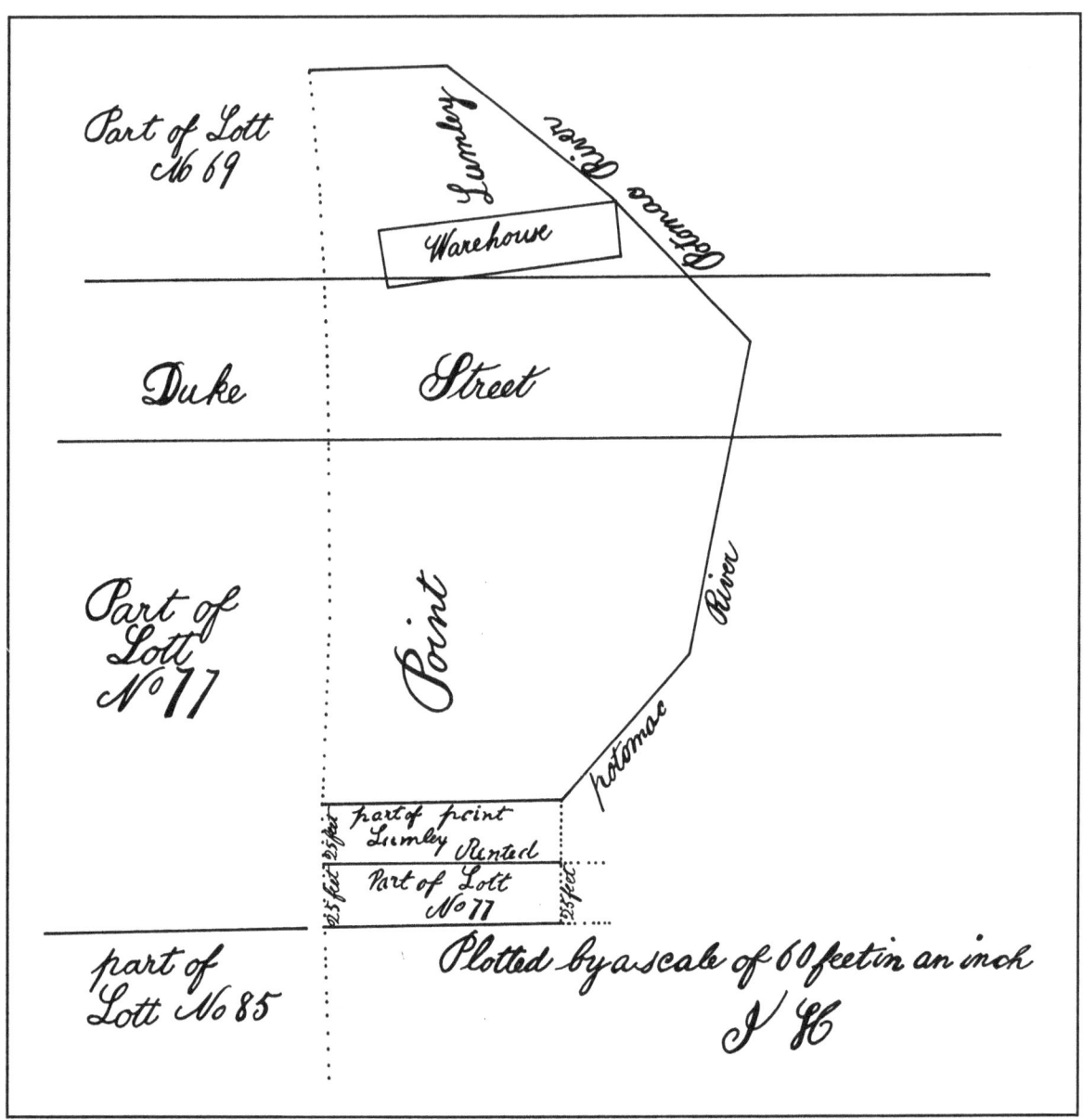

Figure 12 - Plat of Lot Rented to Thomas Fleming, 1774.

Page 77

[Miller Page 93] Rented to William Hartshorn [sic] & Josias Watson the Town Warehouse on Point Lumley on the following terms, vizt to receive the said Warehouse in such order as Andrew Wales the former tenant should put it in conformable to their own agreement the Trustees who are renters of the said house to make the roof tight & to put on weather boards where wanted, also to underpin the said house where wanted to make good & sufficient doors and good lock & hinges where wanted--a pair of steps to be affixed to the West door, the attic story to be secured with props where wanted & necessary a new roof to be put on said house when necessary, but in that case the upper room or the attic story not to be contracted or made less; and the said house during the said term to be kept in tenantable repair, in consideration of which the said William Hartshorn [sic] & Josias Watson are to pay the sum of forty pounds per annum. The said rent to commence from the first day of January last past note that the Trustees agreed to take away the dormer window or door from the north side of the roof & to put in two small windows without glass, but shutters to each, on the [Miller Page 94] south side of the roof no wider than the distance between two rafters the same house by this agreement is to be in their possession ten years unless a subsequent agreement take place--this the Trustees take to be the agreement between them & the parties tho only rented this 29th day of March 1774.

    William Ramsay John Muir
    John Carlyle   Harry Piper
    John Dalton   Thomas Fleming
    Robert Adam   Jonathan Hall

At a meeting of the trustees 22nd day of Jany 1775
The Trustees then present proceeded to make a fixture of the rents or charges that ought to be laid on vessels loading or discharging at Point West. That is to say:

Page 78

every sea vessel to pay 2/, say two shillings for every twenty four hours--
every person landing lumber of any kind if not taken away from the said wharf within forty eight hours to for every thousand staves, one shilling for every day for every thousand shingles Six pence for every day, for every cord wood one shilling for every day oyster shells one shilling per hundred bushels & all other article in proportion, & Mr Thomas Fleming appointed wharf master.

Rented to Thomas Moxley, 36 feet in front on Oronoko street on the west of Capt. Conway's [Miller Page 95] lot distinguished in the plat dated Feby 24, 1774, **B** and 72 feet deep, for sixty three years, paying annually & every year, on the following terms, vizt for the first twenty one years three pounds twelve shillings p. annum--for the second term of twenty one years--seven pounds four shillings p. annum, and for the last term of twenty one years fourteen pounds eight shillings p. annum.

Also rented to the said Thomas Moxley 36 feet square to the North & behind Capt. Conway's lot **B** for which he is to pay For the said term of sixty three years as follows. Two pounds five shillings p. annum for the first term of twenty one years, four pounds ten shillings per annum for the second term of twenty one years, and nine pounds pounds [sic] p. annum for the last term of twenty one years. That the rent for the said lotts commence from the 1st Jany. last past & pay 1st Jany. 1776.

Ordered that John Graham be Surveyor of the streets & landings from King street northerly and that Josia[h] Watson be surveyor from the said street southerly both the said Surveyors to join their hands in repaving King street & that an order be issued for that purpose

Page 79

[Miller Page 96] an indulgence was granted on the 18 of July 1759 to John Carlyle & John Dalton in the infancy of this town that for their cutting down and making a road to the River in Cameron street they had the permission not only to themselves but to their heirs to occupy & hold one haf [sic] of the said street for them to make use of for their own emolument now know ye not only for the present time but for futurity That the said John Carlyle & John Dalton signing at this time with our brother Trustees do disclaim not only for ourselves but for our heirs from henceforth, any right or claim in consequence of the said order.

  Harry Piper John Dalton
  Thomas Fleming Robert Adam
  W^m. Ramsay John Muir
  John Carlyle

At a meeting of the Trustees March the 14th 1778
Present W^m. Ramsay John Muir
    John Carlyle Thomas Fleming
    Robt. Adam

Several Trustees being dead & others removed they proceeded to the choice of two Trustees & made choice of Robert McCrae & Richard Conway, Trustees for the Town of Alexandria, of which notice is to be given them under [Miller Page 97] the hands & seals of the Trustees.

  William Ramsay John Muir
  John Carlyle Thomas Fleming
  Robert Adam

At a meeting of the Trustees the 17 day of September 1778
Present William Ramsay Thomas Fleming
    John Carlyle Robert McCrae
    Robert Adam Richard Conway
    John Muir

Page 80

They agreed to record the following conveyance
"This Indenture Indented & made this seventeenth day of September one Thousand seven hundred & seventy eight witnesseth===
That whereas a peice of sunken ground to eastward of Water street opposite to Lot number fifty one and adjoining to King street on the north side and to Lot fifty six on the south below the

Proceedings of Board of Trustees, Town of Alexandria, 1749-1780

Bank & on the east side of Water street aforesaid unsold and unocupied formerly the property of Philip Alexander of Stafford County but condemed by the Act of Afsembly at the Capitol in Williamsburg in the year one thousand seven hundred & forty eight the money arising from the sale of the lots to be paid to the original proprietors viz.ᵗ Philip Alexander, [Miller Page 98] John Alexander & Hugh West; but the said Philip Alexander being unwilling to abide by the sales of his part of the said Lots agreed with & received from Lawrence Washington[101], Nathaniel Chapman, William Ramsay, John Carlyle & John Dalton to give up all his right title & interest to his part of the said land for the sum of two hundred Pistoles which were paid to him by the Gentlemen aforesaid, who sold & disposed of the said lots in conjunction with the Trustees they the said Washington, Chapman, Ramsay & Carlyle & Dalton receiving the money for their own uses arising from the sale of the said Philip Alexander's part, now as the shore water & other privilidges, opposite to the lands of the said Philip Alexander was invested in him, but by the said sale devolved on the said Washington, Ramsay, Chapman, Carlyle & Dalton, the said William Ramsay & John Carlyle being the only surviveing partners of the Purchase of the said land from Philip Alexander do by these Presents as proprietors of the Said sunken ground or water and also as as [sic] Trustees of the said Town of Alexandria for & in consideration of the sum of one hundred

---

Page 81

pound to them in hand paid by Mefrs. John Fitzgerald & Valentine [Miller Page 99] Peers of Alexandria, Merchants, to give grant alienate & sell to the said Fitzgerald and Peers all their right & interest to the said sunken ground to the sole use & benefit of them the said John Fitzgerald & Valentine Peers & their & such of their heirs for ever. And the said William Ramsay & John Carlyle do hereby warrant & defend the same to be the property of the said Fitzgerald & Peers from theirs heirs forever And do also in as full and ample manner as they can give up their right & title to the said mentioned sunken ground, as purchasers under Philip Alexander aforesaid. In Witnefs whereof they have hereunto put their hands & seals the day & year above written.

Sealed and delivered
In presence of
    Robert Adam
    John Muir
    Thomas Fleming
    Robert Macrea

W.ᵐ Ramsay
John Carlyle
Richard Conway

---

[101] The Library of Virginia, Archives and Records Division, Legislative Petitions, Alexandria, A456, 20 NOV 1778. *Petitioners, under the law of 1748 for the erection of a town at Hunting Creek Warehouse, built in 1775, a warehouse on Philip Alexander's land which became property of the town. They have lately rented parcels of this land to Thomas Fleming, and parcels at Point West to Thomas Moxley, Richard Conway, Robert Mease and Robert Adam for a period of 63 years, with final reversion to town. They have built a warehouse on the south side of Oronoco Street at an expense of £700. Notwithstanding these leases and buildings, Oronoco Street is 66 feet wide, and the county and town wharf gives a clear space of 18,000 square feet. There is a certain piece of sunken ground adjoining land bought by the town for establishment of a town at Hunting Creek, and belonging to Philip Alexander, but purchased from him by Major Lawrence Washington, Nathaniel Chapman, William Ramsay and Messrs. Carlyle & Dalton, for 200 pistoles...* Also see Wesley E. Pippenger, <u>Legislative Petitions of the Town and County of Alexandria, Virginia, 1778-1861</u> (Westminster, Md.: Family Line Publications, 1995), p. 1.

Proceedings of Board of Trustees, Town of Alexandria, 1749-1780

At a meeting of the Trustees the Twenty sixth day of September 1778
       Present
[Miller Page 100]
  William Ramsay Thomas Fleming
  John Carlyle   Robert Macrae
  Robert Adam   Richard Conway
  John Muir

Roger Chew and Jacob Cox are appointed Overseers of the streets & landings in Alexandria.
  Thomas Fleming Wm. Ramsay
  Robert M'Crae   John Carlyle
  Richd. Conway   Robert Adam
         John Muir

Page 82

At a meeting of the Trustees the 8th day of March 1780 in order to settle these accounts.
Present
  William Ramsay John Muir
  John Carlyle   Thomas Fleming
         Robert Macrae
  Robert Adam   Richard Conway

Ordered that an account exhibited by Me*f*rs. Carlyle & Dalton amounting to thirty eight pounds eleven shillings & four pence admitted to record, also an account exhibited by Mr. John Carlyle amounting to eighty six pounds five shillings ordered to be recorded.

Also an account exhibted by William Ramsay ballance one hundred & twenty five pounds three shillings & eight pence, also an account exhibited by Thomas Fleming ballance Twenty five pounds three shillings.

Memorandum That Lott N Cor West point sold to Mr. McCrae & Mease was transferred to Mr. Robt. Adam.
  Wm. Ramsay   Thomas Fleming
  John Carlyle   Robert M'Crae
  Robert Adam   Richd. Conway
  John Muir

Page 83 [Miller Page 101]

The Town of Alexandria in Acc.t with Carlyle & Dalton

Dr.

Date		£ S D	£ S D
1754	To cash p. Jos. Anderson for ditching the streets	7.	
	To Sundry expenses to remove the Court house, viz.t		
	To Cash pd. Cap.t J. Bowman carrying papers to Williams.bg	3.11.6	
	To do to Rich.d Monday fixing a courthouse in town	2. 0	
	To do to Tho.s Smith going with papers to Williams.bg	2. 3.	
	To do for cutting a road	2. 3.	
	To do John Carlyle's expenses to Williams.bg	6.19.	24. 4.6
1759	To do expended on acc.t of the modeling scheme viz.t		
Feb.y 11	To do to Henry Gunnell carrying papers to Winchester	. 9.7½	
14	To do a treat a Summer's 2½ G rum & sugar	.19.1	
	To do rum & sugar at a muster	.12.6	
	To do pd. to Coll. West to watch our Burgefses Mefrs.) Mayson & Johnson)	10.	
	To do to W.m Sewel exprefs to W.msburg.	4.10.	
	To do expenses at Jas. Donaldsons	.15.	
	To do at W.m Adams	1. 1.	
	To do at John Summers	2.10	
	To do at Capt. Douglafses	5.	
	To do by John Baylifs in Prince William	5.	30.17.2½
			£55. 1.8½
1773			
June 25	To Cash pd. John Meales for Mr. Templeman		£7.
			£62. 1.8½

Page 84 [Miller Page 102]

The Town of Alexa. in Acct. with Carlyle & Dalton   **Cr.**

Date		£ S D	£ S D
1773	By Cash from Geo. West	1.12.3	
	By Sum due p. last settlement in this book	7.19.4	
April 13	By Cash of Andrew Wailes	13.18.7	
	By ballance due to Carlyle & Dalton & carryd to acct. with John Carlyle on the other side	38.11.6½	62. 1.8

Errors excepted
p. John Carlyle who
made oath of its being a true copy of an Acct. kept
by Mr. John Dalton, Decd.

Page 85 [Miller Page 103]

Dr.   The Town of Alexandria in Acct. with

Date		£ S D	£ S D
1774	To Carlyle & Dalton balance brot. forward		38.11.6
May 9	To sundry repairs on the long warehouse vizt.		
	To my two Servants 8 days each	5. 8.	
	To 1 m 8d nails & 250 20d	17. 6.	
	To scantling	1.	
12	To 250 & 100 20d nails	4. 2.	
	To cash to Henly & Cate for Plank	1. 8.9	
	To do to Mr. W. Wilson for nailes	17. 6.	
	To 1100 three feet shingles & wagon hire	7.10.	
	To smiths work for locks & hinges	1. 5.	
17	To wagon hire for the steps	3.	
1775		12. 6.	
Feby. 21	To expenses with the Jury vs. Mr. Rd. Arrell 12/6		
	To cash pd. Capt. Elzey Attorney	2.	
	To Clerks notes pd. Francis Adams p. do	15.	
	To a blank Book 29 paper	7. 4.	29. 5.5
	To ballance due the Town in hand of John Carlyle		20. 4.1
			£88. 4.1

Page 86 [Miller Page 104]

	John Carlyle	Dr.	Cr.
Date		£ S D	£ S D
1774	By Cash at twice of Andrew Wailes [sic]	4.18.	
June 10	By Capt. Conway 5 years rents	9.	
	By Thos. Moxley 5 do	29.5.	
	By Mr. Watson & Co. 1775 WR £15	24.18.	
	1776 WR 20	20.	88. 1.
	By Contra Balle £20.4.1		

1780
May 17 Deduct 400 Tobacco p. Mr. W. Payne) 3.6.8
sherriff serving 2 juries vs. Arrell) 16.17.5

Errors Excepted & Sworn to by   £88. 1.
    John Carlyle

Page 87 [Miller Page 105]

The Trustees of Alexandria in Acct. with

1773	To inlarging repairing in the Town &)	
	County wharf at the upper point)	150.
	To an acct. of expenses going to Wmsburg)	
	on acct. of removing the Cthouse &c)	11.12.
		£161.12.
	To ballance due the Town remaining in	
	the hands of Mr. Ramsay	125. 3.10
		£286.15.8

Page 88 [Miller Page 106]

		William Ramsay	**Do.**	**Cr.**
1773		By cash of And[w.] Wailes [sic] in part of the Long Warehouse rent rec[d.] at sundry times	7. 3.6	
1774		By Capt. Rothery Wharfage	1.15.	
1775		By cash of M[r.] Fleming for wharfage	5.18.	
		By Me*f*rs. Watson & Hartshorne	35. 2.	
1777				
Mar. 31		By Andrew Wailes bbl[s.] long warehouse	24.18.1	
		By Thos. Fleming 6 Yr. Ground rent	3.15.	
		By Rob[t.] Adam 5 yr. Ground rent	35.18.9	
Jan[y.] 1		By Rob[t.] T. Hooe to the 20th May 1776	12. 4.6	
1778				
Jan[y.] 1	By Do	1 yr.	20.	
1779				
Jan[y.] 1	By Do		20.	
1780				
	By Do		20.	186.15.8
	By Me*f*rs. Fitzgerald & Pears, a Water Lot			100.
	Errors excepted & sworn to by M[r.] Ramsay			£286.15.8

Page 89 [Miller Page 107]

The Trustees of Alexandria in Acc.t for Wharf

Date		£ S D	£ S D
	To Cash for filling up the wharf	.15.	
	To Cash pd. Mr. William Ramsay he accounts for	5.18.	6.13.
	Ballance due in the hands of Mr. Fleming who swore to this account		25. 3.
			31.16.

The Trustees of Alexandria in acct. for wharfage with

To commifsion on collecting £89.5 a 5 p. cent	4. 9.3	
To copying the records of the town of Alexandria	50.	
Ballance due from James Adam	34.15.9	
	89. 5.0	

Page 90 [Miller Page 108]
age with Thomas Fleming   **Do.**   **Cr.**
date

1775 Jan y. 22	By Cash from	Capt. Lightburn	--.16.--	
Mar. 6	By ditto	Capt. Baker	3. 6.	
7	By ditto	Capt. Snowball	1.16.	
April 7	By ditto	Capt. Roberdeau	14	
15	By Do	Capt. Sanford	8	
27	By Do	Capt. Mathers	8	
June 10	By Do	Capt. Harper	10	
July 15	By Do	Capt. Stayman	1. 6.	
do 15	By Do	Capt. Conway	14	
Do	By Do	Capt. Rothery	10	
Aug. 27	By Do	Capt. Conway	2. 4.	
Nov. 20	By Do	Capt. Conway	2	
1778				
April	By Do	Capt. Conway	8.16.	
Sept. 16	By Do	Robt. Adam & Co.	1.16.	
Oct. 7	By Do	Edward Owens	3. 6.	
	By Do	Benj. Stolman	5. 6.	£31.16.

James Adam   **Cr.**

1778 Decr. 22 By Cash from Capt. Richard Conway	3. 0.0	
1779		
March 1 By William Hunter for 60 days wharfage	9. 0.0	
May 1 By Cash from Capt. Richard Conway	3. 6.0	
25 By Cash from James Muir Wharfage for Capt. Montgomery	1.19.0	
Oct. 1 By Cash from Capt. Richard Conway for wharfage	3. 0.0	
16 By Cash from Mr. Watson 76 days wharfage of the ship Jane	22.16.0	
By William Hunter for wharfage for the ship Jane	46. 4.0	89. 5.0

       Errors excepted & sworn to by James Adam

Page 91 [Miller Page 91]

At a Court held for the County of Fairfax, 20 May 1793.

Dennis Ramsay, Mayor of the Town of Alexandria, presented in Court this book, containing the several Entrys & proceedings of the Trustees of the said Town and the said entrys & proceedings, having been severally, signed by the respective Trustees from time to time appointed for said Town and the said Dennis Ramsay & Robert Mease being sworn to declare the truth respecting their knowledge of the said Trustees book, depose & say, that they are well acquainted with the handwriting of several of the said Trustees, and particularly the handwriting of William Ramsay, John Carlyle, John Dalton, Harry Piper, John Muir, Robert M'Crae, Thomas Fleming, and Richard Conway, and that the signatures of the same to the said Entrys & proceedings are in the true handwriting of the said Trustees, And it appearing to the satisfaction of the Court that the said book, is the same book, that was kept by the Trustees of the said Town, is on the motion ordered to be recorded=

      Test P. Wagener

APPENDIX

LAWS OF VIRGINIA
OCTOBER 1779 - 4TH OF COMMONWEALTH

CHAP. XXV

An act for incorporating the town of Alexandria in the county of Fairfax, and the town of Winchester in the county of Frederick.[102]

Towns of Alexandria and Winchester incorporated.

FOR incorporating the town of Alexandria in the county of Fairfax, *Be it enacted*, That it shall be lawful for the freeholders and house-keepers who shall have been resident in the said town three months next preceding such election, to meet at some convenient place in the said town yearly, on the second Tuesday in February, and then and there to nominate, elect, and choose by ballot, twelve fit and able men, being freeholders and inhabitants of the said town, to serve as

Officers, how elected.

mayor, recorder, aldermen and common councilmen for the same; the persons to elected shall within one week after their election, proceed to choose out of their own body, by ballot, one mayor, one recorder, and four aldermen, and the remaining six shall be common councilmen, whose authority shall continue one year, and until others are chosen and qualified in their stead, and no longer, except such of them as shall be re-elected. That the mayor, recorder, aldermen, and common councilmen so elected, and those thereafter to be elected, and their successors shall, and are hereby made a body corporate and politick by the name

Style of corporation of Alexandria.

of mayor and commonalty of the town of Alexandria, and by the said name to have perpetual succession with capacity to purchase, receive, and possess lands and tenements, and all goods and chattels, either in fee or any lesser estate therein, and the same to give, grant, let, sell or assign; and to plead and be impleaded, prosecute and defend all causes, complaints, actions, real, personal or mixt; and to have one common seal and perpetual succession: That the person who shall be elected the first mayor of the said town, shall, within one week after his election, take an oath or make solemn affirmation before some one

Mayor, recorder, &c. how qualified.

justice of the quorum in the commission of the peace for the said county of Fairfax, for one due and faithful execution of his office; and every succeeding mayor shall be qualified to his office before the mayor for the time being. Every recorder, alderman, and common councilman, before he shall be admitted to execute his respective office, shall take an oath or make solemn affirmation

How long mayor eligible.

before the mayor for the time being for the due and faithful execution of his office. No person shall hold or execute the office of mayor within the said town for more than one year, within any two years.

Judicial and ministerial powers of mayor, recorder and

The mayor, recorder, and aldermen for the time being and their successors for ever, are hereby declared and constituted justices of the peace within the said town, and to have power to appoint constables, surveyors of the streets and highways, and to hold a court of hustings once in every month, within the said town; and to appoint clerks, a serjeant and other proper officers, from time to

---

[102] <u>Hening</u>, Vol. X, pp. 172-76.

aldermen.

Powers of serjeant.

time, where there shall be occasion. The said serjeant shall have the same powers in serving process, levying executions, and making distress on delinquents in civil and criminal prosecutions within the limits of the said town, as the sheriff of the said county is by law invested with, and to settle and allow reasonable fees, not exceeding the fees allowed in the county courts: That they, or any four or more of them (whereof the mayor or recorder for the time being shall be one) shall have jurisdiction, and on the second Thursday in every month hold pleas of actions, personal and mixt, arising within the said town; so as the demand in such action, personal or mixt, does not exceed ten pounds current money, or one thousand pounds of tobacco; may adjourn from day to day, and as a court of record give judgment and award execution thereon, according to law. Also that the mayor, recorder, and aldermen of the said town, shall have, use, and exercise all the powers, jurisdictions, and authorities out of court touching or concerning any crime or offence which any justice or justices of the peace of a county now have, or can or may use and exercise, and in the same manner to summon a court of justices of the county for the examination and trial of any criminal; and that as well in civil as criminal cases the authority and jurisdiction of the mayor, recorder, and aldermen of the said town, shall extend half a mile without and around the limits of the said town.

Limitation of jurisdiction.

Provided always, and be it farther enacted, That it shall not be lawful for the said court of hustings to take cognizance of, or hold plea in any action, personal or mixt, except the debt was contracted or cause of action originated within the said town or limits aforesaid. The mayor, recorder, aldermen, and common councilmen shall have power to erect and repair work houses, houses of correction, and prisons, or other publick buildings for the benefit of the said town; and to make bye laws and ordinances for the regulation and good government of the said town: Provided such bye laws or ordinances shall not be repugnant to, or inconsistent with, the laws and constitution of this commonwealth; and to assess the inhabitants for the charge of repairing the streets and highways, to be observed and performed by all manner of persons residing with in the same, under reasonable penalties and forfeitures, to be levied by distress and sale of the goods of the offenders, for the publick benefit of the said town; with power to hold and keep within the said town annually two

Market days.

market days in every week of the year, the one on Wednesday and the other on Saturday, and from time to time to appoint a clerk of the market, who shall have assize of bread, wine, beer, wood, and other things, and generally to do and perform all things belonging to the office of the Clerk of the market within the said town.

Officers, how removable for misconduct.

In case of misconduct in office of mayor, recorder, aldermen, or common councilmen, or either of them, the others shall have power to remove him, or any of them: Provided, that such person or persons shall not be removed unless seven of the aldermen and common councilmen concur therein.

Vacancies, how supplied.

In case of vacancy in the office of mayor or recorder within one year, the eldest alderman shall succeed thereto. Vacancies in the office of alderman within the year shall be supplied from the common councilmen in regular succession of seniority as they were chosen by the inhabitants of the said town; and the vacancies in the office of common councilmen within the year shall be supplied from the body of the freeholders within the corporation, by ballot of the mayor, recorder, aldermen, and common councilmen.

<table>
<tr><td>Penalty for refusing to execute office, to which elected.</td><td>Every person elected to the office of mayor, recorder, alderman, or common councilman, and having notice of such election, refusing to undertake and execute the same, it shall be lawful for the mayor, recorder, aldermen, and common councilmen for the time being, seven of them concurring therein, to impose such fines upon the person or persons refusing, as they in their discretion may think proper, so that the mayor's fine shall not exceed forty pounds, recorder's thirty pounds, alderman's thirty pounds, and common councilman's twenty pounds; and to award execution for such fines, to be applied to the use of the corporation; and others shall be elected in the room of those so refusing, in manner directed by this act for supplying vacancies in those offices. That the</td></tr>
<tr><td>Common council, how summoned.</td><td>mayor, recorder, and two of the aldermen for the time being, shall have power, so often as they find occasion, to summon a common council of the said town, and that no assembly or meeting of the inhabitants shall be deemed a common council, unless the mayor, recorder, and at least two aldermen and four common councilmen be present. No law, order, or regulation shall be binding and valid, nor shall the same be revoked or altered, or fine imposed for a breach thereof, unless seven of the aldermen and common council men assembled, concur</td></tr>
<tr><td>Property heretofore vested in trustees of Alexandria, transferred to corporation.</td><td>therein. *And be it farther enacted*, That all the property, real and personal, now held by, and vested in, the trustees of the said town of Alexandria, for the use and benefit of the inhabitants thereof shall be, and the same is hereby transferred and vested in the corporation for the publick benefit of the said town. In all courts of law and equity this act shall be construed and taken most beneficially and favourably for the said corporation.</td></tr>
</table>

And be it farther enacted, That the town of Winchester in the county of Frederick shall be, and the same is hereby declared to be made corporate in the same manner, to all intents and purposes, as the said town of Alexandria; and that the freeholders and house-keepers thereof shall be entitled to the same privileges and in like manner, and under the like conditions and limitations; shall have the power of electing twelve able and fit men, to serve as mayor, recorder, aldermen, and common councilmen for the same. The mayor of the town of Winchester first elected shall, before some justice of the quorum in the commission of the peace for the county of Frederick, take the oath of office. The Mayor, recorder, and aldermen shall have the same jurisdiction in civil and criminal cases; and shall, on the second Thursday in every month, hold pleas of actions arising within the said town of Winchester, and the limits herein after mentioned, in like manner as the mayor, recorder, and aldermen, and common councilmen of the town of Alexandria. The mayor, recorder, aldermen, and common councilmen of the town of Winchester, by the name of mayor and commonalty of the town of Winchester, shall in every instance have the same powers, rights, and privileges, and be subject to the same penalties, limitations, and manner of proceedings as the mayor, recorder, alderman, and common councilmen of the said town of Alexandria; and their jurisdiction shall extend to and over the out-lots belonging to the said town of Winchester.

[Marginal notes for second paragraph: "Town of Winchester incorporated, in the same manner as Alexandria."; "Style of corporation."; "Jurisdiction."]

CHRONOLOGY

1742 Fairfax County (Truro Parish) is established from part of Prince William County.[104]

1749 Established at Hunting Creek warehouse on the Potomac River in Fairfax County, a town called Alexandria, on 60 acres of land.[105]

1752 The Fairfax County courthouse and prison are removed from Spring Field (near Tyson's Corner) to the Town of Alexandria.[106] First session of the court in new location convened on 3 MAY 1752, situated on the north side of Market Square, nearly opposite Carlyle House.[107]

1757 Loudoun County formed from Fairfax County.[108]

1762 Boundaries of the Town of Alexandria are extended westward.[109]

1772 Further settlement of the Town of Alexandria is encouraged; marsh lots are ordered drained at the owners expense.[110]

1779 Town of Alexandria incorporated; the mayor, recorder and aldermen are constituted justices of the peace and are to hold a Court of Hustings once in every month.[111]

1779 Certain sales and leases by the Trustees confirmed; boundaries of the town enlarged with certain lots laid off by John Alexander; extension of time to build upon lots.[112]

1782 The Court of Hustings at Alexandria is declared a court of record, and as such is to receive probate of wills and deeds, and grant administrations, provided the testator or intestate resided in the Town of Alexandria at death.[113] In 1783, Hustings Court's power was expanded to include all actions within its jurisdiction not exceeding twenty pounds in money or two thousand pounds of crop tobacco. Water and Union streets are extended.[114]

1785 Citizens of Alexandria petition the General Assembly to drain the marsh adjoining the town and that certain lands of Charles Alexander be condemned for use of public buildings.[115]

1785 An act for regulating the streets in and adjoining the town of Alexandria.[116]

1786 Boundaries of the town extended to include newly improved lots.[117]

---

[104] Hening, Vol. V, p. 207, "An Act, for dividing the county of Prince William."

[105] Ibid., Vol. VI, p. 214; Chap. 84, "An act for erecting a town at Hunting-Creek warehouse, in the county of Fairfax;" Winfree, pp. 443-6, 462.

[106] Harrison, Fairfax, Landmarks of Old Prince William, A Study of Origins in Northern Virginia (Richmond: Old Dominion Press, 1924; reprint ed., Baltimore: Gateway Press, Inc., 1987), p. 321.

[107] Virginia Gazette, 30 APR 1752; FDB D:360; TM:19.

[108] Hening, Vol. VII, p. 148, "An Act for dividing the County of Fairfax."

[109] Ibid., Vol. VII, pp. 604-7, "An Act for enlarging the town of Alexandria, in the county of Fairfax."

[110] Ibid., Vol. VIII, pp. 613-15, "An act to encourage the further settlement of the town of Alexandria, in the county of Fairfax."

[111] Ibid., Vol. X, pp. 172-6, "An act for incorporating the town of Alexandria in the county of Fairfax, and the town of Winchester in the county of Frederick."

[112] Ibid., Vol. X, pp. 192-93, "An act to confirm certain sales and leases made by the trustees of the town of Alexandria, and to enlarge the said town."

[113] Ibid., Vol. XI, pp. 156-58, "An act for giving certain powers to the corporation of the city of Richmond, and for other purposes."

[114] Ibid., Vol. XI, p. 44, "An act to empower the mayor, recorder, aldermen and common council of the town of Alexandria to lay a wharfage tax, and to extend Water and Union-streets."

[115] Virginia Journal and Alexandria Advertiser, 27 JAN 1785.

[116] Hening, Vol. XII, p. 205; Virginia Journal and Alexandria Advertiser, 18 AUG 1785.

[117] Hening, Vol. XII, p. 362, "An act to extend the limits of the town of Alexandria."

1789 Virginia legislature adopted an act offering to cede ten miles square, or any lesser quantity of territory within the state, to the United States for the permanent seat of the general government.[118]

1789 Paving of some of the most frequented streets.[119]

1789 Legislation for moving the Fairfax County courthouse outside the city limits of Alexandria and more near the center of Fairfax County, at "Ravensworth," on the lands of William Fitzhugh, or within 1 mile of the Cross Roads, at Price's Ordinary, to secure 2 acres for a new site.[120]

1790 By November the facility was unfit to transact business, the court takes up temporary quarters over the market on the courthouse lot at Market Square.

1791 Boundaries of the District of Columbia to include a portion of Fairfax County and the City of Alexandria.[121] Corner stone set at Jones Point, near Alexandria, on April 15, 1791.

1794 Court of Hustings in Alexandria to be held on the Friday after the third Monday in every month.[122]

1796 Boundaries of Alexandria extended from parts of Fairfax County: on the north to Montgomery Street, south to the line of the District of Columbia.[123] The time for holding court is changed to the first Monday in every month.[124]

1796 Paving of streets, and concern for stagnant water and other nuisances.[125]

1797 Jurisdiction of the mayor and commonalty extended to paving of streets and to vessels lying at any wharf; rope walk within the town limits to be discontinued.[126]

1798 Part of Loudoun County added to Fairfax County, and a place for holding courts in Fairfax to be fixed by April or May.[127] Tithable persons within the town of Alexandria are exempted from payment of that part of the levy of the county of Fairfax towards costs of building a new courthouse for use of the said county.[128] Richard Ratcliffe donates 4 acres for a new courthouse complex, deed not recorded until 1799.

1800 Seat of the District Court over Prince William, Fairfax, Loudoun and Fauquier counties to be set at the town of Dumfries.[129]

---

[118] Ibid., Vol. XIII, pp. 43-4, "An act for the cession of ten miles square, or any lesser quantity of territory within this state, to the United States, in Congress assembled, for the permanent seat of the general government," passed 3 DEC 1789.

[119] Ibid., Vol. XIII, p. 94, "An act to authorise the raising of a sum of money by lottery, for the use of the town of Alexandria," passed 9 DEC 1789; Virginia Journal and Alexandria Advertiser, 23 SEP 1790.

[120] Ibid., Vol. XIII, p. 79, "An act for altering the place of holding courts in the county of Fairfax," passed 4 DEC 1789.

[121] Richardson, James Daniel, ed., A Compilation of the Messages and Papers of the Presidents, 1789-1897 (Washington: Government Printing Office, 1896-1899), Vol. I, pp. 100-2.

[122] Shepherd, Samuel, comp. The Statutes at Large of Virginia, From October Session 1792, to December Session 1806, Inclusive, In Three Volumes (New Series), Being a Continuation of Hening (Richmond: S. Shepherd, 1835-36; reprint edition New York: AMS Press, Inc., 1970), Vol. 1, p. 310.

[123] Ibid., Vol. II, pp. 40-1, "Acts of the Session of November 1796."

[124] Ibid., Vol. II, p. 37.

[125] Ibid., Vol. II, p. 40, "An ACT concerning the town of Alexandria," passed 16 DEC 1796.

[126] Shepherd, Vol. II, pp. 122-3, Laws of Virginia, December 1797, Chap. 60, "An ACT extending the jurisdiction of the mayor and commonalty of the town of Alexandria, and for other purposes," passed 8 JAN 1798.

[127] Ibid., Vol. II, p. 107.

[128] Ibid., Vol. II, p. 191, Laws of Virginia, December 1798, Chap. 85, "An ACT to exempt the tithables in the town of Alexandria, from a certain part of the county levy," passed 31 DEC 1798.

[129] Ibid., Vol. II, p. 432, Laws of Virginia, December 1802, Chap. 37, "An ACT to amend "An act appointing commissioners to fix the place for holding a court for the district composed of the counties of Prince William, Fairfax, Loudon [sic] and Fauquier," passed 14 JAN 1803.

1800 In April, Fairfax County convenes its first session in the new location in the Town of Providence (now City of Fairfax). Act passed for laying off the Town of Alexandria into wards.[130]

---

[130] Caton, James Randall, comp. Legislative Chronicles of the City of Alexandria (Alexandria: Newell-Cole Company, Inc., 1933), p. 43.

An Act
for Erecting a Town at Hunting
Creek Warehouse in the County of Fairfax[131]

Whereas it has been represented to this present General Assembly That a Town at Hunting Creek Warehouse on Potomack River would be Commodious for Trade and Navigation and tend greatly to the Ease and Advantage of the Frontier Inhabitants,

Be it therefore Enacted by the Governor, Council, and Burgesses of this present General Assembly, and it is hereby enacted by the Authority of the same, That within four Months after the passing of this Act Sixty Acres of Land, parcel of the Lands of Philip Alexander, John Alexander, and Hugh West, situate, lying, and being on the South side of Potomack River above the Mouth of Great Hunting Creek and in the County of Fairfax, shall be surveied and laid out by the Surveyor of the said County, beginning at the Mouth of the first Branch above the Warehouses, and extend down the Meanders of the said River Potomack to a Point called Middle Point, and thence down the said River Ten poles, and from thence by a Line parallel to the dividing line between John Alexander's Land and Philip Alexander, and back into the Woods for the Quantity aforesaid, And the said [Sixty] Acres of Land, so to be surveyed and laid out, shall be and is hereby vested in the Right honourable Thomas Lord Fairfax, The honourable William Fairfax, Esquire, George Fairfax, Richard Osborne, Lawrence Washington, William Ramsey [sic], John Carlyle, John Pagan, Gerrard Alexander, and Hugh West of the said County of Fairfax, Gentlemen, and Philip Alexander of the County of Stafford, Gentleman, and their Successors in Trust for the several purposes herein after mentioned, And the said Thomas Lord Fairfax, William Fairfax, George Fairfax, Richard Osborne, Lawrence Washington, William Ramsey, John Carlyle, John Pagan, Gerrard Alexander, Hugh West, and Philip Alexander are hereby constituted and appointed Directors and Trustees for designing, building, carrying on, and maintaining the said Town upon the Land aforesaid, And the said Trustees and Directors, or any six of them, shall have power to meet as often as they shall think necessary, and shall lay out the said sixty Acres into Lots and Streets, not exceeding half an Acre of Ground in each Lot, and also to set apart such Portions of the said Land for a Market Place and Public Landing as to them shall seem convenient, and when the said Town shall be so laid out, the said Directors and Trustees shall have full Power and Authority to sell all the said Lots by Public Sale or Auction, from Time to Time, to the highest Bidder, so as no Person shall have more than two Lots, And when any such Lots shall be sold, any two of the said Trustees shall and may upon payment of the purchase Money, by some sufficient Conveience or Conveiences, Convey the Fee Simple Estate of such Lot or Lots to the Purchaser or Purchasers, And he or they, or his or their Heirs or Assigns respectively, shall and may forever thereafter peaceably and quietly have, hold, possess, and enjoy the same, freed and discharged from all Right, Title,

---

[131] Winfree, pp. 443-446, 462-463, including following note: *(Hunting Creek) C.O.5/1395, ff. 74-75. Cited by title in 6 Hening, 214. Signed May 11, 1749; see C.J. II, 1056 and J.H.B. (1742-1748), 405. Manuscript notes on 75 ro. indicate that the act was read the third time and passed by the House of Burgesses and Council on April 22 and May 2, 1749, respectively. Signed by Nathaniel Walthoe, Clerk of the General Assembly, William Randolph, Clerk of the House of Burgesses, John Robinson, Speaker of the House of Burgesses and William Gooch, Governor of the Colony. Attested by William Randolph, Clerk of the House of Burgesses. Endorsements on 74 vo. indicate that the act was Number 26; that it was passed May 11, 1749, and that it was "received" on March 19, 1750, with President of Council Lee's letter of November 6, 1749. Additional endorsements note that it was sent to Mr. Lamb on May 21, 1750; and that it was returned February 8, 1751, with no objection. There is also an annotation indicating that the great seal of Virginia was removed by "S.G."*

Claim, Interest, and Demand whatsoever of the said Philip Alexander, John Alexander, and Hugh West, and the Heirs and Assigns of them respectively, and all persons whatsoever claiming by, from, or under them, or either of them.

Provided nevertheless That the said Trustees and Directors, after deducting sufficient [money] to reimburse the Charge and Expence of surveying and laying out the said Lots, shall pay, or cause to be paid, to the said Philip Alexander, John Alexander, and Hugh West, all the Money arising by the Sale of the said Lots according to their respective Rights therein.

And Be it further Enacted by the Authority aforesaid That the Grantee or Grantees of every such Lot or Lots to be sold or Conveyed in the said Town shall, within two years next after the Date of the Conveiance for the same, erect, build, and finish on each Lot so conveied one House of Brick, Stone, or of Wood, well framed, of the Dementions of twenty feet Square and nine feet Pitch at the least or proportionably thereto if such Grantee shall have two Lots contiguous, with a Brick or Stone Chimney, And the said Directors shall have full power and Authority to establish such Rules and Orders for the more regular placing the said Houses as to them shall seem meet, And if the Owner of any such lot shall fail to pursue and Comply with the Directions herein prescribed for the building and finishing one or more House of Houses thereon, then such Lots upon which such Houses shall not be so built and finished shall be revested in the said Trustees, and shall and may be sold and conveied to any other Person or Persons whatsoever in the Manner before directed, and shall revest and be again sold as often as the Owner or Owners shall fail to perform, obey, and fulfil the Directions aforesaid, And the Money arising from the Sale of such Lots as shall be revested and sold as aforesaid shall be by the said Trustees, from Time to Time, applied to such Public Use for the Common Benefit of the Inhabitants of the said Town as to them shall seem most proper, And if the said Inhabitants of the said Town shall fail to obey and pursue the Rules and Orders of the said Directors in repairing and amending the Streets, Landings, and Public Wharfs, they shall be liable to the same penalties as are inflicted for not repairing the Highways in this Colony.

And for continuing the Succession of the said Trustees and Directors until the Governor of this Colony shall incorporate some other Persons, by Letters Patent under the Great Seal of this Colony, to be one Body, Politic and Corporate, to whom the Government of the said Town shall be committed,

Be it further Enacted that in Case of the Death of the said Directors or of their refusal to Act, the Surviving or other Directors, or the major part of them, shall Assemble and are hereby impowered from Time to Time, by Instrument in Writing under their respective Hands and Seals, to nominate some other Person or Persons being an Inhabitant or Freeholder of the said Town in the place of him so dying or refusing, which new Director or Directors so nominated and appointed shall from thence forth have the like power and Authority in all things relating to the Matters herein contained as if he or they had been expressly named and appointed in and by this Act, and every such Instrument and nomination shall from time to time be recorded in the Books of the said Directors.

And Be it further Enacted by the Authority aforesaid That the said Town shall be called by the Name of Alexandria.

And Be it further Enacted by the Authority aforesaid that it shall not be lawful for any Person whatsoever to erect or build, or cause to be erected or built, in the said town any wooden Chimney, And if any wooden Chimney shall be so built contrary to this Act it shall and may be lawful for the Sherif of the said County of Fairfax, and he is hereby required from time to time to cause all such Wooden Chimneys to be pulled down and demolished.

And Be it further Enacted by the Authority aforesaid That no Person whatsoever residing within the said Town shall keep any Swine running at large within the Bounds thereof, but that it shall and may be lawful for any Person whatsoever to kill or destroy the same and immediately give Notice to the Owner or Owners thereof.

Provided always that nothing in this Act shall be construed to prohibit Persons driving Hogs for Sale in or through the said Town or to prohibit Persons residing near the said Town from letting their Hogs run at large.

INDEX

Surname Unknown
- Harry 67
- Jack 78
- Matt 78

A

Acts of the General Assembly: ... 3, 133, 148, 149, 154, 161, 162, 166, 173, 183, 193

ADAM
- Ann/Anne 10, 22, 26, 95, 108
- Catherine 30
- Elizabeth 49, 95
- James .. 8, 22, 49, 95, 109, 150, 179, 180
- Jane 5, 10, 22, 95
- John 5, 10, 22
- Mary 10, 22
- Robert ... 5, 9, 10, 15, 16, 22, 25, 26, 42, 43, 45-47, 76, 91, 95, 96, 108, 137-141, 145, 147-155, 158-174, 178, 180
- W. 159

ADAMS
- Francis 176
- Samuel 72
- William 72, 175

ADDISON
- Anthony 113

ALEXANDER
- Catharine 20
- Charles 186
- Frances 16
- Garrard/Gerard/Gerrard .. 3, 5, 16, 20, 21, 29, 35, 120-125, 127, 128, 134, 136-140, 142, 145, 189
- John 1, 3, 16, 35, 78, 89, 91, 99-116, 120-122, 124, 125, 126, 137, 142, 145, 146, 149, 150, 173, 186, 189
- Lucy ... 99, 102, 107, 108, 111, 113, 114
- Mariamne 88
- Mary 20
- Philip .. 3, 20, 76, 88, 126, 132, 137, 143, 144, 146, 149, 173, 189
- Robert 88
- Susanna 35
- William 101, 102, 108
- William T. 99, 102, 106-114, 116

Alexandria Lots: 1, 3, 151, 189
- 1 .... 4, 120, 122, 125, 142, 145
- 2 .... 4, 120, 122, 125, 142, 145
- 3 ..... 5, 121, 122, 125, 142, 143, 145
- 4 .... 5, 121, 123, 125, 142, 145
- 5 .... 5, 6, 132, 142, 145
- 6 .... 145, 150
- 7 .... 6, 145
- 8 .... 6, 8, 132, 142, 145
- 9 .... 6, 132, 142, 145
- 10 .... 7, 132, 142
- 11 .... 7, 142, 145, 150
- 12 .... 7, 142, 145, 150
- 13 .... 7, 142, 145, 150
- 14 .... 6, 7, 127, 142, 145
- 15 .... 7, 8, 132, 142, 145
- 16 .... 8, 132, 142, 145
- 17 .... 9, 139, 142, 145
- 18 .... 9, 142, 145, 150
- 19 .... 9, 142, 145, 150
- 20 ... 9, 15, 120, 133, 142, 145, 154, 159
- 21 .... 9, 120, 133, 142, 145
- 22 .... 13, 132, 142, 145
- 23 .... 14, 127, 142, 145
- 24 .... 14, 121, 142, 145
- 25 .... 14, 142, 145, 150
- 26 ... 15, 120, 125, 142, 145, 154, 159
- 27 .... 16, 120, 122, 125, 142, 145
- 28 .... 16, 17, 127, 142, 144, 145
- 29 .... 16, 17, 127, 142, 144, 145
- 30 .... 20, 142, 145, 163
- 31 ..... 20, 21, 120, 122, 125, 142, 145
- 32 ..... 20, 21, 120, 122, 125, 142, 145
- 33 ..... 21, 22, 121, 123-125, 142, 145
- 34 .... 23, 127, 142, 143, 145, 165
- 35 .... 24, 92, 132, 142, 143, 145
- 36 .... 24, 120, 122, 125, 142, 143, 146
- 37 .. 24, 25, 120, 122, 125, 142, 143, 146
- 38 .... 25, 121, 122, 125, 142, 143, 146
- 39 .. 25, 27, 121, 122, 125, 142, 143, 146
- 40 ... 23, 28, 91, 121, 122, 125, 143, 146
- 41 .... 29, 120, 122, 143, 146
- 42 .... 29, 120, 122, 143, 146
- 43 .... 29, 131, 146
- 44 .... 29, 131, 146
- 45 .... 29, 36, 121, 122, 146
- 46 .... 23, 31, 32, 120, 122, 146

47	23, 31, 33, 120, 122, 146	100	81, 149
48	34, 121, 122, 143, 146	101	81, 149
49	35, 121, 122, 125, 146	102	81, 149
50	30, 35, 90, 121, 133, 143, 146	103	82, 149
51	36, 120, 122, 143, 146, 172	104	82, 149
52	36, 38, 120, 122, 143, 146	105	82, 149
53	39, 121, 143, 146	106	82, 149
54	40, 121, 133, 143, 146	107	82, 149
55	40, 41, 88, 121, 143, 146	108	82, 149
56	42, 45, 47, 120, 143, 146, 154, 172	109	84, 149
57	42, 45, 47, 120, 143, 146, 154	110	84, 149
58	42, 45, 47, 122, 143, 146, 154	111	86, 149
59	49, 121, 143, 146	112	87, 89, 149
60	50, 121, 124, 133, 140, 146, 148	113	88, 149
61	50, 133, 146	114	89, 149
62	52, 54, 120, 124, 143, 146	115	36, 89, 149
63	52, 54, 120, 124, 143, 146	116	90, 150
64	55, 56, 122, 133, 143, 146	117	91, 150
65	55, 56, 122, 133, 143, 146	118	91, 150
66	58, 59, 122, 143, 146	119	91, 150
67	58, 59, 122, 123, 133, 143, 146	120	91, 150
68	60, 65, 122, 123, 142, 146	121	24, 92, 150
69	60, 120, 143, 146, 152, 153	122	92, 150
70	60, 61, 120, 143, 146	123	92, 150, 163
71	61, 121, 143, 146	124	93, 150, 163
72	55, 63, 64, 122, 134, 135, 146	125	93, 150, 163
73	63, 64, 122, 134, 135, 146	126	93, 150, 163, 164
74	64, 65, 122, 143, 146	127	94, 150
75	64, 65, 122, 143, 146	128	94, 150
76	60, 65, 122, 123, 142, 146	129	94, 150
77	66, 67, 120, 143, 146	130	95, 150
78	66, 120, 143, 146	131	95, 150
79	66, 67, 121, 143, 146	132	95, 150
80	67, 122, 133, 143, 146	133	95, 150
81	67, 71, 122, 133, 143, 146	134	96, 150
82	72, 77, 122, 123, 142, 146	135	96, 150
83	72, 77, 122, 123, 142, 146	136	96, 150
84	73, 122, 123, 137, 142, 146	137	96, 150
85	75, 149	138	96, 150
86	75, 149	139	96, 150
87	76, 149	140	97, 150
88	76, 149	141	97, 150
89	76, 149	142	97
90	77, 149	143	99
91	77, 149	144	99
92	78, 149	145	100
93	78, 149	146	100
94	78, 149	147	100, 101
95	78, 149	148	101
96	66, 79, 149	149	101
97	80, 100, 149	150	101
98	80, 149	151	102
99	80, 149	152	102

153	103
154	103
155	104
156	84, 86, 105
157	106
158	107
159	107
160	107
161	107
162	108
163	108
164	108
165	109
166	109
167	110
168	110
169	110
170	111
171	111
172	111
173	111
174	112
175	112
176	112
177	113
178	114
179	115
180	115
181	116
Boundaries	147, 152, 186, 187
Building Upon	186
Leases Confirmed	186
Marsh	186
Sunken Ground	172
Surveying and Staking	150, 190

Alexandria:
- Board of Trustees 1, 3, 118, 119
- Court House 29, 186-187
- Court of Hustings 183, 186
- Hustings Court 1, 4, 110
- Incorporation of 186
- Library 119
- Market . . 29, 131, 146, 156, 184, 186-189
- Prison 29
- Settlement of 186, 189
- Tithables in 187
- Town Boundaries 129, 130
- Town Records 1, 179, 181, 186, 190
- Trustee . . 1, 3 9, 11, 13-17, 20, 21, 23-25, 27-29, 31, 35, 36, 38, 39-42, 45, 47, 49, 50, 52, 186, 189, 190

ALLISON
- Ann 31-33, 40, 76, 88
- John 6-8, 26, 34, 110, 116
- Mary 28
- Patrick 27, 28, 89
- Rebecca 8
- Robert . 6, 8, 23, 26, 28, 31-33, 40, 51, 76, 77, 86, 88, 91
- William 34, 35

ANDERSON
- Colbert 103
- Elizabeth 93
- Jos. 175
- Robert 5
- William 38, 93

Animals:
- Hogs and Swine 138, 166, 190, 191

ARELL
- Christiana 60, 63, 101
- David . . . 49, 63, 100, 101, 109, 110, 112
- Dolly 71
- Eleanor 34, 39, 50, 60, 61, 63, 77
- Mr. 177
- Phebe/Phoebe 63, 100, 109
- Richard 34, 39, 50, 60, 61, 63, 64, 71, 77, 84, 92, 100, 150
- Samuel . 30, 63, 64, 69, 71, 102, 104, 109, 119

ARMAT
- Sarah 36, 90
- Thomas 36, 89, 90

ASBURY
- Francis 73

ATKINSON
- Guy 33

AWBREY
- Frances 23
- Henry 23
- Thomas 23

B

BADING
- John B. 106

BAILEY
- Elisha 114
- Elisha T. 114
- Jane 114

BAKER
- Barton W. 102
- Capt. 180
- William 64, 65

BARCLAY
    Ann 87
    Thomas 86, 87, 108
BARRY
    Daniel 10, 11, 22
    Mary 10, 11, 22
BAYLISS
    John 175
BEELER
    Benjamin 58
    Christopher 16-18, 58, 59
    Henrietta W. 16-18
    Joseph 16, 58, 59
BEESON
    Edward 68
BEIDEMAN
    Charlotte 63
    Henry 63, 110
BELL
    Anna 72
BENT
    Betsey 11, 51
    Lemuel 10, 11, 51, 106
BIRD
    Catharine 24, 89
    William 6, 24, 89, 92
BLACK
    Alexander 20, 163
    John 92
    Sarah 20
    William 1, 15
BLONDELY
    Jane 115
    Michael S. 115
BLUNT
    Washer 52
BOA
    Cavan 44, 105
BOHRER
    Peter 101, 108
BOLING/BOLLING/BOWLING
    Gerard/Gerrard 113, 126, 152-153
BOONE
    Aloysius 45
    Joseph 45
BOWEN
    Jabez 85
    Obediah 46, 85
BOWMAN
    Capt. 175
BOWNE
    Elizabeth 37
    Matthew F. 37

BOYD
    Ann 55
    John 55, 56
BOYER
    John 43, 44
BOYLE
    Peter 63
BRICE
    John 43
    Nicholas 43
BRIGHT
    Windle 14
BRITTINGHAM
    Ann 42
    Dixon 42
BROADWATER
    Charles 29
BROCKETT
    Robert 10, 32
BROMLEY
    Thomas 145
    William 100
BRONOUGH
    William 72
BROOKE
    John 21
BROOKS
    John T. 23, 24, 81
BROWN
    Mary 54, 79, 80, 109
    Mathew 113
    Samuel M. 53, 54, 79, 80, 108, 109
    William 57, 58
    Windsor 103
BROWNLEY/BROWNLY
    Thomas 9, 139
BRYAN
    Bernard 33
    Charles 36
BRYCE
    Hannah 30, 35, 43, 44
    John 30, 34, 35, 43
    Nicholas 43
    Robert 35, 43, 44
Buildings and Structures: . . 5, 41, 51, 78, 79,
                            83, 161, 186, 190
    Bake House/Oven 5, 64, 75
    Brew House 45
    Brewery 79
    Carlyle House 156, 186
    Carlyle's Gate 139
    Church 156
    Court House . . 28, 29, 128, 131, 134, 141,

     148, 156, 175, 177, 186-187
 Distillery 78, 79
 Fence 76, 90
 Ferry Landing 8
 George Tavern 28
 Grammar School 139
 House . 11, 13, 14, 16, 17, 22, 24, 26, 30,
  41, 42, 45-47, 49, 50, 56, 57, 65, 67, 72,
  75, 83, 85-88, 90, 99, 101-103, 105,
    116, 130, 162, 165, 190
 House of Correction 184
 Kitchen 90
 Loft 51
 Long Warehouse 176, 178
 Market House 156
 Materials 171, 176
 Methodist Episcopal Church 73
 Necessary 28, 90
 Outhouse 16, 17
 Pier 10, 44, 45
 Presbyterian Meeting House 73
 Price's Ordinary 187
 Prison 29, 131, 184, 186
 Public Landing 152, 172, 174
 Pump 78
 Quaker Meeting House 112
 Repairing of 155, 171, 177
 Requirements of 190
 School House 155, 158, 159
 Shed 161
 Smith Shop 136
 Smoke House 28, 90
 Stable 22, 28, 51
 Stone Warehouse 79
 Store/Store House . . . 22, 48, 66, 90, 137
 Tenement 101, 183
 Tobacco Stand 7
 Town House 159
 Town Warehouse . 160, 161, 165, 166, 171
 Warehouse . . . 3, 7, 8, 11, 29, 44, 45, 53,
   106, 132, 135-137, 140, 141, 147,
   154-156, 160-162, 164, 165, 171, 173,
     176, 186, 189
 Wharf . 11, 42, 44, 45, 66, 75, 78, 79, 139,
  147, 154, 158, 163, 164, 167, 173, 177,
    179, 187, 190
 Work House 184
BURNES/BURNS/BYRN/BYRNE
 Patrick 28, 52, 116
BURNETT
 Charles 95
 George 95
 Mary 95

BUSHBY
 John 7, 150
 Mary 72
 William 7, 72
Businesses:
 Abraham Morehouse & Co. 79
 Bank of Alexandria 20, 21, 26, 33
 Carlyle & Dalton 158, 166, 175, 176
 Chapman & Co. 143, 146
 Colin Dunlop & Son 21
 Fisher & Bragg 72
 Henly & Cate 176
 John Murray & Co. 47, 75
 John Sutton & Co. 92
 Joseph Janney & Co. 83
 Nathaniel Chapman & Co. 126
 Robert Adam & Co. 180
 Robert Hamilton & Co. 52
 Saunderson & Rumney 49
 Sutton, Mandeville & Co. 92
 Thomas Patten & Co. 75
 Watson & Co. 177
 William Baker & Co. 64
 William Lowrey & Co. 93, 94
 Williams & Cary 94
 Wilsons & Co. 92
BUTCHER
 Ann 59, 114, 115
 John 34, 39, 59, 87, 112, 114, 115
BUTT
 Adam 50
 Jacob 50, 63

C

CAMPBELL
 Matthew 7, 22
CANNON
 John 107
 Sarah 107
CAREY
 Joseph 77, 78
CARLIN
 Sarah 86, 102
 William 86, 102
CARLYLE
 George W. 29
 John . 3, 5, 8, 9, 13, 14, 16-18, 20, 21, 24,
  25, 27-31, 35, 36, 38, 42, 45, 47, 50,
  52, 54, 58, 59, 92, 93-95, 120-124,
  126-143, 145-167, 169-177, 181, 189
 Mr. 16, 80, 143
 Sarah 29

CAROLAN
    James 21
CARR
    Overton 113
CARROLL
    Charles 109
CARSON
    John 25
    Thomas 25, 93, 163
CARTLICH/CARTLISH
    Charles 28, 29, 106
CARY
    Joseph 51, 55, 56, 77, 93, 94
CASEY
    John 25
CAVENS
    James 39
CAVERLEY/CAVERLY
    Joseph 75
    Peter 63, 100
CAZENOVE/CASANOVE
    Anthony C. 33
    Peter 87, 88
CHALLONER
    John 80, 109
CHAMP/CHAMPE
    John 47, 122, 139, 146
    Mr. 143
CHANDLER
    Walter S. 95
CHAPIN
    Benjamin 57
    Dr. 55, 57
    Gurdin 57, 83, 105
    Hiram 57
    Margaret 57
CHAPMAN
    George 66, 67
    Mr. 122, 143, 146
    Nathaniel . 66, 67, 120, 126, 143, 146, 173
    Pearson 66, 67
CHEW
    John 9, 102
    Joseph 16
    Margaret 102
    Mercy 13, 16
    Mrs. 151
    Roger 13, 174
CHICHESTER
    Richard 38
    Sarah 38
CHRISTIE
    James 27

CLAPHAM
    Josias 13, 131, 132, 142, 145
CLARK/CLARKE
    Elizabeth 71
    Michael 71
    Richard 30, 63
    Sarah 30
CLEMENTSON
    George 103
CLIFFORD
    Jeremiah 7
    Monica 7
    Nehemiah 8
COATES
    Lydia 86
    Samuel 86
COCHRAN
    George 68
COLTART
    Katharine 15, 91
    Mr. 78
    Roger 15, 81, 91
CONN
    Amelia T. 83
    Casina 36, 42
    Catharine 80
    Gerrard T. 82, 83
    Philip 80, 86
    Thomas 36, 41, 42
CONNELL
    James 24, 132, 142, 143, 145, 167
CONNELLY
    James 92, 150
CONWAY
    Capt. 180
    Hannah 84, 85
    John 84, 85
    John S. 85
    Joseph 84, 85
    Lucy 85
    Mary 10, 13, 15, 84, 85
    Richard   4, 6, 10, 11, 13, 15, 85, 168, 171-
                            174, 177, 180, 181
    Robert 84, 85
    Susanna(h) 85
    Thomas 82, 84, 85
COOK
    Sarah 82
    Whiting 82
COOKE
    Elizabeth 87
    John 22
    Lewis 86, 87

Stephen	65, 106
Thomas	73

COOPER
- Ann . . . 17
- Elizabeth . . . 17
- Joel . . . 17
- Samuel . . . 17
- Sarah . . . 17

COPITHORN
- John . . . 137

COPPER
- Christiana . . . 111
- Cyrus . . . 27, 28, 111
- Elizabeth . . . 28, 111

CORYELL
- George . . . 68

Counties:
- Berkeley . . . 9, 51, 90, 103
- Botetourt . . . 44
- Fairfax . . . 1, 4, 9, 11, 15, 22, 29, 50, 124, 128, 131, 132, 148, 153, 156, 164, 181, 183, 187-189
- Fauquier . . . 31, 72, 85, 187
- Frederick . . . 9, 10, 40, 72, 103, 186, 186
- Gloucester . . . 49, 50
- Hampshire . . . 43, 58, 59
- Henrico . . . 9, 81, 102
- King George . . . 99, 107-109, 111-116, 132
- Loudoun . . . 9, 34, 37, 43, 46, 47, 61, 63, 67, 84, 87, 88, 114, 187
- Middlesex . . . 8, 67
- Northumberland . . . 84, 85
- Prince William . . . 3, 15, 21, 26, 60, 65, 75, 85, 107, 156, 175, 186, 187
- Richmond . . . 26, 65, 104
- Shenandoah . . . 43
- Stafford . . . 16, 22, 35, 49, 50, 60, 61, 66, 67, 78, 89, 99, 100, 101-103, 105, 107-110, 132, 149, 173, 189
- Westmoreland . . . 4, 52, 54-56

COUTER
- Angel H. . . . 34, 35
- Catharine . . . 35

COX
- Jacob . . . 58, 99, 174

CRAFFORD
- Thomas . . . 126, 152, 153

CRAIG
- James . . . 36
- Richard . . . 71
- Samuel . . . 87, 90

CRAIK
- Adam . . . 61
- Dr. . . . 47
- James . . . 48
- Sarah . . . 61

CRAMMOND
- William . . . 51

CRAMPHEN/CRAMPHIN
- Richard . . . 52, 53

CRANDEL/CRANDLE
- Thomas . . . 44

Creeks and Runs:
- Four Mile Run . . . 3, 23
- (Great) Hunting Creek . . . 3, 132, 138, 173, 186, 189
- Wills' Creek . . . 16

CROWE
- Lanty . . . 24, 26, 105

CURRIE
- Ann . . . 106
- James . . . 106

CURTIUS
- Jacob F. . . . 35

CUTLER
- Elizabeth . . . 15, 91
- Elizabeth K. . . . 15

D

DABNEY
- John B. . . . 51, 66, 80
- Roxa . . . 51, 66, 80

DADE
- Baldwin . . . 6, 71, 75, 79, 80, 89, 94, 109
- Catharine/Catherine . . . 6, 71, 89, 94, 109
- Francis . . . 1, 140

DALL
- James . . . 32, 38

DALRYMPLE
- John . . . 8

DALTON
- Catharine . . . 24
- Jane . . . 25
- Jenny . . . 25
- John . . . 5, 13, 14, 16-18, 21, 24, 25, 29, 35, 51, 67, 71, 72, 73, 96, 120, 122, 124, 127-143, 146-156, 158-173, 176, 181
- Mr. . . . 16, 143
- Robert . . . 14

DALYELL
- John . . . 91

DANDRIDGE
- Bartholomew . . . 91

DAVEY
- David . . . 115

199

DAVIS
   Samuel 100
   Thomas 50, 100
DAWE
   Philip 39
DEBLOIS
   George 47
   Lewis 46, 47
   Lydia 47
DENEALE
   George 36, 104
DEVILBISS
   Christian 63
   Mary 63
DICK
   Elisha 5, 73, 83, 106
   Hannah 73, 83, 106
DIDIER
   Henry 115
DIGGES
   Charles 4, 140, 141, 152
   George 4
   Thomas 4
   William 4, 16, 65
DIXON
   John . . 5, 23, 28, 31, 40, 55-57, 122, 143, 145
   Mr. 142
DOINGS
   Joshua 114
DONALDSON
   Elizabeth 35, 73, 83, 89
   James 175
   Robert 73, 83
DOUGHERTY
   Robert 103, 104
DOUGLASS
   Capt. 175
   Charlotte 69
   Daniel 69
DOWNEY
   Elizabeth 94
DOWNMAN
   William 26
DOYLE
   Mr. 101
DUFF
   John 29
DULANY
   Benjamin 14, 109, 112
   Elizabeth 14, 109
DUNCAN
   Elizabeth 86

   George 30, 71, 86
DUNDAS
   Agnes 88
   John 6, 14, 15, 24, 36, 88, 89
DUNLAP
   John 33, 37, 64, 82
DUNLOP
   Colin 21, 22
   James 22
duPONT
   Victor 33
DUVALL
   Ann 26
   Nancy 26
   William 26
DYSON
   Hannah 38
   Joseph 37, 38, 45
   Mary 37

E

EARLE
   Henry S. 58
EARP
   Caleb 41
EASTON
   David 48, 61
   Sarah 61
EDELIN
   Edward 110
EHRMIN
   Elizabeth 80
   John 67, 79, 80
EICHENBRADE
   Magdalena 106
   William 105, 106
ELLIS
   Nugent 54
   William 54
ELLISON/ELLISTON/ELLESTON
   Cuthbert 85
   Henry 51
   Mary 84, 85
ELTON
   Anthony 77
   Beersheba 77
   Isabel/Isabella 23, 77, 105, 116
   John 76, 77, 85, 105, 106
   Joseph 77
   Martha 77

Mary 77, 105
Samuel 77
Susannah 77
Thomas 77
William 77, 106
ELZEY
   Capt. 176
ESTAVE
   Andrew 64
EVANS
   Drusilla 10
   Ephraim 65
   Robert 10, 49
EWING
   Thomas 27

F

FAIRFAX
   Col. 158
   Family 137
   George . 120, 123, 128, 130, 143, 151, 189
   George W. . . 7, 23, 36, 42, 43, 45-47, 52,
      54, 60, 64, 67, 71, 73, 123, 124, 127,
      129-139, 146, 153, 154
   Sarah 43, 46, 47
   Thomas 88, 189
   W. 152
   William . . 42, 45, 47, 120, 123, 128, 129,
      131-133, 136, 137, 143, 146, 189
Fairfax County:
   Circuit Court Archives . 1, 23, 36, 68, 76,
      77, 93, 116
FALCONER
   Abraham 53, 54
   Sarah 53, 54
FARRELL
   William 49
FAW
   Abraham 86, 87, 115, 116
   Mary A. 87, 115
FAXON
   Josiah 44
FENDALL
   Mary 38
   Philip 38
   Philip R. 139
FIELD
   John 38, 39, 103
FINLEY
   Amelia 24, 25, 32
   David 24, 25, 31, 32
   Hugh 103, 104

John 103, 104
Susanna(h) 103, 104
William 110
FISHER
   Thomas 115
FITZGERALD
   Jane 4, 37-39, 51, 60, 65, 112
   John 4, 36-39, 51, 60, 65, 76, 78, 99, 112,
      173
   Mr. 178
FITZHUGH
   H. 143
   Henry 61, 121, 146
   Mr. 143
   William . . 4, 49, 121, 122, 145, 146, 156,
      187
FITZPATRICK
   Mary 105
   Thomas 104, 105
FLEMING
   Andrew 17
   Betty 66, 79, 80
   Mr. 159, 178, 179
   Thomas . . . 66, 75, 79, 80, 147, 149, 152,
      153, 155-169, 171-174, 178, 180, 181
FLETCHER
   James 82, 110
   John W. 53, 68, 69
   Mary 69
Flour and Grain Trade: 161
FOLEY
   Dennis 104, 105
   Elizabeth 105
FORBES
   John 46
FOREST/FORREST
   Elizabeth 14
   Joseph 14
   Uriah 87, 88
FORTNEY
   Jacob 18, 28, 41
FOWLER
   George 13
FRANCE
   Philip 109
FRENCH
   Mr. 80
FULLMER
   Joseph 114

G

GABARD
    John 93
GANTZ
    Adam 34, 35
    Mary 34
GARDNER
    Henry 10
GARVEY
    Ann 13
    Lucas 13
GEORGE II, King 3, 130
GHEQUIERE/GHEQUIRE
    Bernard 37, 38
GIBBONEY
    Hugh 113
GIBSON
    John 20, 22, 91
GILL
    John 48, 76, 91
GILPIN
    George 34, 38, 43, 45, 52-54
    Jane 52-54
    Katherine 43
    William 16
GLADDEN/GLADDING/GLADIN
    Mr. 142
    William 126, 153
GLASSFORD
    John 20
GOOCH
    William 189
GOODRICK
    John 89
GOODS
    George 101
GOOSE
    Adam 34
GORDON
    David 25-27
    Sarah 26
GRAHAM
    John 16-18, 82, 149, 172
    Mary 17, 18
Grand Lodge of Virginia 116
GREEN
    Charles 23
    Jesse 28
    Job 106
    John 22
    Jonas 158
    Lydia 106
GREENWAY
    Joseph 14, 49, 76
    Rebecca 14, 76
GRETTER
    Elizabeth 36, 89, 90
    Gretter 36
    John 36, 90
    Margaret 36
    Michael 36, 89, 90, 93, 149
GREYSON
    Benjamin 139
GRIMES
    James 60, 67, 100
    Sarah 100
GULLATT
    Elizabeth 17
    James 17
GUNNELL
    Henry 175

H

HAGUE
    Francis 73
HALL
    Elizabeth 53, 54
    Jonathan 52, 54, 76, 162-171
    Robert 27, 34
    Sarah 53, 54
    William J. 47
HALLADAY
    James 76
HALLEY
    William 106
HAMILTON
    Esther 82
    Eunice 37
    John G. 103
    Robert 52, 54, 75, 81, 82, 102
    Susanna 86, 87
    Theodorus J. 37
HAMP
    Benjamin A. 31, 33, 39, 41, 56
HAMPSON
    Bryan 32, 48
HANNAH
    Nicholas 71
HANSON
    Mary 52, 53, 113
    Samuel 52, 53, 113
    Thomas 113
HARLE
    Robert 23

HARMAN
Jacob 55, 59
HARPER
Capt. 180
Charles 44, 45, 47, 48
Edward 44, 47, 48
Elizabeth 44, 47
Frances R. 44, 45
John . 11, 26, 37, 38, 42-48, 71, 76, 79, 80
John W. 41
Mary 44, 45, 48
Peggy 44, 48
Samuel 57, 76, 77
Sarah 77
William 76, 80
HARRISON
Ann 67
Barbara 49
Dorothy H. 61
Fairfax 156
H. 143
Joseph 57
Joseph W. 57
Mr. 146
Nathaniel 60, 61, 120, 147
Richard 55-57, 64, 67
Robert H. 61
Samuel 49
Sarah 61
Thomas 50, 133, 140
HARTLEY
James 69
HARTSHORNE
Hannah 80
Mr. 178
Rachel 80
Sarah 80
Susanna 86
Susannah 59
William . . 5, 35, 39, 44, 47, 48, 55-57, 59,
66, 67, 71-73, 75, 83, 86, 87, 89, 100,
101, 107, 108, 110, 111, 112, 171
HARWOOD
Rachel 75
Risden B. 75
HAWKINS
Alice 83, 108
John 64, 83, 108
HAWN
John 63
HAYES
Andrew 60

HEADLEY
George 26
Henry 26
Sarah 26
HEDRICK
Thomas 94
HENDERSON
Alexander 15, 20
Archibald 20
Robert 45, 75
HENDRICKS
James 40, 90
John 26, 86, 87
Kitty 90
HENLEY
David 64
HENNINGER
Ann 28
Frederick 28
HEPBURN
Agnes 7, 8, 88, 93
William . . . 6-8, 15, 24, 36, 88-90, 93, 110
HERBERT
George 101
Jenny 25
John C. 29
Sarah 5, 20, 21, 26, 29, 30
Thomas 25
William . . 4, 5, 10, 14, 20, 21, 25, 26, 29,
30, 78, 99
HERLIHY (see also "Hurlihy")
Maurice 9
HESS
Barbara 50
Jacob 49, 50
HEWES
Aaron 65, 112
HICKMAN
John 48, 103
Mary 48, 103
Rebecca 48, 103
William 48, 72, 103
HICKS
William 5, 121, 122
HINEMAN (see also "Hyneman")
Ann 42
Nancy 42
HITE
Frances 9, 10
Jacob 9, 10, 86, 149, 154, 159
HODGSON
William . . 10, 26, 37-39, 47, 48, 72, 87-89

HOLLIDAY
  James 76
HOLLINGSWORTH
  Jesse 58, 59, 65
  Stephen 58
HOOE
  Robert T. 22, 55-57, 64, 66, 67, 178
  Seymour 102, 108
HOOF/HOOFF
  Lawrence 26, 36, 39, 90, 104
HOOKS
  Ann 37, 40
HOPKINS
  John 83
HORNER
  John 51
HOUGH
  John 43, 46, 47, 73, 114
  Mahlon 43
  Samuel 43
  Sarah 46, 47, 114
  William 43, 114
HOYE
  William 44, 45
HUGHES
  Aaron 48
  Catharine 97, 150
  Hugh 9, 94, 150
  Isaac 6, 78, 96, 150
  John 78, 96, 149, 150
  Nathan 16-18, 158
  Rachel 16, 18
  Ruth 97, 150
  Sarah 78
  Thomas 91
HUNTER
  Christiana . 30, 49, 57, 58, 100, 101, 108,
                                           110
  Dr. 159
  Edward R. 57
  George 66
  John . 8, 64, 67, 75, 80, 102, 132-141, 147-
              152, 156, 157, 158, 159
  John C. 67, 75
  Kitty 49, 95
  Nathaniel 64
  Nathaniel C. 64, 65
  Sarah A. 65
  William 5-8, 15, 22-24, 30, 34, 44, 49, 57,
        58, 60, 76, 83, 91, 95, 100-102, 108,
                                      110, 180
HURLIHY (see also "Herlihy")
  Jane 104

Maurice 8, 104
HYNEMAN (see also "Hineman")
  George 42

I

INGLE
  Joseph 40
INGLIS
  Ann 106
  Samuel 106
IRISH
  George 53, 54
IRVIN/IRVINE
  James 5, 10, 11, 22
  Thomas 37
  William 107
ISABEL
  Jonah 114, 115

J

JACKSON
  Joseph 116
  William 116
JAMIESON
  Andrew 5, 75
JAMISSON
  Mr. 35
JANNEY
  Elisha 52-54, 111, 115
  John 35, 111, 113
  Joseph 38, 83, 103
JENIFER
  Daniel 55, 57, 61
  Mary 61
JENKES
  Crawford 37
  John 37
  Joseph 37
JENNINGS
  Daniel 3
JOHNSON
  Mr. 175
JOHNSTON
  Archibald 153
  Elizabeth 56
  George . . 5, 9, 13, 16, 35, 52, 54, 61, 67,
        71, 73, 77, 79, 130, 131-141, 147-149,
                                151-154, 158
  Samuel 56, 77
  W. 158

JOLLY
- John 57, 93, 94
- Rachel 93, 94

JONES
- Charles 22, 24, 89, 107, 116
- David 100
- Dorothy 61
- John 34
- John C. 61
- Notley 1
- Robert 96, 150

JUDGE
- Andrew 93
- Rebecca 93

K

KEATING
- James 105

KEITH
- James . 20, 21, 33, 44, 47, 48, 60, 99, 113
- Smith 115

KENNEDY
- David 48, 51, 71
- James 31-33, 48, 51, 83, 113
- Letitia 32, 33, 48, 113

KENNER
- Hannah 44
- James 44

KETCHAM
- Daniel 79

KEYGER (see also "Kyger")
- George 58, 59
- Mary 58, 59

KIDD
- James 89

KILMER
- Kenton 137

KINCAID
- James 116

KIRK
- Bridget 75, 76
- George 119
- James 75, 79, 84, 88
- Robert 75

KIRKPATRICK
- Elizabeth 15, 91
- Henrietta 15, 91
- John . . 15, 78, 81, 147, 149, 152-155, 157, 159, 160, 162
- Katharine/Katherine 15, 91
- Thomas . 10, 11, 15, 81, 91, 150, 154, 159, 160, 167

KORN
- John 54, 105, 106
- Rosannah 54

KYGER (see also "Keyger")
- George 58
- Mary 58

L

LAKE
- Richard 35, 36

LAMB
- Mr. 189

LAMPHIER/LANGPHIR
- Going 64, 152

LATIMER
- Alexander 21

LAURIE
- James 84, 149

LAWRASON
- Alice 49, 104
- James 49, 53, 71, 104, 112

LAWSON
- James 21

LEAKE
- Richard 152, 156-159

LEAP
- Jacob 63

LEE
- Ann 104
- Anne 4
- Arthur 65, 104, 105
- Charles 76, 82, 85, 90, 95, 96, 109
- Edmund J. 4, 65
- Francis 149
- Francis L. 81
- Hariot 104
- Henry 4
- Lucinda 104
- Ludwell 20, 21, 30, 81
- Mr. 189
- Sally 104
- Sarah 65
- Thomas 85

LEIGH
- Benjamin W. 84

LEMOINE
- John 64

LEWIS
- Hannah 59
- Mordecai 5, 57, 59

LIGHTBURN
- Capt. 180

LIMRICK
   John 17, 35
   Susannah 17
LINDON (see also "Lyndon")
   Roger 9, 120, 133
Liquors: 175
LITTLE
   Charles 9, 29, 93, 106
LITTLER
   Nathan 103
LOCKWOOD
   John 66, 80
LOMAX
   John 8, 10, 13, 104
   Rachel 8, 10, 13
LONGDEN/LONGDON
   Adam 41
   Dorothea 41
   Elizabeth 41
   John 37, 40-2
   Ralph 41
LONGMARCH
   Christian 35
Lotteries: 139, 152, 156, 158
LOVE
   Charles 51
   Samuel 61
LOWNES
   James 48
   Sarah 48
LOWRY
   Olivia 94
   William 93, 94
LOXHAM
   Robert 157
LUMSDON
   John 37, 38
LUTZ
   Michael 111
LYLE
   Elizabeth 14
   Martha 14, 17, 18
   Mary 14
   Robert 14, 17, 18, 39, 49
LYLES
   Henry 34, 35
   Sarah 35, 46, 68
   William 34, 35, 46, 68, 69, 78, 99
LYNDON (see also "Lindon")
   Roger 142, 145
LYNN
   Adam 26, 30, 102, 107, 112, 113
   Catharine/Catherine . . . 30, 102, 107, 113

   Elizabeth 102, 107
   Mary 107

M

M'CRAE/M'CREA/MACRAE/MACREA(see
   also McCrea)
   Allan/Allen 15, 120, 139, 142, 145
   Robert 169, 173, 174, 181
   Mr. 142
M'LEOD
   James 84
   Robert 84
MADDEN
   Hannah 31, 33, 40, 52, 91, 92
   Michael . 23, 28, 31, 33, 40, 51-53, 75, 79,
                                 80, 91, 92
MANDEVILLE
   John 24, 92
   Jonathan 24, 92
   Mr. 35
MANN
   Bernhard 67
   Johanna 67
MARSTELLER
   Christiana 50, 54, 111
   Magdalena 54
   Philip 14, 50, 54-56
   Philip G. 50, 54, 111
   Samuel A. 119, 126
MASON
   Ann 29, 39, 41
   Charles 29, 121, 122, 146
   George . . 39-41, 100, 121, 132, 133, 135,
                   136, 138, 139, 143, 146, 158
   John 116
MASSEY
   Elizabeth 53, 54
   Joseph 53, 54
   Lee 77
MATHERS
   Capt. 180
MATTART
   Jacob 86, 87
MAY
   Dorothy 37
   Joseph 37, 85
   Richard 87
   Robert 21
   Sarah 20
   Thomas 20, 21
MAYER
   Christian 56

MAYSON
  Charles 29
  Mr. 175
McALISTER
  Elizabeth 86
  John 86
McCABE
  Henry 88
  Jane 88
McCARTY
  Daniel 23, 77
  Dennis 72
McCAUGHEN
  Hugh 17
McCAUSLAND
  Marcus 48
  Mary A. 48
McCLANACHAN
  Ann 85
  John 85
McCLEAN
  Archibald 78
McCLEERY
  Isabella 34
  William 34, 35
McCLENACHAN
  Ann 77
  James 77
McCONNELL
  Alexander 37, 63, 64
  Mary 37, 64
McCRAE/McCREA/McRea
  Agnes 46
  Allan 15
  Ann 55
  John 15
  Nancy 30, 43-45, 55, 77
  Robert . 6, 8, 15, 30, 36, 43-47, 55, 56, 76,
      77, 90, 91, 93, 172, 174
McCUE
  Henry 10, 13
McDERMOTT
  Martin 39
McGUIRE
  James 23
McHENRY
  James 10
McINTOSH
  John 65
McIVER
  Colin 51
  John 51, 90
  Margaret 51

McKENZIE
  Alexander 53, 54
McKINZEY
  William 106
McKNIGHT
  Charles 35, 36
  William 35, 36, 85, 105, 110, 116
McLEAN
  Archibald 78
  Daniel 92
  Samuel 93
McLEOD
  Daniel 38
  James 84, 149
  Robert 84
McMACHEN
  Ann 10
McMUNN
  Elizabeth 60
  George 51, 60
McPHERSON
  Daniel 52, 68
  Elizabeth 52
  Isaac 52, 53, 68, 113
  Jane 52
  Martha 68
  Tacey 113
MEAD
  Samuel 5, 132, 142, 145
MEALES
  John 175
MEASE
  Betty 32, 33, 40, 44, 45
  John 31
  Matthew 43, 44, 46, 48
  Robert . . 30, 32, 33, 36, 40, 43-47, 55, 56,
      76, 77, 90, 169, 173, 174, 181
MENDENHALL
  William 115
MERCER
  George 40, 67, 68, 133
  J. 68
  James 68, 69
MILLER
  Godfrey 110
  James 31, 56
  John 56
  Joseph 103
  Mordecai 71, 89
  T. Michael . . . . iii, 1
  Warwick P. 119, 160
  William 31, 87

MILLNOR
  William 80
MILLS
  John 55, 57, 102
MINCHIN
  J. 83
MITCHELL
  Hugh 40
  William 69
MITCHUM
  Thomas 82
MONCURE
  John 50, 122, 133, 146
MONDAY
  Richard 175
MONTGOMERY
  Capt. 180
MOONEY
  Neil 5, 105
MOORE
  Cleon 112
  Gay M. 119
MOREHOUSE
  Abraham 75, 76, 78, 79
MORRISON
  James 72
MORTON
  John 57
MOSS
  John 72
MOXLEY
  Daniel 33
  Thomas 171, 173, 177
MUIR
  Elizabeth 35, 73, 83, 89
  James 25, 26, 180
  John . 9, 15, 16, 23, 35, 39, 51, 73, 80-83,
      88, 89, 137, 138-141, 147-149, 151-153,
           155, 158-162, 164-174, 181
  Robert 73, 88
MUMFORD
  John 46
  John P. 46, 85
MUNCASTER
  Elizabeth 111
  John 67, 111
MUNDAY
  Elizabeth 101
  William . 14, 101, 121, 127, 142, 145, 162,
                           164
MUNSON
  James D. . . . . iii, 1, 119

MURE
  Thomas 16
MURRAY
  James 26
  John 46, 47, 68, 71, 75, 85
  John B. 46, 85
  Margaret 13, 106
  Patrick 13, 106
  Patty 68
MYLER
  Elizabeth 10
  James 10

N

NEBLON
  John J. 116
  Margaret 116
NEILSON
  Hugh 106
NEVIN
  Duncan 14
Newspapers: 149
  Alexandria Advertiser & Commercial
    Intelligencer 65
  Columbian Mirror and Alexandria
    Gazette 38, 43, 65, 105
  Maryland Gazette . 16, 22, 28, 50, 88, 137,
                    139, 148, 151, 154
  Pennsylvania Gazette 148
  Times and Alexandria Advertiser . . 32, 116
  Times and District of Columbia Daily
    Advertiser 91
  Virginia Gazette . . . 1, 16, 17, 21, 78, 148,
                       151, 156, 186
  Virginia Gazette and Alexandria
    Advertiser 29, 73, 87
  Virginia Gazette and General Advertiser . 58,
                            67
  Virginia Gazette and Richmond (Daily)
    Advertiser 104
  Virginia Gazette and Weekly Advertiser . 58
  Virginia Journal and Alexandria
    Advertiser 5, 8, 23, 30, 43, 48, 64, 68,
      75, 77, 83, 91, 102, 104, 116, 186, 187
  Virginia Journal and Alexandria Gazette . 52
NEWTON
  Jane 106
  Mr. 57
  William 40, 94, 106
  Willoughby 52, 54, 124
NICKELS/NICKOLLS
  Isaac 87

NORWOOD
    John 39, 40

O

O'MARA/O'MEARA
    Michael 44, 45

Occupations:
    Alderman 42, 183, 185, 186
    Archivist 1
    Attorney 56, 176
    Attorney at law . . . 16, 61, 76, 81, 96, 102
    Attorney in fact 25, 55-57, 64, 72
    Baker 41, 42, 54, 105
    Biscuit Baker 106
    Blacksmith 34, 115
    Brewer 42, 43, 46, 101
    Bricklayer 82, 93
    Butcher 34, 39, 42, 87, 110
    Cabinet Maker 105
    Captain . . 43, 44, 46, 47, 63, 64, 83, 134,
        135, 137, 160, 168, 171, 175, 177, 178,
        180
    Carpenter 8, 14, 21, 40, 72, 165
    Cartwright 39
    Chain Carrier 152, 153
    Clerk . 23, 27, 50, 116, 120-122, 126, 128,
        133, 136, 137, 140, 159, 162, 176, 183,
        184
    Clerk of Market 184
    Clerk of the General Assembly 189
    Clerk of the House of Burgesses 189
    Collector 78, 137
    Colonel 35, 46, 49, 52, 54, 57, 68, 83, 93,
        130, 137, 139, 141, 143, 145, 146, 151,
        159
    Commissioner 14, 116
    Common Councilman 183, 185
    Cooper 100
    Coppersmith 39
    Cordwainer 76
    Counselor at law 109
    Cryer 120
    Doctor . . 5, 47, 48, 55, 57, 65, 146, 152,
        159
    Escheator 22
    Farmer 109
    General 87, 89
    Governor 189
    Gunsmith 100
    Hatter 34, 39, 47, 48, 59
    House Carpenter 56, 57, 77
    Innholder 16-18, 34, 39
    Innkeeper 16, 17
    Ironmaster 20, 21
    Joiner . . 9, 14, 23, 34, 64, 100, 101, 103,
        165
    Justice of the Peace 29, 131, 183, 184, 186
    Major 104, 126, 129, 173
    Mariner 16, 17, 27, 53, 72, 95, 106
    Mayor . 42, 66, 75, 119, 181, 183, 185-187
    Merchant 4-8, 10, 13-17, 20-23, 25-27, 30,
        31, 34-41, 43, 46, 47-49, 51, 52, 54-59,
        64, 65, 71-73, 75-79, 81, 88, 90, 93,
        96, 99-101, 103, 104, 112, 115, 139,
        173
    Minister 6, 64, 73, 77, 122
    Overseer . . 134, 136, 139, 147, 152, 161,
        167, 174
    Painter 7
    Peruke Maker 50
    Physician 55, 56, 58, 64
    Recorder 42, 183, 185, 186
    Ropemaker 93
    Sail Maker 71
    School Master 155
    Sergeant 53
    Serjeant 183
    Sheriff 9, 51, 106, 136, 177, 184, 190
    Ship Builder 66
    Ship Carpenter 63, 147
    Ship Master 51
    Shoemaker 39, 76, 109
    Shop Keeper 87
    Silversmith 39, 116
    Store Keeper 54, 76
    Surveyor . 3, 152, 153, 162, 164, 172, 183,
        189
    Tanner 82, 93
    Tavern Keeper 8
    Taylor 41, 102
    Tobacconist 99
    Treasurer 156
    Watchmaker 24, 71, 92
    Wharf Master 171
    Wheelwright 63
    Yeoman 58, 59, 78

ORNEY
    Capt. 160

ORR
    John 80, 149, 162, 163
    John D. 37, 105
    Lucinda 105

OSBORN/OSBORNE/OSBURN
    Richard 3, 120-124, 189

OWENS
    Edward 30, 180
OWNBREAD
    William 105, 106

P

PAGAN
    John . . 4, 9, 14-17, 34, 35, 39-42, 45, 49,
        50, 55, 56, 60, 61, 66, 67, 120-124,
        127-131, 142, 143, 145, 146, 154, 189
    Mr. 142
PANCAS
    Jonathan 60
PANCOAST
    David 87, 104
    Mary 87
PARKER
    Richard 90
PARSONS
    Elizabeth 104, 110, 115
    James 82, 83, 104, 110, 115, 116
    John 110, 115, 116
    Mary W. 116
    Mrs. 116
PASCHALL
    Stephen 78
PATON
    John 39
    Mary 114, 115
    William 114, 115
PATTEN
    Mary 37, 67, 80
    Thomas 11, 37, 66, 67, 75, 80
PATTERSON
    John 36, 38, 152
    Susanna(h) 36, 95
    Thomas 95
    William 17, 95, 109
PATTINSON/PATTISON
    John 156-159
PATTON
    James 25, 31, 32, 113
    Mary A. 31, 113
    Thomas 85
PAYNE
    W. 177
PEARCE
    Alexander 34, 44
    Margaret 34, 44
PEARS
    Mr. 178
PEERS

    Eleanor 37, 38
    Margaret 38, 99
    Peggy 112
    Valentine 36-38, 78, 99, 112, 173
PENS
    Jacob 63
PENTECOST
    Dorsey 58, 59
PERIN/PERRIN
    Joseph M. 30, 91, 116
    Mathurin 30
PERRY
    Alexander 81
    Jane 81
    Mr. 81
PETER
    Elizabeth 30, 36
    John 22
    Robert 30, 36
    Ruth 22
PETERKIN
    Thomas 65
PETIT
    John 115
    John B. 115, 116
    Margaret 115, 116
PEYTON
    Frances 32
    Francis 14, 30, 40, 52, 53, 103
    John 49, 50, 121, 124, 133, 146
    Mary B. 49
    Sarah 32, 53, 103
    Valentine 49
PIPER
    Anthony 40
    Harry . 5, 23, 28, 40, 55-57, 81, 121, 122,
        143, 146, 149, 151-155, 159-161,
        163-167, 169-172, 181
PIPPENGER
    Wesley E. . . . . iii, 1, 119
Places:
    A. Jamieson's Woodyard 75
    Adam's Pier 10
    Annapolis, Md. 75, 139
    Arlington 119
    Baltimore Co., Md. 6
    Baltimore, Md.   11, 27, 28, 32, 34, 39, 48,
        54-56, 58, 77, 89, 94, 109, 115, 116
    Beaufort Co., N.C. 17, 95
    Belvoir 137
    Bladensburg, Md. 10, 52
    Boston, Mass. 47, 64, 85

Brandon, Md.	60
Brew House	45
Cadiz, Spain	55
Carlyle	24, 92
Cecil Co., Md.	20
Cedar Grove Farm	132
Charles Co., Md.	21, 22, 37, 49, 61, 66, 77, 106, 113, 139
Charleston, S.C.	78
Chester Co., Pa.	16, 21
Co. Cumberland, Great Britain	40, 56
Co. Galloway, Scotland	25
Colchester	8, 20, 22, 139
Cumberland Co., England	23
Cumberland Co., Pa.	93
District of Columbia	187
Dorchester Co., Md.	100
Dumfries	64, 65, 85, 92, 139, 187
England	137
Fairgirth, Scotland	40
France	3
Frederick Co., Md.	34, 63, 84, 87
Fredericksburg	8, 27, 68, 91
Georgetown, Md.	14, 22, 30, 86-88, 95
Georgia	44
Germany	106
Glasgow, Scotland	20-22
Great Britain	3, 14, 84
Gunston Hall	41
Hall Catt	40
Ireland	3, 54, 99
Jones Point	187
Kilmarnock	92
Kilmarnock, Scotland	22
Kirkenbright, Scotland	25
Landing	141
Landing, Cameron St.	138
Leesburg	43, 88
Liverpool	51
London, England	68
Long Ordinary	16-18
Lower Merion, Pa.	78
Marsh	129, 130, 162
Maryland	4, 16, 38, 46, 55, 64, 71, 75, 100
Middlesex Co., Great Britain	24
Middle Point	189
Montgomery Co., Md.	22, 87, 88, 95, 160
Montgomery Co., Pa.	20, 21
New Castle, Del.	21
New Jersey	79
New York	33, 64, 77, 85, 109
Newcastle Co., Pa.	93
Newcastle, Del.	20
Orange Co., N.C.	103
Pasture	129
Philadelphia, Pa.	5, 31, 38, 39, 43, 46, 47, 51, 56, 57, 59, 61, 64, 67, 75, 78-80, 86, 90, 99, 100, 103, 106, 109, 115
Point Lumley	66, 129, 135, 136, 140, 147, 161, 162, 165, 167, 169, 171
Point West	147, 162, 167-169, 171
Port Tobacco, Md.	106
Presbyterian Burying Ground	77
Price's Ordinary	156, 187
Prince Georges Co., Md.	4, 8, 10, 16, 25, 53, 60, 63-65, 71, 82, 94, 107, 108, 110, 113
Providence, R.I.	85
Public Landing	164, 189
Queen Anne's Co., Md.	54
Ravensworth	187
Richmond	186
Rope Walk	187
Rosegill	67
Salisbury	132
Sandy Spring Monthly Meeting	160
Scotland	40
Shuter's Hill	21, 30
Somerset Co., Md.	85
Spring Field	186
St. Kitts, Island of	13
Stratford	4
Sussex Co., Del.	28
Truro Parish	186
Tyson's Corner	186
Upper Marlborough, Md.	139
Upper Merion, Pa.	78
Upper Point	177
Urbanna	104
Warburton, Md.	4
Warrenton	85
Washington Co., Md.	83
Washington, D.C.	82
West Indies	13
West Point	147, 173
West's Point	161
Westmoreland Co., Pa.	58, 59
Whitehaven	9, 23, 40, 51, 55
Whitehaven, England	55-57, 72
Wilkes Co., Ga.	6, 8
Williamsburg	3, 173, 175, 177
Wilmington, Del.	20
Winchester	175
York Co., Pa.	28, 55, 63, 79

PLEASANTS
  Mary 39, 103
  Samuel 38, 39, 103
PLUMMER
  John 41
POLLARD
  Joshua 51
  Thomas 51
POMERY
  Elizabeth 115
  Walter 114, 115
  William 91
PORTER
  Catey 58, 59
  Francis 126
  Mr. 142
  Sarah 32, 33, 37, 40
  Thomas 32, 33, 37, 40, 85
Potomac River .. 4-6, 8, 9, 15, 42, 43, 45, 46,
     52, 56, 57, 78, 79, 100, 132, 137, 139,
            140, 154, 159, 169, 172, 189
POTTER
  Sarah 82, 149
POTTS
  Elizabeth 20, 21, 30
  John 20, 21, 30, 78, 94, 99, 149, 150
POWELL
  Leven/Levin 21, 68, 69
  Sarah 69
  William H. 68, 83
PRATT
  Shubael 71
PRICE
  Jane 35, 114
  Mary 87
  Oliver 35, 114
  Thomas 87

Q
Quakers 112

R
RAE (see also "Rea")
  Jonathan 23, 127, 165
RAMSAY
  Amelia 28, 31, 33, 40, 91
  Andrew 21
  Ann 9, 23, 26, 31, 51, 76
  Anne 23, 51, 76
  Anthony . 16, 91, 127, 142, 145, 150, 153

  Betty 31, 32, 40, 80
  Catharine 21
  Clarissa 33
  Dennis . 23, 26, 28, 31-33, 40, 51, 82, 91,
                       109, 119, 181
  Edward 56, 57
  Edward M. 39, 59, 101
  Elizabeth 94
  Hannah 31, 40, 91, 92
  Jane 23, 26, 31, 32, 40
  Jane A. 24, 33
  John 33, 94
  Mary 39
  Mr. 145
  Naomy 58, 59
  Sarah 28, 31, 40, 91
  Susannah 94
  Thomas 94
  William .. 3-5, 7, 9, 14-17, 20, 21, 23-26,
       28, 29, 31, 33, 35, 39-42, 45, 47,
       49-51, 55-57, 60, 61, 64, 66, 67, 71, 73,
       76, 80, 91, 120-124, 127-141, 143, 145,
       146-157, 159-162, 164-167, 169-174,
                  178, 179, 181, 189
RANDOLPH
  William 189
RATCLIFFE
  Locian 113
  Richard 113, 114, 187
RATTLE
  Anne 85
  James 85
REA (see also "Rea")
  John 142
  Jonathan/Johnathan 143, 145
REDMAN
  Thomas 60
REED
  Elizabeth 93
  Thomas 93
RESLER
  Jacob 50
REYNELL
  John 86
REYNOLDS
  John 10, 103
  Sarah 103
  William 17, 72
RHODES
  William 72
RICHARDS
  Ann/Anne 23, 28, 53, 69, 90
  George 85

Nancy 28, 32, 90
Thomas   23, 28, 31, 32, 36, 52, 53, 69, 90, 92

RICK
   John 34
RICKETTS
   John T. 106
   Mary 106
   Mr. 57
   Thomas 40
RIDDLE
   Frances R. 45
   Joseph 32, 33, 38
RIGDON
   Edward 84
   Elizabeth 84
RIGG
   John 42
RING
   Constance K. . . . . iii, 1, 27
ROBERDEAU
   Capt. 180
   Daniel 75, 78, 79
   Jane 78, 79
ROBINSON
   John 189
   Joseph 71
   Matthew 26
   Mr. 14
   Peter 150
ROGERS
   Giles 72
   John 72
ROSS
   D. 52
   David 53
   Hector 22, 139
ROTHERY
   Capt. 178, 180
ROWAN
   Patrice C. 79
   Patrick 149
ROZIER
   Eleanor 108
   Henry 82, 94, 108, 149, 150
RUMNEY
   John 26, 37, 38
   Mr. 14, 49
RUMSEY
   James 34
RUTHERFORD
   Mary 90
   Robert 8, 90, 150

RUTTER
   Mr.? 37

S

SADLER
   Henry 109
SALKELD
   Elizabeth 27, 28
   Henry 25, 27, 28, 121, 122, 143, 146
SANDERSON
   Mr. 14
SANDFORD/SANFORD
   Betty 99
   Capt. 180
   John 99
   Lawrence 13
SAUL
   Joseph 114-116
   Mary 115
SAUNDERS
   Hannah 56
   John 57, 77, 85-87, 99, 100, 105, 112
   Joseph 56, 57
   Mary 86, 87, 100
SAUNDERSON
   Mr. 49
SCHECKEL/SHECKLE
   Dederick/Diederick 28, 38, 41, 42
SCHIESS
   Sebastian 55
SCOTT
   C.R. 25
   Charles R. 32
   David M. 104
   David W. 85
   John 17, 95
   Richard M. 33, 85
SEBASTIAN
   Benjamin 34, 35, 63, 162
SEEKRIGHT
   Aminadab 60
SEMPLE
   Elizabeth 22
   John 21
   William 22
SEWEL/SEWELL
   Elizabeth 50, 51
   William 50, 51, 133, 175
SEXSMITH
   Matthew 33
SHAKESPEARE
   Mr. 101

SHAW
   Eleanor 18, 23, 24
   Elizabeth 23
   Isabel/Isabella 23, 77, 105
   Thomas 23
   William 18, 23, 105
SHEAFFER
   Henry 27, 28
   Mary 28
Ships:
   Jane 180
   Vessel 147, 164, 171, 189, 190
SHORT
   Ann/Anne 52, 71
   John 52, 53, 71
SHREVE
   Benjamin . 39, 47-49, 53, 86, 87, 103, 112
   Hannah 48
   Susanna(h) 49, 53, 87, 103, 112
SHROPSHIRE
   William 80
SHUGART
   Zachariah 79
SIMMONDS/SIMMONS
   Jane 42
   Samuel 41, 42, 49, 50, 51, 81
SIMMS
   Charles 32, 81-83, 95, 102
   Jesse 14, 30, 33, 38, 45, 95
   Thomas 22
SIMPSON
   Elizabeth 36, 90
   William 36, 90
SKELTON
   Joseph 21, 124
SLACUM
   Catherine 100
   Gabriel 100
   George 45, 49, 66, 68, 108
SLIMMER
   Christian 43, 44, 55, 59, 63, 86
   Mary 55, 59
SMITH
   Alexander 10, 33, 37, 38, 40, 69, 89, 112, 113
   Hugh 33
   James 39
   Jesse 38
   Johnson 111
   Mary 114
   Nathaniel 16, 17, 72, 127, 142, 145
   Rachel 33, 38, 40
   Samuel 114

   Sarah 116
   Thomas 175
   William 9, 27, 28, 116
SMOCK
   Robert 75, 79
SNOWBALL
   Capt. 180
SPADDEN
   Ann 28
   Robert 28
SPANGLER
   George 60
   Paltzer 55, 79
SPEAKE
   Josias M. 53, 100
SPENCER
   Mary 28
   William 27, 28
SPROUSE
   William iii
STABLER
   Mary M. 160
STAYMAN
   Capt. 180
STEEL
   John 23, 24
STEIBER
   Michael 50
STEPHEN/STEVENS
   Adam 35, 121, 133, 141, 143
STEPHENS
   Dr. 146
STEPHENSON
   Richard W. 73
STETSON
   Charles W. 3
STEUART
   Andrew 99
   Betty 31
   Charles 99
   James 31
STEWART
   Andrew 10, 78, 99
   Betty 31, 32, 80
   Cicily 115
   Elizabeth 114
   James 31
   James M. 31
   John 114, 115
   William G. 108
   William R. 31

STOLMAN
    Benj. 180
STORRS
    Joshua 9
Streets: ... 105, 129, 130, 151-153, 161, 164,
        167, 172, 174, 183, 184, 189, 190
    (Alley) . 14, 17, 20, 33, 39, 41-44, 46, 49,
        54-58, 63, 65, 67, 68, 72, 73, 75-77, 79,
        80, 85, 90-92, 94, 104, 110, 112, 168,
        169
    Allison's Alley 76
    Cameron 24, 25, 27-29, 91, 107, 110, 116,
        138, 172
    Chapel Alley 72
    Ditching of 175
    Duke .. 60, 61, 63-68, 71-73, 82, 83, 103,
        104, 110, 112
    Fairfax 6-8, 13, 14, 16, 20, 21, 25, 29, 31,
        34, 38, 39, 43, 46-50, 55, 56, 58, 64,
        65, 71, 72, 76, 77, 80, 96, 97, 100,
        108-110
    Fit for Travel 151
    King .. 31, 34-36, 38-41, 88-90, 107, 110,
        115, 167, 172
    Montgomery 187
    Oronoco .. 4-7, 94-97, 168, 169, 171, 173
    Paving of 172, 187
    Pendleton 95-97
    Pitt 81-84, 86-96, 101, 110
    Prince .. 42, 44, 45, 47, 49, 50, 52, 54-56,
        58-60, 84, 86, 87, 88, 91, 105, 106, 110,
        113, 114
    Princess 8-10, 13, 14, 93, 94
    Queen .. 15-17, 20, 21, 23, 24, 87, 92, 93,
        154
    Regulation of 186
    Royal . 7, 9, 14, 17, 20, 23, 24, 27-30, 35,
        40-42, 50, 59, 60, 65, 72, 73, 78, 80,
        81, 96, 101, 109, 110
    St. Asaph 87, 100, 102-107, 110-116
    Union .. 42-44, 52, 60, 61, 66, 75, 76, 78,
        99, 107, 186
    Water .. 5, 6, 8, 9, 15, 24, 29, 31, 32, 36,
        42, 43, 45, 46, 52-55, 61, 63, 66-68,
        75, 76, 78, 79, 97, 99, 107, 108, 139,
        140, 154, 172, 173, 186
    Wilkes 99-102, 107-111
    Wolfe 75-82, 102, 103, 110-112
STROMAN
    Elizabeth 28
    Henry 28
STROTHER
    William 40, 121, 133, 146

STRUTFIELD
    William 23
STUART
    David 113
    Eleanor 113
    William G. 101, 102
SUCKLEY
    George 72
Suits:
    Alexander v. Birch 3
    Birch v. Alexander 3
    Marsteller v. Coryell 84
    Richard Arell v. Town of Alexandria .. 61
    U.S.A. v. Herbert Bryant, Inc. 119
SULLIVAN
    Honora 105
    John 104, 105
SUMMERS
    Isabel/Isabella 77, 105, 116
    John 175
    William 51, 53, 77, 94, 105, 115, 116
Surveys and Plans: 66, 68, 110, 126, 129-131,
        148, 150, 162, 168, 169
SUTTON
    Ann 24, 92
    John 24, 92, 112
    John D. 24, 92
SWEIG
    Donald 137
SWIFT
    Ann 64
    Jonathan 37, 38, 64
SWOPE
    Adam S. 56
    Eve 56
    Jacob 56
    Michael 55, 56, 79
SYDEBOTHAM
    William 10, 52, 53
SYMMER
    Andrew 16
SYMMERS
    Mr. 139

T

TALBUTT/TALLBUTT
    McKinsey 23
TALIAFERRO
    John 113
TARBUCK
    Ann 95, 150

John 17, 95, 150
TARTSEPAUGH/TATSEPAUGH
   Peter 71
   Susannah 71
Taxes:
   Wharfage 179, 186
TAYLOR
   Elizabeth 6
   Jesse 6, 23, 86, 89, 102, 116
TEMPLEMAN
   Mr. 175
   W. 157
   William 27, 76, 158, 159
TERRET/TERRET
   Amelia 65
   Mr. 143
   Pearson 64, 65, 122, 146
   William H. . 58, 59, 64, 65, 122, 123, 133, 146
THOM
   William 77
THOMAS
   Joseph 8, 57
   Rachel 8, 57
   Samuel S. 84
THOMPSON
   Ann 79
   Edward K. 46, 47
   Jonah 20, 24, 25, 47, 48, 68, 69
   Joseph 72, 79
   Margaret 48, 69
   Samuel 72
   Thomas 72
THOMSON
   Thomas 16
THORN
   Michael 43, 44
THORNTON
   Joseph 42
THUMBLER
   George 63
   Margaret 63
TOBIN
   Thomas 43, 45
TOWNSEND
   Platt 64
TRESIZE
   Thomas 87
TRESSELER/TRESSLER/TRISTLER
   Ludowick 60
   Lewis 115
TURNER
   Charles 88

TURNING/TWINING
   Nathaniel 13

U
UHLER
   Catharine/Catherine 41, 42
   Valentine 41, 42
USHER
   Abraham 39

V
VALETTE
   Betty 66, 80
   Eli 66, 80
VEITCH
   Betsey 69
   Richard 69
Virginia House of Burgesses 189
Virginia Land Office Patents 4
VOWELL
   John C. 44, 45, 53, 87, 89, 99
   Margaret 53, 89
   Mary 53, 89
   Thomas 44, 45, 53, 87, 89

W
WAGENER
   Andrew 103
   P. 181
   Peter 104
   Sinah 104
WAITE
   Jane 72
   William 72
WALES (see also "Wells")
   Andrew . . . 17, 18, 42, 43, 45-48, 52, 53, 101, 160, 161, 164, 165-167, 171, 176-178
   Margaret 17, 18, 42, 43, 45-48, 101
WALKER
   Henry 61
WALTER
   William 64
WALTHOE
   Nathaniel 189
WANTON
   Mary 87
   Philip 87, 111, 115

WARD
- Celia . . . 8
- William . . . 7, 8, 111

WASHINGTON
- Ann . . . 81, 102
- Augustine . . . 55, 56, 122, 133, 143, 146
- Bushrod . . . 3, 81, 102
- George . . . 36, 87, 89, 91, 149, 150, 154
- George A. . . . 83
- Hannah . . . 104
- Lawrence . . . 3, 36, 38, 120, 122, 124, 127-130, 143, 146, 173, 189
- Martha . . . 91

WATERS
- William . . . 72

WATSON
- Elizabeth . . . 61
- James . . . 61
- Jane . . . 45, 47, 58, 83, 104, 105
- Joseph . . . 76, 84, 86
- Josiah/Josias . . . 7, 43-48, 58, 59, 82, 83, 86, 104, 105, 107, 108, 171, 172
- Mr. . . . 178, 180

WEATHERLY
- Jesse . . . 100

WEBB
- Hannah . . . 84, 85
- John . . . 85

WEBSTER
- Catharine E. . . . 102
- Elizabeth . . . 102, 107
- John S. . . . 107
- Mary . . . 107
- Philip . . . 30, 102, 107

WEIGHTMAN
- Elizabeth . . . 9
- Richard . . . 9, 57

WELDON
- John . . . 139

WELLS (see also "Wales")
- Andrew . . . 160, 161

WEST
- Ann . . . 6, 7, 67, 71, 146
- Anne . . . 122
- Col. . . . 175
- George . . . 8, 9, 72, 73, 122, 126, 133, 137, 146, 150, 153, 176
- George W. . . . 6
- Hugh . . . 3-8, 14, 21, 25, 27-29, 31, 36, 38, 50, 52, 54, 58, 59, 60, 65, 72, 73, 121-124, 126-133, 137, 138, 142, 145, 146, 150, 173, 189
- J. . . . 142
- John . . . 3, 7, 8, 29, 63, 64, 67, 71, 120, 122, 125, 126, 129, 132-136, 140, 142, 146, 150, 152, 153, 165
- Mary . . . 63, 64
- Mr. . . . 143
- Roger . . . 5, 120
- Sybil . . . 7
- Thomas . . . 6, 7, 10, 11, 13, 15, 24, 71, 106
- William . . . 6, 8, 72, 122, 146, 150

WESTON
- Lewis . . . 63

WHALIN
- Dennis . . . 94

WHEATON
- Elizabeth . . . 37, 77
- John R. . . . 37, 77

WHEELER
- Israel . . . 103

WHITE
- Betty . . . 10
- John . . . 26, 92
- Thomas . . . 10, 11, 17, 28, 87

WHITING
- Carlyle F. . . . 29
- Mary . . . 50
- Thomas . . . 49, 50

WILKINSON
- Jane . . . 112
- Thomas . . . 112

WILLIAMS
- James . . . 75
- Thomas . . . 93, 94

WILSON
- Chloe . . . 86
- Cumberland . . . 22
- Daniel . . . 71, 133
- Elizabeth . . . 32
- George . . . 41
- James . . . 22, 31, 32, 68
- Joseph . . . 86
- Mr. . . . 78
- W. . . . 176
- William . . . 5, 15, 20-22, 43, 44, 55, 56, 81, 91

WINFREE
- Waverly K. . . . 3, 138

WINN
- Owin . . . 122

WINSOR
- Olney . . . 37

WISE
- Elizabeth . . . 13, 30, 49
- John . . . 10, 13, 30, 35, 36, 49, 50

Peter .. 14, 30, 42, 49, 71, 82, 83, 90, 107, 110, 114, 116, 149, 167

WISEMILLER
Jacob 106

WOLFENDEN
John 39

WOOD
Draper L. 165

WOODROW
John 106
Mary 106

WORMELY/WORMLEY
Ralph 8, 67, 121, 143, 146

WORRELL
Elizabeth 51
Morris 51

WRIGHT
Ann 44, 45, 81, 95
James 113
Sarah 113
William 43-45, 81, 94, 95, 99

WROE
Absolom 71

Y

YATES
William 8, 132, 142, 145

YOST
John 100
Rebecca 100

YOUNG
Ann 42
Catherine 41
David 37, 40-42
Dorothea 41
Elenor 71
James 15
John 106
Joseph 77
Mary 82
Notley 82
Thomas 41, 42
William 41, 71

Z

ZIMMERMAN
Elizabeth 114
Lodowick/Ludvick 71
Mary 71
Tobias 34, 113

Other Heritage Books by Wesley E. Pippenger:

Alexandria (Arlington) County, Virginia Death Records, 1853-1896

Alexandria City and Arlington County, Virginia Records Index: Vol. 1

Alexandria City and Arlington County, Virginia Records Index: Vol. 2

Alexandria County, Virginia Marriage Records, 1853-1895

Alexandria Virginia Marriage Index, January 10, 1893 to August 31, 1905

Alexandria, Virginia Marriages, 1870-1892

Alexandria, Virginia Town Lots, 1749-1801, Together with the Proceedings of the Board of Trustees, 1749-1780

Alexandria, Virginia Wills, Administrations and Guardianships, 1786-1800

Alexandria, Virginia 1808 Census (Wards 1, 2, 3, and 4)

Alexandria, Virginia Death Records, 1863-1896

Alexandria, Virginia Hustings Court Orders, Volume 1, 1780-1787

Connections and Separations: Divorce, Name Change and Other Genealogical Tidbits from the Acts of the Virginia General Assembly

Daily National Intelligencer *Index to Deaths, 1855-1870*

Daily National Intelligencer, *Washington, District of Columbia Marriages and Deaths Notices (January 1, 1851 to December 30, 1854)*

Dead People on the Move: Reconstruction of the Georgetown Presbyterian Burying Ground,
Holmead's (Western) Burying Ground, and other Removals in the District of Columbia

Death Notices from Richmond, Virginia Newspapers, 1841-1853

District of Columbia Ancestors, A Guide to Records of the District of Columbia

District of Columbia Death Records: August 1, 1874-July 31, 1879

District of Columbia Foreign Deaths, 1888-1923

District of Columbia Guardianship Index, 1802-1928

District of Columbia Interments (Index to Deaths), January 1, 1855 to July 31, 1874

District of Columbia Marriage Licenses, Register 1: 1811-1858

District of Columbia Marriage Licenses, Register 2: 1858-1870

District of Columbia Marriage Records Index, 1877-1885

District of Columbia Marriage Records Index, October 20, 1885 to January 20, 1892: Marriage Record Books 21 to 30

District of Columbia Probate Records, 1801-1852

District of Columbia: Original Land Owners, 1791-1800

Early Church Records of Alexandria City and Fairfax County, Virginia

Georgetown, District of Columbia 1850 Federal Population Census (Schedule I) and 1853 Directory of Residents of Georgetown

Georgetown, District of Columbia Marriage and Death Notices, 1801-1838

Husbands and Wives Associated with Early Alexandria, Virginia
(and the Surrounding Area), 3rd Edition, Revised

Index to District of Columbia Estates, 1801-1929

Index to Virginia Estates, 1800-1865
Volumes 4, 5 and 6

John Alexander, a Northern Neck Proprietor, His Family, Friends and Kin

Legislative Petitions of Alexandria, 1778-1861

Pippenger and Pittenger Families

Proceedings of the Orphan's Court, Washington County, District of Columbia, 1801-1808

The Georgetown Courier *Marriage and Death Notices:*
Georgetown, District of Columbia, November 18, 1865 to May 6, 1876

The Georgetown Directory for the Year 1830: to which is appended, a Short Description of
the Churches, Public Institutions, and the Original Charter of Georgetown, and
Extracts of the Laws Pertaining to the Chesapeake and Ohio Canal Company

The Virginia Gazette and Alexandria Advertiser:
Volume 1, September 3, 1789 to November 11, 1790

The Virginia Journal and Alexandria Advertiser:
Volume I (February 5, 1784 to January 27, 1785)

Volume II (February 3, 1785 to January 26, 1786)

Volume III (March 2, 1786 to January 25, 1787)

Volume IV (February 8, 1787 to May 21, 1789)

The Washington and Georgetown Directory of 1853

Tombstone Inscriptions of Alexandria, Volumes 1-4

www.ingramcontent.com/pod-product-compliance
Lightning Source LLC
Chambersburg PA
CBHW081222170426
43198CB00017B/2687